£3

THE SPOILS OF WAR

By the same author

DE GAULLE
ESCAPE FROM GERMANY

THE SPOILS OF WAR

THE RISE OF WESTERN GERMANY SINCE 1945

AIDAN CRAWLEY

THE BOBBS-MERRILL COMPANY, INC.

Published in the United States by the Bobbs-Merrill Company, Inc.
Indianapolis   New York
Published in Great Britain by William Collins Sons & Co., Ltd.

ISBN 0-672-51358-7
Library of Congress catalog card number 73-1728
Manufactured in the United States of America

First U.S. printing

Contents

Acknowledgements

I have received generous help from the British Foreign Office and the German Embassy in London, from several government departments in Bonn and, above all, from the staff of the British Embassy there. The Minister, Mr Brooks Richards (now Ambassador in Saigon) and Mr Lance Pope (Councillor), besides offering the warmest hospitality, were indefatigable in arranging for me to meet people. General Francis Bowes-Lyon, G.O.C. Berlin until the end of 1970, was equally kind. Mr Cullingford, the Labour Attaché and Mr Francis Kenny, one of the original British architects of the present West German trade union system and now a consultant in Bad Godesberg, provided between them a unique fund of knowledge on the development of West German Industrial Relations.

The Office for the Defence of the Constitution in Cologne, the Press Bureau of the Federal Government, the Central Statistical Office in Wiesbaden offered every facility. I am grateful to the Ministry of Defence in London for allowing me to see the Handbook for Military Government in Germany, the circulation of which is still restricted.

Herr Herbert Blankenhorn and Herr Karl Gunther von Hase, successively German Ambassadors in London, made many helpful suggestions. Dr Rudolf Völlmer, the Labour Attaché, kindly read part of the text.

I must also thank Dr Anton Kurze, the Town Clerk of Aachen, and his staff for much information about the rebuilding of their city. The B.B.C. were kind enough to arrange for a special showing of a television programme dealing with West German industry and to send me the transcript of Lord Chalfont's interview with Chancellor Willy Brandt.

Among the many individuals who spared time to see me I should like to thank in particular Dr Hermann J. Abs, Lord Annan, Brigadier Sir John Barraclough, Sir William Barnetson, General

Sir Alec Bishop, Dr Carl Blessing (who has since died), Dr Franz Burda, Dr Wilhelm Fehse, Dr Hans Globke, Dr Max Grundig, General Ulrich de Maizière, Count Peter Munster, Herr Herbert Pavel, Dr Carlo Schmid, Lord Shawcross, Sir Christopher Steel, Field-Marshal Sir Gerald Templer, Herr Hans Oskar Vetter, Dr Lüdger Westrick, Prinz Casimir Wittgenstein, Herr Peter von Zahn.

Without the unstinted service provided by the staff of the London Library, the Royal Institute of International Affairs, the Wiener Library and the Library of the Ministry of Defence, this book could not have been written.

Above all, I am deeply grateful to Professor Werner von Simson, Dean of the Faculty of Jurisprudence at Freiburg University, who not only read the manuscript, but made many corrections of fact and challenged several assumptions. Neither he, nor anyone else I have mentioned, bears any responsibility for the final text.

My secretary, Mrs Patricia Woodall, and Mrs Anna Phillips have shown infinite patience in typing and retyping the manuscript.

CHAPTER I

Prelude to Defeat

Not until Russian guns reverberated across the Oder in January, 1945, did the ordinary people of Germany feel the first, chill presentiment of defeat. Although General Zhukov was overrunning East Prussia and General Eisenhower was fighting his way towards the Rhine, although the German offensive in the Ardennes had failed, the public still listened to what their radio told them. Their Minister of Propaganda, Dr Goebbels, was so convincing that he almost compelled them to have faith in a secret weapon – the successor to the V1 and V2 – that would turn the scale in Germany's favour.

Even the ten thousand British and American air force prisoners at Stalag Luft 3, a camp near Sagan in Silesia, did not dare to believe that the collapse was imminent until they heard, on 23rd January, the sound of Russian guns twenty miles to the east. Apparently Hitler felt that prisoners were valuable in the desperate game he was playing, for on the evening of the 26th the camp was informed that everyone would start marching westwards in a few hours' time. No arrangements had been made for food or billets, and as it was bitterly cold, with the temperature frequently dropping to forty degrees of frost at night, the men knew that they would have a struggle to keep alive. Furthermore they would have to carry their own food. 'A large consignment of Red Cross parcels had arrived at the camp a few days earlier so we spent the next few hours making sledges with wood taken from the walls, floors and ceilings of our barracks,' wrote one of the prisoners.[1]

'At intervals through the night we quit the camp, company by company, stopping at the Food Store on our way out. Not everything in a Red Cross parcel was useful for a march, so we rifled

[1] The official but confidential history of Royal Air Force escapes from prisoners of war camps was written by Aidan Crawley in 1946. It included a description of the marches made by prisoners in 1945. An abridged version of the history was published by Collins and by Simon and Schuster under the title *Escape from Germany*, in 1956.

half a dozen parcels to fill one with what was most useful – chocolate, coffee and cigarettes were the best currency for barter and had priority. As a result, by the time the tail of the column reached the gate they were confronted by an extraordinary sight. The snow around the Food Store for hundreds of yards was literally carpeted with discarded tins and already a stream of civilians from Sagan were scavenging all they could carry. Thousands more tins had been tossed into a little compound which held sixty Russian prisoners who sang to us as we passed by. They told us they had never seen so much food in their lives before.'

As soon as the column of ten thousand British and American airmen reached the main roads it was literally engulfed by refugees. Some had already travelled many hundreds of miles from east Prussia and even the Ukraine which, until this year, had retained a colony of many thousands of German families. 'What surprised us most was the way they travelled,' wrote the same prisoner. 'There was not a car, lorry or even a bicycle to be seen – only a seemingly endless line of covered wagons and carts drawn by horses or mules. We were suddenly back a hundred years, living again the scenes described so vividly by Sergeant Burgoyne in his diary of the retreat of Napoleon's army from Moscow which many of us had just been reading. For this was not merely a retreat, but the migration of a vast peasant population. Each wagon represented a family or the remnants of a family with the old couple, shrouded in black shawls, sitting motionless on the driving seat, small grand-children and pregnant mothers lying on the mattresses in the cart behind and the elder children walking alongside the spare mules and horses which were tethered to the wagon's end.

'They were a pitiful sight, frozen, hungry, shoes and clothes falling apart, dragging themselves along to an unknown destination, hoping only that it might be beyond the reach of the Russian army. It was so cold that even in the day-time any drink mixed with cold water froze solid before it was possible to carry it to one's mouth. At night men and women could keep alive only by huddling together in a wagon or, if they were lucky, in the aisles of a church. Those who fell asleep in the snow were dead within a few minutes.

'Yet their fellow countrymen gave these fugitives no welcome. Every village in Silesia had already received its quota of refugees from the west who had been evacuated earlier in the war as the

result of allied bombing. The inhabitants of these villages wanted
no further overcrowding. It had not yet sunk into their consciousness that within days they themselves would have to move. As the
wagons rattled slowly down a village street, doors were slammed
and windows hastily shut. On the pavement stood only the burgomaster and the village elders determined to see that the column did
not stop. When night fell and the refugees could go no farther
village officials would herd them into the main square or perhaps
into a churchyard, and stand guard to see that no one escaped.

'At the time we prisoners did not know how vast the migration
was, or that we were a part of its vanguard. Literally millions of
people were on the move. We did realise, however, that we were
seeing the disintegration of Germany. Within an hour of taking the
road prisoners and refugees had become indistinguishable. We were
bound together by one common thought – to keep together so as to
keep alive. Frostbite took toll of our guards, who were mainly
middle-aged reservists, and many fell out that first morning. Those
who could still walk trudged along, their backs bent, their eyes
fixed on the snow at their feet. When their weapons became too
heavy they put them on our sledges, which was generally the last
they saw of them. The refugees gladly let us climb on to their
wagons and, as they had nothing with which to barter, we gave
them what food we could spare.

'The people we met in the villages were beginning to be afraid.
When we went into their houses to barter – twenty cigarettes for
a loaf of bread, five for a pound of potatoes – the family would
crowd round and ply us with questions. How far away were the
Russians? How were they behaving? Should the villagers stay
where they were or join the column? Occasionally an officer or a
brown-shirted burgomaster would call us "terror bombers" or
"child murderers" and shout out that we were not allowed to talk
to civilians. Once a guard knocked from a woman's hand a cup of
tea she was handing me. She turned on him like a viper and said
that her son was a prisoner in England and was being well treated.
She would give me tea whatever he might do.

'The S.S. were dreaded by the German civilians almost as much
as the Russians. Some S.S. commanders were such fanatical Nazis
that even now they were prepared to carry out Hitler's orders and
execute summarily anyone guilty of "defeatism", which meant

refusing to burn food stocks, blow up road bridges or prepare for last ditch resistance. Detachments of S.S. were constantly retreating through our column and sometimes they would threaten to shoot if we did not get out of their way. One day three of them strode up to a group of us brandishing revolvers and accusing us of stealing a goose they had cooked for supper. Fortunately not a trace of it could be found. We ourselves never saw an S.S. unit larger than a platoon and mostly they seemed weary and dispirited. Twice I watched an S.S. corporal go to a house and ask for water and each time the housewife, having seen his uniform, slammed the door in his face. He meekly retreated.

'The great trek of which we formed part meant more than the disintegration of the comfortable village life of Eastern Germany. It was also the end of an aristocratic tradition which had begun with the forcible conversion of the Prussian Slavs by the Teutonic knights in the thirteenth century. The Junkers had survived the First World War and both under the Weimar republic and under Hitler had resumed their traditonal rôle of forming a bastion against the Poles and the Slavs to the east of them. Now we saw their splendour crumbling away. One evening we came to a town called Muskau whose neat avenues and imposing buildings suggested a principality. At one end stood a vast palace which, we learned, belonged to the family Von Arnim. Count von Arnim himself was at home and although I did not meet him we all felt his authority. For the first time on the march we were provided with billets, occupying his riding school, stables, pottery, laundry and a glass factory in the town whose furnaces were still alight and seemed to frozen prisoners the nearest thing to paradise they could imagine. The vast stables housed a unique collection of carriages and coaches dating from the sixteenth century; some of the loose boxes which had been built for race-horses, were equipped with hot and cold water both of which were still running; the house was a museum of pictures and furniture.

'In the evening, while some of the senior officers were being shown the treasures of the house by Von Arnim, others drifted out into the town and, to their astonishment, found themselves invited into homes and given dinner. It was still a feudal society and we were the beneficiaries of its final flicker. The Count had taken us in, his tenants would do the same. They were not merely polite but genuinely friendly. For the first time our attempts to barter were refused. Schnapps and wine were produced and, while the prisoners ate and drank, their clothes were dried and sometimes even mended. Conversation was restrained without being stilted. These Eastern Germans had realised at last that the war was lost. The knowledge had come as a shock, but I never heard any of them complain or criticise their government. They were proud and the dignity with which they faced approaching catastrophe compelled admiration. No doubt the foreboding of a misfortune even greater than ours was a common bond, and fear of the Russians made them treat us as allies rather than enemies – yet we felt that their sympathy for us was real and instinctively we reciprocated it.

'Their first question was almost always the same. How had we been treated? We looked bedraggled, but we could honestly reply that, as far as it lay within their power, the German air force and army had behaved correctly. Their relief was obvious. Muskau was on the high road to the Eastern Front and inevitably the talk veered towards the Russians. In every house we entered there were cripples and, since Muskau had escaped bombing, it was not difficult to guess where they had come by their wounds. The description of what they had endured through the Russian winters made our little trek seem like a picnic. Gradually the conversation would approach the present and again, the first question was always the same. How were the Russians behaving? Should the inhabitants of Muskau stay where they were or join our column? Having heard during the march how the Russians were raping and looting as they advanced, we advised them to leave.

'Soon we too were on the move again, this time separated from the column of refugees. We entrained in cattle trucks and travelled slowly across Germany to a camp a few miles from Bremen. There, for two months, we waited, watching the allied air offensive and listening to the news over the radio. Day after day through February and March, hundreds of British and American bombers would blacken the sky above us as they made their way unopposed to Hamburg or delivered their attacks on Bremen. The explosions from the ten thousand pound bombs shook our camp and at night the blaze lit up the whole sky. It did not surprise us to learn later that Hamburg had suffered an even more terrible fire-storm than Dresden, that cars had melted and people been roasted in the streets. To us it seemed impossible that any building in either city should remain standing and unlikely that any inhabitant would survive.

'But the Germans were still retaliating. One night in February an extraordinary explosion within a mile or so of our camp was followed by a bright light rising vertically into the sky. Next morning the B.B.C. announced that several V2's had landed in London. And although no German aircraft ever challenged the massed bombers as they droned overhead, more than once we saw aircraft of a quite extraordinary speed flying low towards the British front line. They were the Arado and Messerschmidt jets, taking off from the autobahn and strafing our troops as they crossed the Wesel or the Rhine. These were the first operational jet air-craft in the world and nothing that the allies possessed could match them. Had they been designed as fighters and had the Germans had enough petrol to launch serious attacks against our bombers, these machines could have inflicted enormous losses even at that late stage of the war.

'On the morning of 9th April, after the British had crossed the river Wesel at Verden, fifteen miles away, we were ordered to march out on to the Luneburge Heide, the great heath which stretches from Bremen to the Elbe. The area commander, although entirely cut off from his divisional headquarters, was a fanatical Nazi and had decided to fight to the last. Our German Camp Com-mandant was still more frightened of him than of us.

'For the next three weeks, as we wandered slowly in a north-easterly direction, we watched anger turn to bewilderment and bewilderment to despair in the people around us. For the first few days, as we crossed the Luneburge Heide, the troops who streamed by us were hostile. They had come from Holland, where they had seen little fighting, and could not believe what was happening. We watched them digging in their eighty-eight millimetre guns along the roadside and learned later that they had fought them well enough to knock out eight of our leading tanks.

'But as the news of the advance of the Russians came over the radio the will to fight suddenly evaporated. We listened to Goeb-bels telling the people of Germany how to carry out Hitler's "scorched earth" policy, how to organise the Werewolves and how, as a last resort, the retreat into the Redoubt round the Bertchesgarten would be accomplished. We could see no sign of compliance with his orders. We found that some burgomasters had deserted their villages, but through fear for their lives rather than loyalty to Hitler. In the country districts life seemed normal and there was no sign of any deliberate destruction.

'The weather was perfect and, having equipped ourselves with perambulators in exchange for coffee, we walked light. Firewood was plentiful and our camp at night had all the appearance of a giant fair. We cut turf to build shelters, slept on straw and ate more food than we had seen for years. Very occasionally a Nazi would stand and revile us, but he was now a figure of fun or of silent derision.

'We passed a training school where boys of fifteen to seventeen were being taught infantry tactics. They were rushing about, lying down and firing blank cartridges like public school boys on a field day. When they recognised our uniforms they dropped their rifles and came rushing across to bombard us with frightened questions. Their one anxiety was not to have to fight at all, let alone become Werewolves. Their officers did not interfere with them as they talked to us.

'By 21st April, we were scattered along the beautiful valley of the Trave river, some miles to the south of Lubeck, living in farms and refusing to march farther because an outbreak of typhus was reported in the city. Our guards were dwindling and although one or two were still capable of shooting an unarmed man, most were more anxious to know how they would be treated when taken prisoners themselves. Every village was full of refugees from all over Germany. Landowners from East Prussia were serving as woodmen and their wives as scullery-maids; whole families from bombed towns were living in a single room. But there was still plenty of food and the main concern was about property. Would the British loot the villages? Would farmers remain in possession of their land? Would anyone get paid? Above all, would they be protected from the Russians?

'On 26th April, we were invited to billet ourselves on an estate called Trenthorst-Wulmenau belonging to a Mr Raemtsma, a large cigarette manufacturer who was also a director of the Hamburg-American Shipping Line. He had prudently calculated that the presence of some three thousand British officers was a sound insurance for his property. The estate was magnificently equipped and housed two pedigree herds of Friesian cows each a hundred and fifty strong. There, taking turns with the Polish milkman, we settled down to watch the end.'

Meanwhile Hitler had not given up hope. 'Is it not still possible,' he asked his colleagues on 24th April, 'that any day now – any hour – war may break out between the Bolsheviks and the Anglo-Saxons over their prey, Germany?' For months the Nazi leaders had been waiting for a 'miracle' to save them. The secret weapon had not materialised, and as the Russians drove farther into the heart of Europe the most likely miracle seemed to be a split between the western powers and Russia. When the Russians began their great offensive in January, Göring had pointed out that the Allies had 'entered the war to prevent us from going to the East; not to have the East come to the Atlantic. If this goes on we will get a telegram from the West in a few days.'[2]

The telegram never came, and in April massed air raids on Berlin drove Hitler into the *Führerbunker* under the Chancellery. Although still in command, Hitler was in a state of mental and physical disintegration. His head shook, his hands trembled and he shuffled about like an old man. Dr Goebbels felt that the time had come to study two horoscopes which had been locked away unread at Himmler's Headquarters. One belonged to Hitler and had been drawn up in 1933 on the day that he had become Chancellor; the other was that of the German Republic dated 9th September, 1919. 'Both horoscopes,' wrote Schwerin von Krösigk in his diary, 'had agreed in predicting the outbreak of war in 1939, the victories till 1941, and then the worst defeats culminating in the worst disasters in the early months of 1945, especially the first half of April. There was to be an overwhelming victory for us in the second half of April, stagnation till August and in August peace. After the peace there would be a difficult time for Germany for three years; but from 1948 onwards she would rise again to greatness.'[3]

Goebbels was so excited by these revelations that he broadcast to the German people on 6th April that 'the Führer has declared . . . that a change of fortune shall come . . . The true quality of genius is its consciousness and its sure knowledge of coming change . . . Destiny has sent this man so that we, in the time of great

2 *Führer Conferences on Naval Affairs*. Fragment 24. 1945. Issued by the Admiralty. London.
3 *The Struggle for Europe*. Chester Wilmot. Collins, London; Harper and Row, New York, 1952. Also *End of a Berlin Diary*. W. Shirer. Hamish Hamilton, London; Alfred Knopf, New York, 1947.

external and internal distress, shall testify to the miracle. There is no solution except Adolph Hitler.' A week later, just as the All Clear was sounding at midnight, Goebbels burst into the *Führerbunker* with the sensational news of Roosevelt's death. 'My Führer, I congratulate you. Fate has laid low your greatest enemy. God has not abandoned us . . . A miracle has happened.'[4] But the miracle did not stop the onward roll of the allied armies, nor was there any sign of that other miracle which was to separate West from East.

Yet Hitler was not wholly wrong in predicting divergences between the allies; a rift had opened, not between Russia and the West, but between the Western Powers themselves. At the first meeting of the Big Three at Teheran in the late autumn of 1943 Roosevelt had fallen under the spell of Stalin's squat dignity and enigmatic personality. Although others at the conference were impressed by the dictator's 'cruel, crafty look', Roosevelt was fascinated by the penetrating mind, the mixture of truculence and humour, the blunt demands and icy calculations that suddenly gave way to warm, even uproarious hospitality. Roosevelt not only became convinced that Russian friendship could be won, but believed that he could tame the half-savage dictator by the force of his own personality.

No doubt Roosevelt's optimism was encouraged by practical considerations. He was eager to enlist Stalin's intervention against Japan which, his advisers estimated, might save the United States a million lives. Furthermore, as Russia would emerge from the war as the strongest power on the continent, her co-operation was essential to the President's 'Grand Design'.

This post-war blue-print called for a new United Nations organisation with 'teeth in it'. It was to be based on the Atlantic Charter which assured all nations the right of independence and self-determination. Russia and America, along with Britain and possibly China were to provide the bite; it would be their duty to keep the smaller nations in line, by force if necessary.

Roosevelt's miscalculations sprang from his conviction that Russia had no territorial ambitions. He failed to understand either Russian communism or Russian imperialism, a failure which seems inexplicable in the face of Stalin's tireless demands; his stranglehold on the Baltic states, his seizure of Polish territory, his in-

4 *Goebbels – The Man Next to Hitler*, Rudolph Semmler, Westhouse, London, 1947, p. 192.

sistence on ports and bases in China and, finally, his cool request for a 'trusteeship' over Libya. Apologists explained that Russia was merely asking for what she lost in 1917, or seeking security against a recrudescence of German power. 'Stalin is a realist,' Roosevelt informed the Polish patriot, Mikolajczyk, 'and we mustn't forget, when we judge Russians actions, that the Soviet régime has had only two years of experience in international relations. But of one thing I am certain. Stalin is not an Imperialist.'[5]

This, of course, could not be said of Winston Churchill. The more admiring the American President grew of Stalin, the more critical he became of Churchill. The fact that Britain was a democracy and the Soviet Union a dictatorship seemed to him a trifling difference compared to the fact that Russia was a satisfied power while Britain undoubtedly would attempt to re-establish her hold upon her colonial empire. Roosevelt not only regarded colonies as nurturing the seeds of future conflicts, but as morally indefensible. His son, Elliott, claims that Roosevelt told Churchill bluntly: 'I can't believe that we can fight a war against Fascist slavery, and at the same time not work to free people all over the world from a backward colonial policy.'[6] Later, he remarked to Elliott, 'I've tried to make it clear to Winston – and the others – that while we're their allies and in it to victory by their side, they must never get the idea that we're in it just to help them hang on to their archaic, medieval Empire ideas . . . Great Britain signed the Atlantic Charter. I hope they realise that we mean to make them live up to it.'[7] Secretary of State Hull reflected the same view when he told Congress that a United Nations organisation, operating under the Atlantic Charter, would do away with the need 'for spheres of influence, for alliances, for balance of power, or any of the special arrangements through which, in the unhappy past, nations strove to safe-guard their security or promote their interests.'[8] Like Roosevelt, Hull believed that America 'must and could get on with the Soviet Union' which was possible as long as Washington was 'patient and forbearing.'

Churchill's appraisal of Joseph Stalin was very different. There were

5 *The Pattern of Soviet Domination*, Stanislaw Mickolajczyk, Sampson, Low Marston & Co., London; McGraw Hill, New York 1948, p. 65
6 *As He Saw It*, Elliott Roosevelt, Duell Sloan & Pearce, New York, 1946, p. 97.
7 *As He Saw It*, Elliott Roosevelt, pp. 121–2.
8 *Memoirs*, Cordell Hull, MacMillan, New York, 1947, p. 1467.

times when he fell under the Marshal's spell. Writing to Eden after the Teheran Conference he spoke of 'that great and good man', and at Yalta, bathing in the general euphoria induced by the closing months of the war, he said that he walked through the world 'with greater hope and courage' because of his friendship with the Russian leader. But down from the summit and back in his own country, Churchill took a much cooler view. 'Trying to maintain good relations with a Communist is like wooing a crocodile,' he told Sir Alan Brooke. 'You do not know whether to tickle it under the chin or to beat it over the head. When it opens its mouth you cannot tell whether it is trying to smile or preparing to eat you up.'[9] As D-Day approached he became increasingly anxious about Russian intentions. 'Are we going to acquiesce in the Communisation of the Balkans and perhaps of Italy?' he wrote to Anthony Eden, his Foreign Secretary on 4th May. 'I am of opinion on the whole that we ought to come to a definite conclusion about it, and that if our conclusion is that we resist the Communist infusion and invasion we should put it to them (the Russians) pretty plainly at the best moment that military events permit. We should of course have to consult the United States first.'[10]

The United States was not consulted and no proposal was ever made. No doubt the Foreign Secretary felt that such a move would do more harm than good for he was well aware of the suspicions entertained by Roosevelt and his advisers towards Churchill. 'The Prime Minister is a very great man,' Joseph Davies, a former U.S. Ambassador to Moscow, reported to Washington, 'but there is no doubt that he is "first, last and all the time" a great Englishman. I could not escape the impression that he was basically more concerned over preserving England's position in Europe than in preserving peace.' On this, the Chairman of the American Joint Chiefs of Staff, Admiral Leahy, commented: 'This was consistent with our Staff estimates of Churchill's attitude throughout the war.'[11]

It is not surprising that although Churchill revealed his anxieties about Soviet expansion to his own advisers he did not raise the subject with Roosevelt. Not only did he bear the stigma of Prime Minister of an 'empire', but the war had bled Britain white and

9 *Triumph in the West*, Arthur Bryant, Collins, London, 1959, p. 140.

10 *The Second World War*, Vol. v, Winston Churchill, Cassell, London; Houghton Mifflin, Boston 1956, p. 623

11 *Churchill, Roosevelt, Stalin*, Herbert Feis, Princeton University Press, 1957, pp. 650–2.

rendered her dependent on American financial aid. Churchill could not afford to undermine his delicate relationship with the President by impugning an ally in whom the latter had placed his confidence. Furthermore, public opinion favoured Roosevelt's outlook rather than Churchill's. The resistance of the Russian people and the suffering inflicted upon them had aroused the admiration and sympathy of the whole western world. No other country had paid such a fearful price. The scorched earth policy carried out by Hitler's armies had not only devastated thousands of miles of countryside, and countless cities, but had rendered homeless 25,000,000 people who were living in caves and mud huts. The flooding of the coal mines of the Donetz had paralysed Russian industry and seven million soldiers had died on the battlefield. When an Allied official criticised the undisciplined behaviour of the Red Army in Germany, a Russian officer is said to have replied: 'This is not the Red Army. The Red Army perished on the battle-fields in 1941 and 1942. These are the hordes of Asia whom we have whipped to war so that we might roll back the German on-slaught.'[12]

Roosevelt's faith in Russia and his ardent desire for friendship was shared overwhelmingly by the American and British peoples, and at the Yalta Conference, in February, 1945, three months before the end of the war, many observers felt that this trust had not been misplaced. Stalin was genial and smiling, at times almost senti-mental. 'I am talking,' he declared after dinner, 'as an old man; that is why I am talking so much. But I want to drink to our alliance, that it should not lose its character of intimacy, or its free expression of views. In the history of diplomacy I know of no such close alliance of three Great Powers as this . . .'[13]

Stalin's good humour undoubtedly sprang from the fact that the Red Army was now in a commanding position. All the capitals of Eastern Europe were in its hands and the capitals of central Europe within its grasp. Malinovsky was about to accept the surrender of Budapest and only 80 miles from Vienna – Koniev was less than 120 miles from Prague – and Zhukov 45 miles from Berlin.

With victory approaching, the future of Germany was raised on

12 *Four Power Control in Germany and Austria 1945-46*, Balfour and Mair, Royal Institute of International Affairs, Oxford University Press, 1956, p. 40.
13 *The Second World War*, Vol. vi, Winston Churchill, p. 316.

the agenda. Whatever differences the three leaders had about Europe as a whole, this was a subject on which they had been in rough accord from the very first. Nazism and Prussianism must be rooted out so that the 'Teutonic urge for domination' never again should be allowed to tear the world to pieces. It had long been agreed that the whole of Germany would come under military occupation until a Peace Conference settled the future. If necessary Allied troops would remain for twenty-five years. The country would be divided into three zones, administered separately by the three Powers. The zonal boundaries had been hammered out by a European Advisory Committee and accepted by those concerned. The American sector lay in the south-west; the British in the west, embracing the Ruhr – and the Russians in the east.

The Russian zone was much the largest comprising 40 per cent of Germany's 1937 territory; 36 per cent of its population, 33 per cent of its productive resources. Nevertheless, America and Britain felt that their representatives on the Advisory Council, Mr Gilbert Winant and Sir William Strang, had done well, as it looked as though the Russian army would advance much farther than the sector assigned to it.

It had also been agreed that the city of Berlin, enlarged to a nine-mile radius, would be administered jointly by the three powers. Here the Allied Control Commission would sit, headed by the commanders-in-chief of the three armies, who would act as a co-ordinating committee. Although Berlin lay, like an island, 120 miles within the Soviet zone, the Western Allies had not thought it necessary to demand a guarantee of free access; Mr Winant was convinced that free access was implicit in the undertaking.

At Yalta Mr Churchill pressed for the inclusion of France as one of the occupying powers. Stalin objected on the grounds that 'in this war France opened the gates to the enemy'[14] – a strange observation in view of his own pact with Hitler. But Churchill fought hard, for Roosevelt had remarked, almost casually, that American troops probably would not remain in Europe more than two years. The Prime Minister knew that Britain could not shoulder the burden alone; and in the end Stalin gave his assent on the proviso that the French sector would be carved out of the American and British zones.

14 *Speaking Frankly*, James Byrnes, William Heinemann, London; Harper and Row, New York, 1947, p. 25.

Stalin then raised the subject of German dismemberment to which all three leaders had given their approval in principle. 'At Teheran,' wrote Churchill, 'Mr Roosevelt had suggested dividing Germany into five parts, and he, Stalin, had agreed with him. I, on the other hand, had hesitated and only wanted to split her into two, namely Prussia and Austria-Bavaria, with the Ruhr and Westphalia under international control. The time had now come, he, Stalin, said, to take a definite decision.'[15]

Roosevelt had always favoured a tough peace. Indeed, a few months previously, at Quebec, he had approved the Morgenthau Plan. This notorious proposal, drawn up by the head of the American Treasury, Henry Morgenthau, Jr., severed East Prussia, the Ruhr, Silesia and the Saar from Germany. Its purpose was to strip the country of all means of heavy industry and turn it into a pastoral community. Roosevelt not only had accepted the plan, but persuaded Churchill to initial it as well. Later, when the War Secretary, Mr Stimson, remonstrated with the President at the un-American vindictiveness of the scheme, he had retracted.

Although Churchill later was to cite as one of the 'morals' of his history of the Second World War: 'In Victory: Magnanimity', his own scheme was not much different from the Morgenthau Plan. When he went to Moscow in 1944 he encouraged Stalin to think of a Federation of South German States which meant giving Bavaria, Baden and Württemberg to Austria, a separate Rhineland state; and international control of the Ruhr, the Saar and the Kiel Canal. East Prussia and part of Silesia would go to Poland. The moderate voices of academics, such as E. H. Carr, were lost in the din. Carr, while acknowledging the frightening defects of the German character, insisted that the only way to achieve a lasting peace was to enlist the support of young Germans for the integration of Germany in a new European pattern.

Dismemberment nearly became an accomplished fact at Yalta. Churchill told Eden that he had 'been struck at every point where I have sounded opinion at the depth of feeling that would be aroused by a policy of "putting poor Germany on her legs again".'[16] Although the Prime Minister was further influenced by Stalin and Roosevelt, a Carthaginian peace was not at all characteristic of him; and perhaps this was why he recoiled at the last moment. 'We are

15 *The Second World War*, Vol. vi, Winston Churchill, p. 307.
16 *The Second World War*, Vol. vi, Winston Churchill, p. 306.

dealing with the fate of eighty million people,' he pointed out, 'and that requires more than eighty minutes to consider.' 'I said that we all agreed that Germany should be dismembered,' he wrote in his history, 'but that the actual method was much too complicated to be settled in five or six days . . . Mr Roosevelt suggested asking our Foreign Secretaries to produce a plan for studying the questions within twenty-four hours and a definite plan for dismemberment within a month. Here, for a time, the matter was left.'[17]

The Americans left Yalta convinced that a new day had dawned. Stalin had promised to hold free elections in all the territories liberated by his armies, and had declared enthusiastic support for the embryo United Nations organisation. Yet by the end of March Russia had broken every major pledge. The King of Roumania was given an ultimatum forcing him to dissolve his government and to appoint a communist Prime Minister; members of the Polish underground, invited to Moscow to discuss the formation of a broader government, were arrested and later put on trial; and it was announced that Molotov would not, after all, be able to attend the preliminary meeting in San Francisco to set up the 'United Nations' organisation.

Churchill's worst forebodings seemed to be coming true. The only good news was the fact that Germany's western front had collapsed – American and British troops had crossed the Rhine and were striking deep into Germany, north and south of the Ruhr. The Russian armies, on the other hand, meeting fierce resistance in Silesia and Pomerania, were advancing comparatively slowly on Berlin. For the first time it looked probable that Montgomery's army would get there first.

But on 28th March General Eisenhower altered his plans. He decided to by-pass Berlin and to thrust due east to the Leipzig-Dresden area where he could join hands with the Russians and cut the remaining German forces in half. He confided his plan to Stalin who agreed with alacrity that 'Berlin had lost its former strategic significance.'

Now the rift that Hitler had talked about so long, and was still discussing in his air raid shelter in Berlin was opening. But the disagreement was between Britain and America. Churchill was in a state of consternation. He telephoned to Eisenhower and begged

17 ibid., p. 327.

him to reconsider his decision. His own views on Stalin's aims were, however, so alien to American thought that he could not employ arguments which were really telling; all he could do was to insist that Berlin, as a symbol of German resistance, was still of paramount importance. He telegraphed Roosevelt suggesting that if the Russians captured Berlin, as well as Vienna, they would be able to claim an 'overwhelming contribution' to victory which might make them increasingly difficult to deal with. 'I therefore consider that from a political standpoint we should march as far east into Germany as possible, and that should Berlin be within our grasp we should take it.'[18]

But Roosevelt was dying and military decisions were referred to General Marshall who firmly supported Eisenhower's 'strategic concept'. Marshall believed that politics had no place in war and that 'the single objective should be quick and complete victory.' 'Such psychological and political advantages,' he wired a few days later, 'as would result from the possible capture of Berlin ahead of the Russians should not override the imperative military considerations which, in our opinion, is the destruction, and dismemberment of the German armed forces.'[19]

Roosevelt died on 12th April; Hitler had shot himself on 30th April; Berlin fell to the Russians on 2nd May. On 4th May Eisenhower, whose armies were about to enter Czechoslovakia, conveyed his intention of proceeding to Prague to the Soviet Chief-of-Staff, General Antonov. Although Prague was anyone's prize – just as Berlin had been – the Russians reacted violently. Such a move, they said, would interfere with their own plans; accordingly would General Eisenhower be good enough to halt his armies? Eisenhower gracefully deferred, and Prague was liberated by the Russians on 9th May. 'As a war waged by a coalition draws to its end political aspects have a mounting importance,' Churchill wrote in his history. '. . . It is true that American thought is . . . disinterested in matters which seem to relate to territorial acquisitions, but when wolves are about the shepherd must guard his flock, even if he does not himself care for mutton.'[20]

Hitler's armies surrendered unconditionally at midnight on 8th-9th

18 *The Second World War*, Vol. vi, Winston Churchill, p. 407.
19 *The Struggle for Europe*, Chester Wilmot, p. 693.
20 *The Second World War*, Vol. vi, Winston Churchill, p. 399.

May. Germany, as it had been for three-quarters of a century, had ceased to exist. Half the territory with which she had begun the war was occupied by Russians and Poles. Millions of German refugees who had fled before the Soviet armies were swarming through the countryside of the western sectors. And seven million displaced persons, who had been used as foreign labour, were on the loose, prowling through the villages, looting and murdering. The great cities were in such ruins that Air-Marshal Tedder compared them to Babylon and Carthage. Thousands of bridges were down and miles of railway tracks reduced to twisted metal. Not a single canal, including the great Rhine waterway, was navigable. Although Hitler's last, frenzied order to 'scorch the earth' had not been obeyed by his own people, allied airmen had achieved the same result.

Germany was no longer a nation for there was no longer a government. Admiral Dönitz was recognised as Hitler's successor only long enough for the Allies to see that their terms of surrender were being carried out. A fortnight later he and other members of the defunct Nazi government were in prison. There was not even an administration, except at parish or rural district level, and then only in the remoter areas. Most of the officials were Nazis and they had vanished in the last hours before the surrender. One minute they were seen on the roads in sleek black cars, honking furiously, pulling up at petrol stations and demanding fuel that long ago had run out, and the next they had disappeared. Sometimes they slipped into the gentlemen's lavatory and returned ten minutes later dressed in civilian clothes; other times they drove along until they came to a clump of trees, behind which they made their change. Then they abandoned their cars and melted into the stream of refugees.

Now all was ended; no German authority existed; only allied officers moving into the villages, towns and cities, pasting up notices on town halls and church doors: 'We come as conquerors, but not as oppressors.' Although this was not strictly true, it was the only ray of hope for the Germans.

CHAPTER II

Conquerors but not Oppressors

'It is a mistake to try and write out on little pieces of paper,' wrote Churchill to Eden at the end of 1944, 'what the vast emotions of an outraged and quivering world will be, either immediately after the struggle is over or when the inevitable cold fit follows the hot . . . there is therefore wisdom in reserving one's decisions as long as possible and until all the facts and forces that will be potent at the moment are revealed.'[1]

If Churchill's pronouncement had been the result of cool deliberation there might have been wisdom in it, but he was, in fact, excusing himself to Eden for having virtually no plans at all. Yet the Allies were embarking upon one of the most ambitious projects ever undertaken by victors in a war. For the first time in history the entire structure of a large, complex industrial state was to be reorganised and rebuilt by the conquerors themselves. There was not even to be a puppet German government to carry out the Allies' orders, for the influence of National Socialism had been so all-pervasive and the opposition so feeble that there seemed no hope of finding Germans with sufficient authority. As the Americans and British had already discovered, even when the Allies shared a common political outlook, the difficulties of reaching agreement on how the occupation should be carried out were enormous.

Ever since 1942 high level official committees in both the United States and the United Kingdom had been sitting and discussing the future of Germany. All aspects were considered; legal, economic, military and political. The committees received little guidance from their governments but they put forward some sensible suggestions. It was assumed that Germany would be disarmed and her industries be so limited that she would not again be able to wage war. As far as was practicable, all traces of National Socialism were to be abolished, the laws of Hitler's government rescinded, the party and ancillary institutions disbanded and the

1 *The Second World War*, Vol. vi, Winston Churchill, p. 306.

leaders brought to trial in some form. For the good of Europe and world trade, it was recommended that Germany, whatever her political future, should be treated as an economic whole and that her level of industry should be sufficient to enable her gradually to resume a 'tolerable economic existence.' Almost unanimously the committees were against the dismemberment of Germany into separate states. They favoured a federal or decentralised democratic régime and a Bill of Rights guaranteeing the basic democratic freedoms.

Inevitably, on some points, the committees differed among themselves. The foreign and economic experts in both countries recommended a civil administration for conquered Germany; the United States military departments considered that 'the surrender and recuperation of Germany were purely military matters which would have to be decided at military level.'[2]

In spite of the 'Economic Consequences of the Peace' after the First World War, which John Maynard Keynes had so brilliantly illuminated in his book of that title, Germany was expected to repair the physical damage she had caused, although reparations were to be in kind rather than money. However, there were wide differences of opinion over the amount Germany could provide, not to mention the theories about frontiers and constitutions which were almost as numerous as the committee members.

But detailed planning by government never got beyond an elementary stage. Every time the work of the committee reached the summit it was thrown into confusion by some new decision. First, in January, 1943, came Roosevelt's announcement of 'unconditional surrender' as the only terms on which the war could come to an end. Perhaps Churchill was right in saying that any detailed terms acceptable to all the allies would have 'looked so terrible when put on paper, and so far exceeded what was in fact done, that their publication would only have stimulated German resistance,'[3] but neither he nor Roosevelt ever faced the implications of a decision to which Stalin had only indicated assent by silence.

Until then both Anglo-Saxon leaders had been clear that the war was being fought, not against 'the people' of the Axis nations, but

2 Balfour and Mair. Op. Cit., p. 17.
3 *The Second World War*, Vol. iv, Winston Churchill, p. 617, also Churchill's memorandum to his cabinet colleagues setting out the minimum requirements in Jan. '44.

against 'their guilty and barbaric leaders'. Now their attitude became ambivalent. 'I do not want them (the Germans) to starve to death,' wrote Roosevelt to Hull in August, 1944, 'but, as an example, if they need food to keep body and soul together beyond what they already have, they should be fed three times a day from army soup kitchens . . . the German people as a whole must have it driven home to them that the whole nation has been engaged in a lawless conspiracy against the decencies of modern civilisation.'4 Churchill went even farther and excluded the Germans from the Atlantic Charter which was to assure the future peace of the world: 'The term "unconditional surrender" does not mean that the German people will be enslaved or destroyed. It means, however, that the Allies will not be bound to them at the moment of surrender by any pact or obligation — there will be for instance, no question of the Atlantic Charter applying to Germany as a matter of right . . . "unconditional surrender" means that the victors have a free hand . . .'5

But a free hand is not much use if you cannot agree how to use it and as the war neared its end agreement was farther away than ever. The only guidance given to the British and American officers and officials who were to enforce the terms of unconditional surrender came not from their government, but from the Chiefs of Staff in military orders issued to their commanders in the field. Even these differed between the two countries.

In 1944, while the Western Allies were approaching the Rhine, an attempt had been made to frame joint instructions for the Anglo-American forces. The directive of the Anglo-American Chiefs of Staff to the Supreme Commander ran: 'Military government will be established and will extend over all parts of Germany, including Austria . . . by virtue of your position you are clothed with supreme legislative, executive and judicial authority and power in the areas occupied by the forces under your command.'6

Some advice on how these powers might be executed was given and more detailed instructions, which had been worked upon for many months by the Civil Affairs department of the British and American armies, were incorporated in a 'Handbook for Military

4 *On Active Service in Peace and War*, Henry L. Stimson and McGeorge Bundy, Harper and Row, New York, 1948, Hutchinson, London, 1949, p. 334.
5 *Hansard*, 22nd February, 1944.
6 *Civil Affairs and Military Government North-West Europe 1944-46*, F. S. V. Donnison, H.M. Stationery Office, London, 1961, pp. 191-2.

Government in Germany prior to Defeat or Surrender.' These plans, which were given the code name Eclipse, were reasonably constructive. It was anticipated that local government in Germany would probably have collapsed except at the urban or rural district level and it had to be built up again from there. In general: 'The administration shall be firm. It will at the same time be just and humane . . . you will strongly discourage fraternisation . . . military occupation is intended (i) to aid military operations, (ii) to destroy Nazism . . ., (iii) to maintain and preserve law and order, (iv) to restore normal conditions among the civil population as soon as possible . . .'[7]

An economic 'guide' stressed the need to keep full production and distribution going and to restore the various public utilities and the coal mines to full working order as soon as possible. Productive capacity, apart from munitions, and control of prices and wages were also to be preserved. This was enough to be going on with and General Eisenhower ordered the handbook to be issued to all under his command at S.H.A.E.F. (Supreme Headquarters Allied Expeditionary Forces) on the understanding that further instructions would be forthcoming once surrender had taken place. But he was over-optimistic.

When American troops captured Aachen in September, 1944, military government officials, using the handbook as a guide, sought the help of the clergy in finding men to take over jobs formerly held by Nazis. They therefore followed the advice of the Bishop of Aachen in appointing a new mayor. Unfortunately, the business man whom the Bishop recommended proved to have had an unsavoury Nazi past. The Press got hold of the story, the American public was shocked and Roosevelt, egged on by Morgenthau, publicly denounced the S. H. A. E. F. handbook. Three months later it was replaced by a directive known as J.S.C. 1067 which declared that Germany was 'not to be occupied for the purpose of liberation but as a defeated enemy nation'. No steps were to be taken 'looking forward' to economic rehabilitation, and de-Nazification was to be carried out in such a way that mistakes of the kind made at Aachen could not recur. This new directive was so bleakly negative that Mr Lewis Douglas, one of the distinguished American industrialists who had been co-opted to help plan the future of Germany and who was later Ambassador in London,

7 F. S. V. Donnison, *Op. Cit.*, p. 197.

exploded: 'This thing was assembled by economic idiots. It makes no sense to forbid the most skilled workers in Europe from producing as much as they can for a continent that is short of everything.' Douglas flew to Washington to try to get the plan revised but found that 'fatal bowknots had been tied' and eventually resigned.[8]

The British reluctantly accepted J.S.C. 1067 so long as S. H. A. E. F. was in existence, but once Military Government had been established they went their own way. As neither the French nor the Russians had issued any handbooks at all, it could only be by a miracle of co-operation between the Commanders who were to become the Military Governors that the Occupation could be a joint operation at all. It depended above all on that understanding between the Russians and Americans in which Roosevelt had such implicit trust. As Harry Hopkins, Roosevelt's special adviser, was to say later to his biographer, Robert Sherwood, 'There wasn't any doubt in the minds of the President or any of us that we could live with them (the Russians) and get along with them peacefully for as far into the future as any of us could imagine.'[9] This faith was now to be tested in the city which Eisenhower had considered of no particular strategic importance, Hitler's former capital, Berlin.

'This is more like the face of the moon than any city I have ever imagined,' wrote William Shirer in an article for the *New York Herald Tribune* a few weeks after the capitulation. The destruction made the senses reel, for it was difficult to imagine how anyone had survived the thousands of tons of bombs and shells which had almost erased the huge capital city from the map. Hundreds of streets had been completely obliterated, stations were ghostly shells; the famous Tiergarten a battlefield, the former Imperial Palace roofless, Hitler's government buildings charred remains.

'The spacious avenues, once the pride of the city – the Friedrichstrasse and the Leipzigerstrasse, the Kurfürstendamm and the Unter den Linden – were so covered with debris that bulldozers had to be set to work to clear a passage even for tanks and armoured vehicles. And everywhere came the putrid smell of decaying flesh to remind the living that thousands of bodies still remained beneath the funeral pyres of rubble.'

8 *Diplomat Among Warriors*, Robert Murphy, Collins, London; Doubleday, New York, 1964, p. 308.
9 *Roosevelt and Hopkins*, Robert E. Sherwood, Harper Bros., New York, 1948, p. 370.

But to the 'hordes of Asia,' in dirty tattered uniforms who had moved across Europe in horse-drawn transport, Berlin still seemed a fabulous prize. The Americans, following the Russian maxim that the only way to make a friend was to be a friend, had given the Russians duplicate plates for the printing of Occupation Marks, on the understanding that a strict account would be kept. The Russians, however, had seized the opportunity of printing enough notes to pay their troops months and even years of arrears without seeing fit to mention the matter. The soldiers, quite naturally, went on a wild spending spree and anything they couldn't buy they looted. Silver, jewellery, cameras and particularly Mickey Mouse watches were what they most wanted. Some of them wore five or six watches on a single arm.

Their night life was simple, for they soon developed the habit of breaking into houses and flats and raping the female inhabitants. Indeed, any girl unwise enough to walk about the city, even in day-light, was likely to hear the dreaded cry '*Komm Frau*'. 'A Russian would catch the first girl he saw on the street, grab her by the wrist and with the leering invitation "*Komm Frau*", would drag her into the nearest building and rape her. If no building was convenient he would violate her on the street.[10] And if a German father or brother tried to protect the victim he was promptly shot. Although German women resorted to every trick to make themselves unattractive – unkempt hair, dirty faces, ragged clothes – the Russians were not easy to repel. Two hundred and thirty girls were treated in the same Berlin hospital on a single day.

Zhukov could well have replied, had he been informed, that the German girls were lucky to have a hospital; their counterparts in Russia who had been raped by the Germans had had to fend for themselves. But for the sake of Russian prestige alone he had to restore discipline and get the city into some sort of working order before he could welcome his allies. For under the Yalta Agreement Berlin was not only to be governed by a four-power Kommandatura consisting of the Military Governors of the different sectors, it was to become the headquarters of the Allied Control Council, the supreme authority for Germany as a whole. Zhukov, therefore, had much to do.

His first concern was to provide diversion for his troops. Within two days of entering the city he had ordered cabarets, theatres and

10 *Berlin Command*, Brig. Frank Howley, Putnam, New York, 1950, p. 66.

restaurants to reopen and was soon organising concerts and football matches. At the same time he was replacing the victorious army with second-line occupational troops and putting these to work to restore the electrical supply lines and repair the thousands of breaks in the water and sewage mains.

But Zhukov had other objectives as well. Although Stalin had once told Mikolajczyk, the Polish leader, that communism 'fitted Germany as a saddle fitted a cow', the Russian leader, at least, was quite clear about the purpose of the occupation. What Stalin wanted was not the annihilation of Germany, but a communist Germany, a fulfilment of the revolution which so nearly came about in 1919. In his victory message of 9th May, Stalin had publicly abandoned the idea of dismemberment. Now giant posters were appearing in Berlin, sometimes on ruined walls, sometimes on specially erected hoardings, quoting the speech he had made in 1942 in which he had described the 'rumours' that the Russian army intended to destroy the German State as 'an absurd calumny'. 'It would be ludicrous to identify Hitler's clique with the German people,' proclaimed the huge headlines. 'History teaches that Hitlers come and go, but the German people and the German State remain.'

Stalin had already foreseen that the zones might mean the division of Germany; realising also that the size of the Russian zone could be decisive, he had begun proclaiming that Germany must be treated as an economic whole even before his troops had entered Berlin. From the moment they were in possession 'unification' became the slogan with which he hoped to win all Germans to his side. For the Germans in the Russian zone, therefore, collaboration became the touchstone. Whoever would obey the Russians could eat; whoever would collaborate could become a member of the new élite even if he had previously been a Nazi. 'We are the friends of the little Nazis' shouted the second batch of posters in the city, and the Russian administration soon showed that this was no idle boast.

Zhukov's orders were explicit; first take everything in Berlin and the zone which could conceivably be of use to Russia, then get German industry going so as to supply what Russia needed and, at the same time, organise the zone so that it could fit as quickly as possible into the rapidly expanding Communist world. The Marshal wasted no time.

In the first few days all the horses in the outer suburbs, which had many small holdings, were rounded up and driven away along with seven thousand cows. Most of them came from what were soon to be the Western Zones. Then, still without regard for his allies, he ordered the Russian army to remove every useful piece of equipment they could find in the western sectors of the city. The refrigerator at the slaughter-house, generators from the power stations, machinery from every mill and factory, stoves and pipes from restaurant kitchens, typewriters, desks and filing cabinets were all taken and classified as 'reparations'. The work was done hurriedly by unskilled men and many valuable machine tools were ruined when yanked out with crowbars instead of simply being unscrewed.

Having denuded Berlin, Zhukov set about organising his zone. As the Russians needed the collaboration of the bourgeois factory owners and business men to get industry going, they began by creating four political parties each of which was allowed to establish links with parties or groups in the other zones. This was already familiar strategy in the 'people's democracies' of eastern Europe, where peasant or socialist parties were being allowed to exist until such time as they could be infiltrated or taken over by members of the Communist Party itself. In Germany, therefore, not only the Communist Party, but the Social, Liberal and Christian Democrats were all licensed within a few weeks of the Occupation. Almost immediately, led by the German communists, they held a joint convention, announced a common programme of rehabilitation and set up anti-Fascist committees which at once became a means of general intimidation.

Within this framework the communist take-over began. A new press followed party lines. The Red Army founded the *Tägliche Rundschau* which became the main newspaper of Berlin and each of the other parties was allowed its own journal, published under communist supervision but with just enough freedom to give an illusion of democratic life. The Berlin radio was situated in what was to become the British sector; undeterred, the Russians took it over and remained there even after the British arrived, confident that they could retaliate effectively if any move were made to get them out.

In every town mayors and a council were appointed, with German communists selecting, on instructions, members of the 'democratic' parties who had survived the concentration camps or who had an anti-Nazi record as the chief officers, but retaining control behind this façade themselves. In Berlin, a sixty-seven-year-old architect, Arthur Werner, became mayor with nine councillors from the non-communist parties; the six communists, however, controlled the police and education and really ruled the city.

The Soviet Reparations Commission, the central organisation responsible directly to Moscow and working closely with the army, was dismantling factories capable of producing war materials or reorganising them to supply the Russian army. 'Agitprop', a Russian commercial agency run by Tulpanov, an ex-army Com-missar who formerly had been an engineer and spent much time in Germany in the nineteen-twenties, set about reorganising German industry according to a plan designed to benefit the Russians and at the same time make the transition to a full communist state easier. Factories which had belonged to the Nazi state were nationalised. Those which had been owned by individual Nazis were either given to 'reliable' supporters of the Communist Party or taken over by the workers at communist instigation. Those which remained in the hands of their original owners were so supervised that the proprietors were left in no doubt about the desirability of obeying Russian orders.

Two fundamental reforms were quickly carried out. All bank accounts were blocked, not just temporarily but permanently. However much money a man might own he was only allowed to withdraw three hundred marks. This, at a single blow, ensured the destruction of all private fortunes and put people with very different backgrounds on exactly the same level. To live, everyone had to get a job. Those who had done well under the Nazis were deprived of their ill-gotten gains and those who wanted to succeed under the new régime were totally dependent on the Russians and their German henchmen for their living. If they collaborated, they reaped their reward – extra rations, theatre tickets, higher pay. If they were obstructive they joined the thousands clearing rubble and rebuilding the city. The reform cut back production, stifled new enterprise and kept the standard of living of the Germans in the Russian zone at or below that of neighbouring satellites, but it laid the foundation of the sort of society the Russians wanted to see.

The second measure was a wholesale land reform. This had been planned in detail and was put into effect by Edwin Hornle, a German communist who was flown in especially from Russia. It took the now familiar pattern of a wholesale reduction of large holdings and the creation of new smallholders who, in time, would lend themselves easily to collectivisation as taxation and mechanisation made the size of their farms uneconomic. No one was allowed to own more than two hundred and fifty acres; most owned far less. Excess land and land formerly owned by 'war criminals' or the Nazi state, was confiscated without compensation and some of it given to communal bodies like schools and hospitals, whose members were totally ignorant of farming and therefore dependent upon the party or state officials who planned and supervised their production. Again the effect was to reduce the supply of food just when it was most desperately needed. On the other hand the reform created a kind of peasant proletariat whose lot, even when collectivisation came, might be preferable to that of the factory or mine worker. The new peasants, therefore, might be expected to resist any attempt to revert to a bourgeois society.

Zhukov's tactics were successful. There was never any question of the Russians being popular, but they were obeyed and collaboration was not entirely involuntary. Of course most German communists were enthusiastic, while men like Jacob Kaiser, who had escaped arrest by the Gestapo and led the Christian Democrats in East Berlin, or the liberals Lohr and Kastner, still clung to the belief that all anti-Fascists ought to be able to work together and remained members of the zonal hierarchy for several years.

Every now and then the Russians seemed to falsify their optimism. Individually they behaved towards the Germans with a baffling mixture of waywardness and ruthlessness. No orders about non-fraternisation had been issued and, having put the Germans of their choice into positions of power, Russian officers and officials entertained and befriended them. On the other hand, if any German mayor or worker showed signs of non-co-operation, he or she was at once singled out by the communist-controlled press, named, denounced as a 'Fascist' or 'reactionary', and dismissed. Women who resisted the Russian soldiers might be shot out of hand or given the present of a wrist watch according to the whim of the moment. Drink made the Russians maudlin or trigger-happy and no one knew what to expect.

The Russian attitude towards de-Nazification was at least easy for the Germans to understand. Stalin regarded members of the German armed forces as a captive labour force and deported between two and three million to Russia. Thousands of others captured in uniform were set to work in the ruined German cities. Members of the S.S., caught through denunciation, were often shot out of hand, their bodies left on the street with an X tattooed across their backs by tommy-gun bullets. On the other hand well-known Nazis who were prepared to co-operate made a spectacular jump from the Nazi to the communist hierarchy. At the Moscow Foreign Ministers' Conference in 1947, in reply to Molotov's usual gibe at the ineffectiveness of western de-Nazification, Ernest Bevin was able to cite a list of names: Markgraf, who had been much decorated for his exploits as an S.S. commander on the eastern front, Chief of Police in Berlin; Steidle, formerly an officer in the Wehrmacht, Minister for Labour and Health; Lundwehr, chief Nazi Trade Commissioner in the Balkans, now head of the Economics Department of the Berlin City Government; Augustin the German tank expert, making tanks for the Russians; Ochel, the Nazis' best locomotive engineer, working on the railways. There were a host of others, research engineers for jet engines, submarines, drainage, scientists of all kinds whose names never appeared in any official list. 'As we are unlikely to be affected politically,' commented a Russian officer, 'we use the brains of the Nazis as much as possible.'[11] This suited most Germans.

In the nine weeks in which Zhukov ruled Berlin alone, therefore, he not only made himself master of the city but impressed the Soviet stamp heavily on the Russian zone. The City Council and the twenty Borough Councils beneath it were administered at the dictates of the German communists who, in turn, carried out the orders of their Russian masters. The police, into which thousands of those 'little Nazis' whose allegiance the Russians claimed had been recruited, obeyed the Councils. Russian troops and officials occupied the best buildings, including those into which the Western Allies hoped to move, and controlled such stretches of road and railway as were usable and led into the city. Among the ruins banks, swimming pools, libraries, a telephone service was functioning and plays and films which the Russians thought suitable were being performed or shown at eleven theatres and a hundred and fifty cinemas. The courts were sitting, dispensing laws which were being revised by the Communist Party or giving effect to the

11 *The Eastern Zone and Soviet Policy in Germany* 1945-1950, J. P. Nettl, Oxford University Press, 1951, p. 71.

decrees of the Military Government. And all this resuscitated life was taking place according to Russian time, which meant that it was still light at midnight and dark at seven in the morning. This suited the Russian temperament and, had Zhukov had his way, would have continued indefinitely. Stalin, however, had commitments to his allies which he was not in a position to ignore.

The Western Allies had assumed that the Declaration of Defeat and Assumption of Supreme Authority, which was to be the basis of four-power control, would be made as soon as the fighting was over. British, American and French teams, both for the Control Council and the Kommandatura, were ready and waiting. But first the Declaration itself had to be agreed and, since no right of access to Berlin had ever been granted, Eisenhower and his colleagues found that they had to await the permission of the Russians before they could enter the city. This was not granted until 5th June, a month after the Russians had captured it.

Even then the first meeting was a formality. Elaborate preparations had been made for the reception of the western generals. Flowers had been specially flown in from Russia and bedded out in the grounds round Zhukov's headquarters at Karlshorst on the outskirts of Köpenick; carpenters, plumbers and builders were installing bathrooms and putting the finishing touches up to the moment of arrival. Zhukov expected his guests to stay and had laid on a sumptuous banquet for the evening.

Eisenhower, Montgomery, de Lattre de Tassigny and their staffs arrived before lunch hoping to sign the documents establishing the Control Commission early in the afternoon. The Russians, however, were still haggling over the wording and it was not until around five o'clock that Zhukov invited them across to a building which had been specially prepared. The signing took place under arc lamps and in front of the world's reporters and photographers but when, over drinks, Eisenhower suggested to Zhukov that a small team from the West remain in Berlin to arrange for the arrival of the Control Council, Zhukov refused, saying that the Control Council could not begin to function until all the British and American troops had withdrawn into their own zone. Eisenhower, already annoyed at being kept waiting, left the banquet which Zhukov had prepared almost as soon as it had begun, taking all his colleagues with him.

There was nothing in any agreement to justify the Russian action, but the Red Army was in possession of Berlin and Zhukov's refusal merely emphasised what was to become increasingly apparent – that the Allies could come there only on Russian sufferance. Although Clay, Eisenhower's deputy and soon his successor, re-marked that the Russians seemed to be able to find 'technical reasons at will for breaking any agreement, verbal or written',[12] the Americans brushed aside Churchill's pleas to stand firm and capitulated. Eisenhower did not even get a guarantee of unrestricted entry to Berlin before agreeing to withdraw his troops to his own zone.

But appeasement did not mollify Zhukov. At the next meeting of commanders on 29th June he brusquely announced that no food from the Russian zone would be available to feed the western sectors of Berlin. This was in total contradiction of Allied expectations. Clay and his British counterpart, Sir Ronald Weekes, had been told by their governments that Berlin would be provisioned from its normal sources, although almost all of these now lay under Russian control.

Next the Russians demanded that coal for their sector of Berlin should come from the Ruhr. This was not wholly unreasonable as the coal in their own zone was soft brown coal and they needed hard coal for certain purposes. But while they railed at the British for raising difficulties over transport which the Russians them-selves had created, they made little attempt to keep their own deliveries of brown coal up to schedule. In the end the British supplied almost all the coal for the city.

When Clay and Weekes demanded the use of three railways and two roads to transport the fifty thousand troops they would need for Berlin, Zhukov replied that the demobilisation of the Red Army made this impossible and offered only the single railway line through Magdeburg, the autobahn through Helmstedt and two air corridors. Because they could do nothing about it – short of forcing a passage through the Russian lines – the Western Allies accepted both these humiliating conditions.

But humiliation had only just begun. The movement of the twenty-five thousand United States troops into the American sector of Berlin was timed for 1st July. The day before, General Parks,

12 *Decision in Germany*, Lucius Clay, Heinemann, London; Doubleday, New York, 1950, p. 26.

the American commander, sent an advance reconnaissance party of some five hundred men to prepare the way. In spite of Zhukov's undertaking that no controls or checks would be imposed at the zonal frontiers (the undertaking was never given in writing), the party was halted on the bridge over the Elbe at Dessau where the Russians arbitrarily demanded that the numbers be reduced to thirty-seven officers and a hundred and seventy-five men. Colonel Howley, the Deputy Military Governor designate, argued in vain and eventually selected the stipulated number. Even then they did not reach Berlin.

Colonel Howley described the trip as 'bedlam'. Not only were there innumerable traffic snarls, but the Russians had set up dozens of check points and seemed to delight in creating difficulties. Many of the guards were waving bottles of vodka, so drunk they could hardly stand, but after innumerable toasts the friendliness invariably gave way to officiousness. 'When one particularly obstreperous Red Army officer tried, for no apparent reason, to halt the column at a bridge, an American officer, whose name I have forgotten, but whose deed I will cherish always, jumped from his car and personally deposited the struggling Russian into the ditch . . .'[13]

Howley led his detachment to the Grünewald Forest on the outskirts of the city where the men camped in a protective circle as in the old covered-wagon days on a prairie. General Parks had agreed with General Gortakov, the Russian Military Governor of the city, that the Americans should take over their sector after the Independence Day parade of 4th July. But once again there was a hitch. Just as Colonel Howley was issuing his orders to his Military Government detachment, he was sent for by General Parks and shown a note which the latter had just received from Zhukov which read: 'In view of the fact that Berlin is to be ruled by an Allied Kommandatura . . . your sector will not be handed over to you until the Kommandatura is set up.'[14] It was signed by Zhukov. This time, however, the Americans had had enough. The agreement about the take-over had been made by the Commanders-in-Chief and had been explicit. Howley told Parks that the note was simply a ruse to enable the Russians to finish looting the American sector and Parks agreed with him. They decided to go ahead and take over their six Boroughs as planned.

13 *Berlin Command*, Brigadier-General Frank Howley, Putnam, New York, 1948, p. 43.
14 *Frank Howley*, Op. Cit., p. 48.

Howley knew that the Russians were late risers and ordered his men to move into their offices at daybreak: 'Don't get into a fight, but protect yourselves if you have to. Don't back out and don't make any concessions. If the Russians challenge you tell them you are just obeying orders.'[15] At dawn each little detachment, consisting of three or four Military Government officers and half a dozen enlisted men, entered its borough, woke up the local mayor, took over his house as headquarters, hung out the United States flag and put up posters proclaiming military government and the establishment of American military courts. Then they waited.

The Russians woke at about eleven in the morning and when they discovered the awful fact, ordered the Americans out in some boroughs and began tearing down the United States posters. The Americans sat tight. Howley raced across the city and argued with the Russian general who eventually gave way. For the next week there was an uneasy truce, with Russian and American military government detachments claiming authority in the American sector and the poor German mayors frantically trying to obey conflicting orders. When a Russian officer announced his intention of bringing a detachment of troops to empty the vaults of a bank, Howley brought in tanks to defend it and the Russian stayed away, ringing up later to say that all he really wanted was to empty the contents of his own safe deposit. Once or twice the Americans threatened to shoot when Russian soldiers entered German houses to get at the women. In each case the Russians retreated. Then on 11th July, the Kommandatura was formally instituted and the Russian troops withdrew from the Western sectors, leaving guards only at the gas and electricity centres. It was to take the Americans a long time to have them removed.

And so it went on. Although the Western Allies did manage in the end to get effective control of their sectors in Berlin, it took them many months; the Kommandatura itself never really operated as a unified governing body. The very document on which its constitution rested had been drawn up by Zhukov and included a sentence which laid down that 'all existing regulations and ordinances issued by the commander of the Soviet army garrison and military government of Berlin' should remain in force until specific notice of their cancellation had been given. This meant simply that the Russians could ignore the ordinances of the Kommandatura in

15 *Frank Howley*, Op. Cit., p. 49.

their own zone whenever it suited them by claiming that their actions were in conformity with an ordinance which had been promulgated before the Western Allies arrived. When asked to produce copies of such ordinances they always refused. It also meant that the Berlin City Council and the Borough Councils under it worked to two masters, the Kommandatura and the Russian military government. For the councils were Russian-appointed bodies effectively run by German Communists under Russian instructions.

The City Council also controlled the police force of some twelve thousand men and here again the Russians had established an entrenched position. Markgraf had under him several hand-picked German communists who used the police force as an instrument of Soviet policy. Germans in the western sectors of the city who spoke out against communism or refused to join the communist-dominated trade-union, would suddenly find themselves arrested and brought before the courts where the communists had done their best to install obedient judges. The charge was usually that of obstructing the orders of the Red Army and the sentence often hard labour or even deportation. If the judges proved recalcitrant the Russians resorted to even harsher methods. During the first few months of the Kommandatura's existence five judges, three holding court in the Russian sector, one each in the American and British sectors, were abducted, never to be heard of again.

Russian depredations were not confined to people. Through the Magistrat they tried to confiscate city buses so as to send them to Warsaw and to steal locomotives being used in the western sector. They tore up railway tracks to repair lines in their own zone and raided refugee trains arriving at western terminals, stripping the starving refugees of the last of their belongings. Only when the Americans began to shoot in earnest did the organised looting stop. To Russian protests the Americans replied that if a Russian soldier pulled a gun on an American, the American would be inclined to shoot first; it was part of the American tradition. The only way to avoid killings was for the Russians to assert proper discipline. In the end the Russians agreed to joint patrols and jeeps carrying American, Russian, British and French military policemen became one of the familiar sights of the city. They succeeded in restoring some sort of order. Nevertheless, it could scarcely be argued that the first experience of Russo-American friendship had been reassuring.

CHAPTER III

Retribution

The laurels of victory sit uneasily on democratic heads. The three Western Allies embarked upon the occupation with the avowed intention of punishing the Germans for having surrendered their sovereignty to Hitler, and preparing them gradually for self-government through adult suffrage. The Germans, they were determined, must learn that ultimate power resided in the people. Yet the very nature of military government was a flagrant denial of the principles the Allies were trying to inculcate.

The Allied Control Council was the supreme authority for Germany. This body was composed of the four victorious Commanders-in-Chief who were appointed in the hope that the collaboration they had established in the closing stages of the war could be perpetuated in peace. It wielded absolute power. Eisenhower, Zhukov, Montgomery and de Lattre de Tassigny could consult their governments on matters of general policy, but decisions which they took unanimously affecting Germany as a whole had the force of law. It was true that already the Russians had carried out such far-reaching reforms in their zone that immediate agreement on the form of administration to be applied to the vanquished people was impossible, but it was still hoped that, in the spirit of the 'new dawn' which was Roosevelt's legacy to the world, such differences would be resolved at the summit conference summoned to Potsdam in July. In the meantime Eisenhower and Zhukov had come to a personal arrangement and had announced in the beginning of June that, in the absence of unanimity in the Council, each commander would be supreme in his own zone – words which already had an ominous ring for the Germans.

Eisenhower decided not to move to Berlin, but to make his headquarters in Frankfurt, as he had the task of supervising the transfer of millions of Americans to the Far Eastern theatre of war and facilities in the ruined city were not adequate. The other

Commanders-in-Chief followed suit and remained in their own zones, only travelling to Berlin for the Council meetings. It was agreed that their deputies, Clay, Sokolovsky, Robertson and Koeltz should establish themselves in the capital and bear the brunt of the day-to-day administration.[1]

General Lucius Clay, who was soon to emerge as the most important man in Germany, was an army engineer, an expert in logistics who in pre-war days had supervised multi-million dollar public enterprises. He was a technician who liked to get things done and hoped that too many restrictions would not be placed upon him in the reconstruction. As early as April he had wired to Washington that 'retribution . . . is far greater than realised at home . . . Our planes and artillery have . . . carried the war direct to the homes of the German people . . . We must have freedom here to bring industries back to production.'[2] But Washington was in no mood to listen. Although Truman was both shrewder and more humble than Roosevelt, he was too new a President to make a radical departure from his predecessor's policies; Roosevelt's remark to Stimson that if he had his way he would keep the Germans on the bread-line for twenty-five years still represented American thinking.

The Potsdam Conference, the last summit meeting of the Big Three, began as a meeting between Stalin, Truman and Churchill and ended, after the results of the British general election were known on 26th July, with Mr Attlee in the Prime Minister's chair. It also began with the Americans pressing the Russians to declare war against Japan and ended with the knowledge that the atom bomb was ready for delivery. The bombs were dropped on 9th and 10th August and Japan capitulated four days later. It was soon evident that total victory had hardened Allied hearts.

The Potsdam Agreement, which was published on 2nd August, 1945, in so far as it carried Allied policy towards the Germans any farther, served to strengthen the rigid and negative provisions of the handbook J.S.C. 1067. It was an American-inspired document, drawn up by men who were still living under the late President's influence and designed to tighten the bonds of 'friendship' between the Russians and Americans. It ignored entirely what had hap-

1 Eisenhower and Zhukov were replaced before the end of the year by McNarney and Sokolovsky, and Montgomery by Sir Sholto Douglas in 1946.
2 *The American Occupation of Germany*, J. Gimbel, Stanford University Press, 1968, pp. 5–6.

pened in Berlin since the Russians conquered it, and its clauses were almost wholly punitive.

Although the preamble proclaimed the Allies' intention to prepare the Germans for the 'eventual' reconstruction of their life, the spirit of the document was that of the Morgenthau Plan. Clause 3 stated unequivocally that 'the German people . . . cannot escape responsibility for what they have brought upon themselves, since their own ruthless warfare and the fanatical Nazi resistance have destroyed the German economy and made chaos and suffering inevitable.' Clause 13 laid down that 'in organising the German economy, primary emphasis shall be given to the development of agriculture and peaceful domestic industry'. Most of the other clauses referred to controls, restrictions or prohibitions of some kind to 'ensure the extirpation of Nazism and the reduction of the German standard of life to a level not exceeding the average of other European countries,' a level which statisticians calculated should be 74 per cent of the 1936 figure, regardless of the fact that Germany no longer had access to the food produced by her former eastern provinces and had to support a larger population.

Reparations, dismantling, the trial of 'war criminals,' the removal from positions of responsibility, public or private, of 'all members of the Nazi party who have been more than nominal participants in its activities,' were all provided for. The cession of East Prussia to Russia and Poland was confirmed. After Stalin had excused the Poles for occupying all German territory east of the Oder because all the Germans had 'run away,'[3] the frontier with Germany of the Oder and the western Neisse river was accepted as a *fait accompli*. Ironically, sanction was also given to the 'orderly transfer' of the German population in this and other regions of Eastern Europe. Millions of them were already dead. Almost the only constructive proposal was an instruction that 'Germany should be treated as an economic whole'; it was on this that the Americans and British pinned their hopes.

The fulfilment of the Agreement was left to the Commanders-in-Chief who had now become Military Governors. They duly equipped themselves with all the paraphernalia of government, appointing no fewer than 175 committees in the four zones, staffed by fifty thousand civil servants from the west and only slightly fewer from Russia. But what little hope remained of the Council act-

3 *The Second World War*, Vol. vi, Winston Churchill, p. 327 and p. 567.

ing in unison was immediately dashed by General de Gaulle, who announced that, as France had not been invited to Potsdam, she would not be bound by any of its provisions. Whenever, therefore, a proposal was made in the Council that some organisation be set up to deal with the German economy as a whole, it was met with a French veto. For the French were still bent on the dismemberment of Germany and objected to a centralised organisation of any kind.

As a result, although the Council met monthly, its authority was virtually non-existent. The committees, many of which were in almost constant session, drafted innumerable laws dealing with every aspect of German life from the employment of women in the building industry to limitations on the size of ships, which the Council would duly promulgate; but since there were no central agencies to carry out the Council's decrees, implementation was left to the zonal commanders with the result that many laws were never imposed at all and others only in a sense that differed markedly from one zone to another.

For the Potsdam Agreement had also confirmed that where unanimity could not be reached on questions affecting Germany as a whole, each Commander-in-Chief should retain absolute power in his own zone. Without reference to their Government these Marshals and Generals could determine life or death and exercise complete control over all persons and property. Any German found carrying arms could be court-martialled and shot. Germans could be arrested without warrant and kept in detention without trial. Houses, furniture, and personal belongings could be requisitioned without notice or appeal. Any German could be summarily dismissed from his or her employment or transferred at will from one place to another. Rationing of food was to be continued and prices and wages were to be fixed.

For most Germans, therefore, the end of the war meant the substitution of four military dictatorships for one authoritarian régime, the most obvious difference being that life under the conquerors became even less predictable and more precarious than it had been under Hitler. The bombing and shelling had ceased, yet it is probable that more Germans died in the first two years of the occupation than had been killed in nearly six years of war.

With so many millions on the move in and out of Germany statistics were unreliable and in any case were compiled several years later, but in 1939 it was officially estimated that there were more than ten million 'ethnic' Germans living outside the borders of the Reich and to these must be added those who were settled, sometimes as far east as the Ukraine, during the war. All but a few thousands of these were driven out of their adopted lands in 1945. Yet, when the Federal Government came to compile their own figures, they only put the number of refugees who had reached Western Germany at nine million,[4] including the three million who had fled from the Russian zone, most of whom had always lived within the old German boundaries. When Dr Wenzel, who ran the Protestant Agency for Social Welfare in Berlin, estimated that more than six million Germans had died between May and September, 1945, in Russia, the Russian Zone and Eastern Europe, he may not have been far off the mark.[5]

Probably the heaviest death rate occurred among the Germans driven out of East Prussia, Poland and Czechoslovakia, for in spite of the provisions of the Potsdam Agreement the conditions under which they travelled were appalling. They were herded into cattle trucks and then shunted backwards and forwards for weeks on end. Germans expelled from East Prussia or Czechoslovakia were sent 'home' to Silesia, whence they were immediately expelled again by the Poles.

No one who had seen the way the Poles had been treated during the war could have anything but sympathy for them, yet their revenge was terrible.[6] Few Germans were allowed to work and most found themselves without incomes of any kind. The exchange rate between the mark, which Germans were forced to continue using, and the zloti was fixed so that Germans paid four times the Polish prices for anything they bought. An egg could cost a German twenty-five shillings or three dollars. It was a policy designed to

4 Some recent official publications put the figures at 13,000,000, but this includes children born of refugee parents.
5 *The Rebirth of the German Church* (Stewart Herman, S.C.M. Press; Harper and Row, New York, London, 1946), p. 202. Elizabeth Wiskemann, quoting official German estimates, puts the number of Germans living East of the Oder-Neisse line and in Poland in 1944 at 11,445,000. All but a million of these either fled before the Russian armies or were driven out under the 'exchange of minorities' system agreed at Potsdam. German civilian 'losses' (i.e. deaths) between Potsdam and 1950, she puts at just under 2,000,000 in that area alone. It is not unreasonable to suppose that at least double that number died fleeing before or being overtaken by the invading Russian forces in the much larger area which included the Ukraine, the whole of the Balkans, Hungary and Czechoslovakia
6 The author escaped from a prison camp in Poland in March, 1943, and spent some days in Polish towns and villages.

force all Germans to emigrate. In some towns German suicides were so numerous that they could not be recorded. Corpses were buried naked so that the living could use the clothes taken from them. Law and order had virtually broken down and the trains carrying the German expellees were raided by gangs of young Poles who, if they could not get in by other means, made holes in the roofs of the wagons, jumped down among the Germans and robbed them of their last belongings, including the clothes they wore. Many of these Germans reached Berlin naked. Tens of thousands died of hunger and exposure. At one time it looked as if the Germans would pass through the equivalent of a twentieth-century Black Death. Thousands of corpses still lying under the rubble of German towns produced a plague of rats and flies. In Berlin, an epidemic of malignant boils which necessitated im-mediate amputation of the infected part, produced a thousand hospital cases a day. Malnutrition and infected water brought typhoid, paratyphoid and dysentery; home-brewed alcohol sent hundreds blind; scarlet fever, tuberculosis, venereal disease, oedema and sheer emaciation took a tremendous toll. Health reports were meagre, but the figures available suggested that in 1945 in the British zone and in Berlin, from one in seven to one in five babies died in the first week of their lives and that general mortality was about five times the normal. In Greater Berlin about 60,000 people died between May and July, 1945.

But death was not necessarily the worst that could befall a German in those days. There was still the fear of the knock on the door heralding the departure of father, son or brother to some internment camp with which communication was impossible; still the fear of bereavement or the separation of parents from children through the vagaries of zonal boundaries, and still, for some, and to the Allies' shame, the dread of torture. Above all there was the enduring fact of slow starvation. Which of these a German suffered and to what degree, depended upon the zone which he or she in-habited.

When the war ended no one in the Allied camp questioned the necessity of a thorough purge of the Nazis and their supporters. Many Germans were also in favour of it, either because they had be-longed to that small band of those who had opposed Hitler, or, more commonly, so as to be revenged on those who had brought them to their present misery. Yet, because of the way de-Nazification was carried out, it lost all semblance of purification and became an act of indiscriminate vengeance.

It was the Americans who set the pace. In the American zone everyone over the age of eighteen had to register and answer a questionaire – a *Fragebogen* – which contained 133 questions. Factual answers about membership of organisations could be checked, because in the summer of 1945 a complete card index of the members of the Nazi party and its auxiliaries was found, waiting to be reduced to pulp, in a Munich paper mill. But when it came to remembering every article or other publication written, in whole or in part, since 1923, every speech and lecture delivered, the details of every job held, it was obviously impossible to be accurate; yet the penalties for giving false information were high.

At the beginning most Germans made an effort to tell the truth, largely because failure might make the difference between death and survival. According to the answers given, a German could be classed in any one of five categories, each, except the fifth which meant exoneration, carrying penalties ranging from death to forfeiture of all property and exclusion from every job except that of manual labourer. Few Allied officials spoke German so that they were inevitably a prey to informers who might be using the *Fragebogen* for political purposes, or just individuals paying off old scores. Denunciations became so frequent and so difficult to check that one German advisory committee suggested that anyone wishing to lodge one should pay a deposit of three hundred marks, to be forfeited if the information proved untrue. But as time went on and the Germans saw how many well-known Nazis went free while opponents were penalised, the *Fragebogen* became a music hall joke made worse because, as one Control Commission officer followed another in the scramble to get home, the same form often had to be filled in by the same German over and over again. In all 12,000,000 questionaires were issued in the American zone resulting in 930,000 sentences. Perhaps American zeal can be judged by a comparison of the more serious charges. Of those arrested for Nazi or military crimes the British tried 22,296, the French 17,353, the Russians 18,000 and the Americans 169,282.[7]

By Christmas 1945, quite apart from those who had been thrown into internment camps, the Americans had dismissed from their

7 *The Death & Life of Germany*, Eugene Davidson, Cape, London; Alfred Knopf, New York 1959, p. 128.

jobs 141,000 people, including eighty per cent of the school teachers, half the doctors, and in some towns practically the entire staff of the department of public health. In Heidelberg a hundred and twenty-two out of four hundred and sixty-nine bank employees were sacked. Many of the Germans felt that the sackings were not only wasteful, but foolish and indiscriminate. Dr Blaum, the anti-Nazi Lord Mayor of Frankfurt, declared that the purge was too widespread and was 'depriving him of the tools necessary for the rebuilding of the city,' while Dr Treu, the Lord Mayor of Munich, flatly refused to co-operate. Blaum was reprimanded, Treu dismissed, and the purge continued.

Worst of all were the internment camps into which nearly 150,000 allegedly prominent Nazis, members of the S.S. or the Gestapo and high-ranking officers of the armed forces, were thrown immediately upon capture. Usually they had no clothes other than those in which they stood and no others were provided. They were unable to buy or forage for food because they were not allowed out of the camp. They were not permitted to see their relations or lawyers or to receive gifts. Thousands remained in prison for more than a year, only to find that no charge was to be brought against them.

Ernst von Salomon, a Nationalist who had been implicated in Rathenau's murder between the wars, was arrested (in error as it turned out) and flung into a camp near Natternberg, north of Munich, with a Jewish woman with whom he had lived during the war. He had never joined the Party, but no doubt because he was a famous writer and an old freedom-fighter of the 1920's, the Nazis had left him alone. Now he was to get his deserts. On arriving at the camp men and women were lined up against the wire and then, one by one, taken into a room where the military police systematically beat up the men and raped the women while soldiers peered gleefully in through the windows. Von Salomon's teeth were knocked out and his face streamed with blood. When he staggered to his feet he turned to an officer who had sat passively chewing gum while the beating went on and said: 'You are no gentleman.' This was greeted with roars of laughter. 'We are boys from Mississippi,' the military police declared proudly, and kicked him through the door. Von Salomon spent eighteen months in camp without a single interrogation and came out looking like a skeleton.[8]

8 *Der Fragebogen*, Ernst von Salomon, Rowohlt Verlag, Hamburg, 1951. Von Salomon

This sort of treatment was quite common. 'One day a senior American medical officer dropped into my Berlin office,' wrote Robert Murphy, the United States political adviser to General Clay, 'and said he wanted to show me something if I could spare an hour. We drove to an American internment camp in the suburbs, where the occupants were "little Nazis" awaiting classification. These were former Party members who held insignificant jobs in the Party organisation, including even charwomen in the Nazi offices. It should be remembered that, when the United States forces moved into Germany, their directives prescribed thirty-three automatic arrest categories, mostly on account of membership, high or low, in a Nazi organisation. The commandant of the camp we were inspecting was a serious young American officer who showed us around conscientiously. I was startled to see that our prisoners were almost as weak and emaciated as those I had observed in Nazi concentration camps. The youthful commandant calmly told us that he had deliberately kept the inmates on starvation diet, explaining "These Nazis are getting a dose of their own medicine." He so obviously believed that he was behaving correctly that we did not discuss the matter with him. After we left, the medical director asked me: "Does that camp represent American policy in Germany?" I replied that of course it was contrary to our policy and that the situation would be quickly corrected. When I described the camp's conditions to Clay he quietly transferred the grim young officer to a post for which he was better suited.'

'On another occasion,' continues Murphy, 'we were informed that the Nazi torture camp, equipped with devices to extort confessions, was still operating under American auspices. A zealous American intelligence officer had found out how effectively Nazi devices persuaded Nazis to confess their own misdeeds, and he was chagrined when ordered to close this establishment.'[9]

Murphy may have managed to check some of the worst abuses, but the fact was that neither of these officers was reprimanded and both clearly felt that they were fulfilling the spirit of J.S.C. 1067, the military directive which Roosevelt had stiffened so that the

---

mentioned that Carl Blessing, later President of the Federal Bank was in this same camp. A fortnight before he died in 1971 the author met Blessing and asked him if Von Salomon's account was true. Blessing confirmed every detail and said that he himself had received the same treatment.

9 *Diplomat Among Warriors*, Robert Murphy, Collins, London, 1951, pp. 360-1.

German people should be made to realise they had all connived at Nazi crime.

Hand in hand with de-Nazification went the dismantling of German industry. Under the Potsdam Agreement the Germans were to pay reparations 'in kind' for the damage they had done to other countries and were to be allowed to revive their industries only to a level which would allow them a standard of living equal to the average in Europe. Factories capable of being used for war purposes were therefore to be dismantled and their machinery removed.

As far as reparations were concerned, it had been agreed that the Russians should be the chief beneficiaries and, in the early months of the occupation, the Russians helped themselves both from Berlin and their own zone by taking any machines which they thought might be useful. In the Western Zones dismantling was carried out under an international commission (on which the Russians also sat) and was much slower and more methodical.

Although dismantling went on for four years the total amount of machinery removed from Germany was surprisingly small – perhaps four per cent of their total industrial capacity. As much of it came from industries like steel or chemicals, where, theoretically, surplus capacity had been built up during the war, it must have seemed to the Allies that the Germans had little cause for complaint. Yet dismantling caused more bitterness among the Germans even than de-Nazification. In the western zones it did not begin to get into its stride until the middle of 1946, by which time Military Government was exhorting the Germans to produce more so as to pay for imports and save British and American taxpayers.

The Germans thought it imbecile or worse to destroy shipyards which could have earned foreign currency or chemical works which could make desperately needed pharmaceuticals, merely to conform to an overall 'level of industry' plan which, in any case, was constantly being revised. Nor did it help the elected representatives of a municipality who were losing factories and having to meet rising unemployment, to be told that the total reduction in German industry was small. Perhaps if all dismantling had been carried through by August, 1947, as was originally planned, the outcry would have been less; the Germans expected to be disarmed and dismantling would have appeared to be part of this process. But once the Marshall Plan had been launched and Germany was being urged to join the Western bloc, the contradiction became in-supportable. What was the point of importing ball-bearings from the United States for the German railways while destroying German factories that could make them because they had once supplied Hitler's armies? Did it make sense to fly bull-dozers into Berlin while at the same time blowing up the plants that could have manufactured them on the spot?

German workers struck, sabotaged equipment which was to be removed, and sometimes attacked the foreign workers who were doing the removals. German burgomasters and town councils refused to co-operate. In Baden the entire State cabinet resigned, the President, Dr Wohlleb, saying that 'the existence of the people of Baden and the livelihood of a section of highly qualified skilled workers was at stake.' But although General Clay suspended de-liveries to the Russians in May, 1946, because the Russians refused to fulfil the terms of the Potsdam Agreement, he threatened Ger-mans who struck in the American zone with military action and insisted that dismantling continue. The British backed him up. The machines, they said, were needed by the countries which the Germans had despoiled; yet those countries were crying out not for old damaged machinery, but for new equipment which only a re-suscitated German industry could supply. Some of the machinery sent to eastern European countries was so obsolete that it was sold to the United States for scrap and then transformed into modern machinery which was shipped back to Germany. The worst absurdities occurred in the Ruhr. At the very moment when the British were trying to raise the level of steel production, urging the Germans to mine more coal, they allowed rolling mills, steel plant and coal-mining equipment to be 'dismantled' and hauled away. Four Krupp furnaces, uprooted at a cost of twenty million marks, were valued for reparations at only nine million marks. As time went on the Germans made it a point of honour to replace all the old machines that had been removed with the latest British, American or Swiss equipment.

However illogical their effects, it could at least be argued that de-Nazification and dismantling were part of a deliberate punitive policy which the Germans had brought upon themselves; no such justification could be applied to non-fraternisation.

The Nazis had coined the phrase *Herrenvolk*; now it was the

Allies who were assuming that role. To the cold and hungry Germans, looking in from the outside at the brightly lit windows of the Allied messes, their own country had become a ghetto and they themselves the despised and segregated race. No doubt the rash of special road signs directing motorists, who were normally Allied personnel, to the various regimental headquarters, 'The Officers' Club,' 'The Yacht Club' were necessary, since German signs would have been incomprehensible, but the constant reiteration of the notice 'Entry strictly Forbidden to Civilians' – which could only mean Germans because every Allied visitor was accorded military status – the segregated lavatories, the specially marked queues for Allied officers and other ranks outside the cinemas to which Germans were only allowed to go as Allied guests, the special cubicles reserved for Allied women at the hairdressers would have been frowned upon by the most reactionary colonial administrators and were a replica of all that the Nazis had imposed upon the Poles or other subject races. Clubs, of course, were entirely segregated and no member of the occupation forces was allowed to invite a German to his mess or home – even if the German happened to be the owner.

The occupying forces lived in a world apart. All the best of the undamaged buildings were requisitioned for messes, clubs, barracks or offices. Except in the French zone there was no 'billeting' in the sense of German families being forced to take in Allied personnel; the Allies simply confiscated the accommodation they needed. Generals and high officials lived in the largest villas, or took over palaces, including the Krupp Villa Hugel, near Essen. A secretary who needed a home was ordered to go out and find rooms by turning the Germans out, commandeering their furniture and household utensils. Some relished the experience, many more squirmed at what they were being forced to do, but they had no alternative. Non-fraternisation dictated that no German could share a house with a conqueror or have any private relationship other than that of servant to master, and even after non-fraternisation was relaxed the rules about accommodation held good.

As the occupation got into its stride and American, British and French families were brought into Germany to join husbands and fathers, the plight of the Germans became worse. Official statements that no Germans were evicted until alternative accommodation had been found were simply not true – unless one counted as accommodation cellars and ruined hovels which were already so overcrowded that the occupants had to take turns to lie down and sleep. Single Allied officers usually had two rooms to themselves. According to a reporter on *The New York Times*, one American family displaced eight German families and the requisitioning of 125 houses in the Grünewald of Berlin dispossessed a thousand German civilians.[10] In most cases the standard of living of the Allied families was higher than any they had enjoyed previously. Since Allied labour requirements were a 'first Priority'[11] many British and American families had servants for the first time in their lives. Messes were lavishly staffed and food far more plentiful than in Britain or France. Five course meals, including fish, meat, sweet and cheese, were common in British and French messes whose inmates would have been grateful for two courses of far lower quality in their own countries. Every British officer received soap, chocolate and two hundred cigarettes a week as of right, and could buy as much more as he wanted. Food and drink were fantastically cheap – about a third of what they would have cost under normal circumstances. American rations were unlimited. If the Germans could get their own ration of seven cigarettes a week they were lucky. Soap was *ersatz* and often as hard as pumice-stone, but without its cleansing properties.

What the Allies lacked in accommodation they quickly built. The 'Hamburg Project' was notorious. There were only three more or less undamaged areas in Hamburg, some parts of which were featureless heaps of rubble reminiscent of the Warsaw Ghetto after the Germans had obliterated it. Two of these areas were reserved for the Control Commission and were turned into a sort of garden city. When Victor Gollancz, a well-known British publisher, visited the city in the autumn of 1946 he found more than ten thousand building workers engaged on the project as against three thousand five hundred providing alternative accommodation for the seventeen thousand Germans who had been evicted, and seventeen hundred employed on ordinary repairs for the Hamburg population.[12]

The 'Allied Victory Club,' built on the site of a former cinema and theatre, and comprising everything from a ballroom to a

10 *New York Times*, 16th December, 1946
11 Military Handbook, Chapter 9, Clause 754 (b).
12 *In Darkest Germany*, Victor Gollancz, Gollancz, London, 1947, p. 107.

gymnasium, cost 13 million marks and used enough materials to house at least six thousand German civilians. Dr Karl Arnold, one of the ablest and most respected of Germans who was Lord Mayor of Dusseldorf, wrote: 'the population very much regrets to see that the construction and repair of buildings for purposes of entertainment is carried out by the occupation forces on a scale that would have been remarkable in pre-war Germany . . . On the other hand it is planned to close down factories manufacturing cement and building materials.'[13]

Victor Gollancz, pursuing his lone crusade for more enlightened treatment of the conquered race, described how, during that terrible winter, he spent an afternoon in Hamburg where there were twenty thousand people living in cellars and thousands more paying money to be able to sleep in ruined railway stations and air raid shelters. At the end of the day he returned in a state of deep depression to the office of the British official who had helped arrange his visit. His host, one of the many members of the Control Commission for whom Gollancz had a considerable respect, noticed that he was distressed and asked him why. When Gollancz told him, he replied: 'I wouldn't know anything about that. I come to my office in the morning, do a hard day's work and then go home to the mess and relax. For knowing anything about the life of the Hamburgers I might just as well be in Whitehall.'[14] Not surprisingly, Gollancz found that much of the information about availability of rations and the incidence of sickness bore little relation to the facts. As Michael Balfour, who was also serving in Germany at the time, wrote a little later: 'It was easy to wrap oneself in the magic carpet on which the occupation forces lived and forget that human being were existing all around one in utterly different conditions.'[15]

The contrast between the way of life of governors and governed was greatest of all in the French zone. The example had been set by General de Lattre de Tassigny, the first Commander-in-Chief, who believed that the Germans could best be impressed and re-educated by grandeur on a scale which surpassed anything they had known. 'Our ceremonies and military displays ought also . . . to show the Germans that we too know how to conceive big ideas, to carry out huge schemes, to achieve the beautiful, but by means where

13 *In Darkest Germany*, Victor Gollancz, p. 104.   14 Ditto, p. 98.
15 Balfour and Mair, Op. Cit., p. 113.

man, the individual, was not crushed by the mass he had raised up.'[16]

Accordingly de Lattre had his villa at Lindau specially landscaped, imported the National Opera Company from Paris to play for him and employed students from the Villa Medici, the French art-school in Rome, to design and decorate barracks and compose special military music – all at the expense of the German population off whom the French occupying forces were living. When General Devers, the American commander, came to pay a farewell visit, two thousand Algerian cavalrymen carrying torches lined his route. De Lattre's magnificence provoked protests not only from the Germans, but from his own compatriots who were suffering from cold and hunger in France.

Although at the end of July, de Lattre was recalled and General Koenig, who had led the French column in the relief of Paris, took his place, the tone set by de Lattre survived. Baden-Baden, the most famous of all German spas, remained the seat of French military government. Its best hotels, practically undamaged, were occupied by the French officers and their families who flocked into the zone to take advantage of the 'luxury living.' In the evenings, in the ballroom of the Casino, the municipal orchestra played Viennese waltzes. Since many of the officers and officials had served Pétain, the French left-wing press began to speak of 'the nostalgia of the military for watering places' and to call Baden-Baden 'Little Vichy.'

The American zone consisted of the largely Catholic states of Bavaria, Baden, Württemberg and Hesse. 'The British and the French got the coal, the Russians the wheat fields and we got the scenery,' explained an American officer. Many Germans felt themselves fortunate to be in the American zone as they believed that the lofty idealism of the United States and fun-loving, gum-chewing G.I.'s would protect them from the harshest aspects of occupation. They knew that the Russians would be savage, the French merciless, the British icily aloof. They hoped that the Americans would be more interested in reconstruction than revenge. To their dismay they discovered that not only were the Americans deeply hostile, but in a tearing hurry to go home.

In the early months of occupation the Americans interpreted

16 *The French in Germany 1945–1949*, F. R. Willis, Stanford University Press, California, 1962, p. 75.

their instructions to treat Germany as 'a defeated country' as a licence to do whatever they pleased. They looted with the rapacious-ness of the Russians until they discovered that their P.X. rations were worth their weight in gold; thereafter they got what they wanted through the black market. Although the American army had strict orders not to fraternise, the soldiers refused to comply as far as girls were concerned. The American Military Courts obligingly stretched a point by declaring that venereal disease would not be regarded as proof of fraternisation; however, in order to prevent the courts from becoming a laughing stock, in July the non-fraternisation rule was withdrawn. Venereal disease increased by nearly twenty per cent, assuming the proportions of a medieval plague.

The pursuit of women did not change the attitude of the troops towards the population as a whole. Although American policy stipulated that soldiers must be 'firm but just', indiscipline was wide-spread and more often than not went unpunished. In many parts of the zone officers and men alike rode rough-shod over the local community. In Marburg, a town seventy miles from Cologne, the Rector of the university alleged that 'Marburgers were afraid to walk on the streets at night even before curfew hours.'[17] A girl suffered a fractured vertebra when she jumped from a third-story window to escape from soldiers who had followed her into her apartment; the victims of two attacks were totally blinded. One of the games the soldiers enjoyed most was hooking the ankles of any girl they passed in their trucks with the handle of a cane; when a man came within reach they beat him. The Dean of the Theological Faculty reported that, walking through a narrow street, he would certainly have been struck by troops in a passing lorry had they not at that moment been distracted by a girl.

Realising that many Marburgers who had welcomed the Ameri-cans when they first arrived, had ceased altogether to co-operate by the end of 1945, the American Military Governor of the town asked for a report from the Advisory Political Committee which con-sisted mainly of German Socialists and Christian Democrats. A survey, published some years later gave a précis of the Committee's findings:

17 *Marburg. The German Community under American Occupation*, J. Gimbel, Stanford University Press, 1961, pp. 69–70.

1. The military requisitioning policy, although just in its demands that Nazi homes be requisitioned, was unjust in practice. Some Nazis sat comfortably in their homes 'and laughed'[18] while Occupation forces and Military Government requisitioned the houses and apartments of anti-Nazis. Troops senselessly destroyed property in the requisitioned houses . . . They took along radios when they moved. They confiscated cameras. They tossed porcelain, pictures, furniture and other valuables into the street, occasionally to be soaked with gasoline and burned. In some homes the troops destroyed or took stamp collections, paintings and other works of art. Two cafés that had been requisitioned for troop messes were left stripped of equipment and fixtures. Dumbfounded and bitter, the population of Marburg stood by and watched their last meagre possessions being senselessly destroyed, long after the Allied weapons had achieved total victory.

2. The prisoners whom the American Army released came home half-starved. Released prisoners from the camp at Marburg South reported that they had been beaten.

3. American troops permitted mobs of Germans and displaced persons to loot captured Wehrmacht stocks while the normal ration coupons for shoes, clothing and food could not be honoured by the merchants.

4. The American Army did not maintain law and order as it had during the early days of the Occupation . . . American soldiers, or displaced persons dressed in American uniforms and armed with American weapons, attacked and robbed Germans in their homes or on the streets.

5. Marburgers were forced to cut down their consumption of electric power to a minimum which was almost unbearable while houses requisitioned by the Occupation forces could be seen to have lights burning from top to bottom both by night and by day.

6. Germans reported an unusually large number of accidents involving American vehicles. Pedestrians were run down almost daily. Civilian vehicles had been rammed or forced into the ditches. Many American drivers did not obey civilian traffic policemen.

7. American de-Nazification was based upon a basic misunderstanding of the Nazi régime . . . Many Marburgers agreed with the Military Government in spirit, but they thought Military Government investigators used Gestapo methods . . .

18 J. Gimbel, Op. Cit.

8. The rural population complained about American hunting rights and practices. The troops hunted at night with spotlights and fished with hand grenades. They drove their vehicles over planted fields.

The members of the Committee were restrained in their comments, but they admitted that when a former member of the *Hitler Jugend* said to them: 'You talk of the evils of National Socialism, but Allied Militarism is just as bad,' they found it difficult to reply.

The Marburg survey illustrates not only the fair-mindedness of the Americans, for it was they who published it, but also the peculiar disadvantages under which they laboured in dealing with the Germans; for American culture differs radically from the European. A striking example of this was given by Nicholas Nabakov, who was then serving with American Intelligence in Berlin.[19] One evening he attended an opera in the Russian zone. It was an official occasion and all senior American officers had been invited; however, as opera was not their idea of an evening's entertainment, many had gone only under protest. The performance was given by the Prussian State Opera Company and, as the curtain went up and the orchestra began to play the first bars of Puccini's *Madame Butterfly*, Nabakov was filled with foreboding. As the tale unfolded the American General sitting next to him became more and more indignant. The play, he ejaculated, was an insult to the American army, a slander on an American officer – and how dare Germans put on American uniforms! Convinced that the whole thing was a German plot hatched especially for the occasion, the General lodged a formal protest with General Clay.

By the spring of 1947, the Allied occupation was heading for a disaster of such proportions that it threatened to destroy not only the Germans, but the other nations of western Europe as well; for if Germany became depopulated its neighbours would inevitably be dragged down to a pastoral existence. The deterioration had been going on for more than a year. In February, 1946, the meagre ration in the British zone had been reduced to a level which, according to the correspondent of the *Manchester Guardian*, meant that the daily diet of a German in the Ruhr consisted of 'two slices

19 *Old Friends and New Music*, Nicholas Nabakov, Hamish Hamilton, London; Little Brown, Boston, 1951, pp. 213–15.

of bread, with perhaps a smear of margarine, a spoonful of porridge and two not very large potatoes.' Even this ration often could not be met. Men and women would stand in queues all day only to find that at the end there was no food left. Wuppertal was without bread for ten days; almost the whole population of Hamburg had eaten their bread ration in the first half of March and had nothing left for the second, and this at a time of year when vegetables were scarce and little could be foraged in the countryside.

Mr John Hynd, the British Minister responsible for Germany, said in a speech at Sheffield that it was 'a matter of days whether twenty-three million people were going to starve in the streets,' No one paid much notice because, as the days went by, it was clear that he had been exaggerating; yet if Mr Hynd had said months, rather than days, he would have been right, for the position was to get steadily worse. Ex-President Hoover, who had surveyed the rest of Western Europe the year before, visited Germany during the winter and shocked the world with his report. The picture he painted was ghastly. Western Germany, he said, had sunk to a level of destitution which had not been seen in Europe for a hundred years.

That winter of 1946-47 was one of the coldest on record in Europe, and Germany was still desperately short of coal; a household was lucky if it could scrounge a few lumps a week. In the British and American zones three quarters of all industry had to be shut down for lack of power. Schools were closed and in Berlin two hundred people were recorded as 'frozen to death.' Throughout the British zone cases of hunger oedema had risen by tens of thousands and men and women were fainting daily at their work. For weeks before the Hoover report was published journalists had been describing widespread signs of starvation; 'earth-coloured faces and hollow cheeks,' children begging in the streets and emaciated women harnessed to carts pulling piles of wood or felling trees; and always the endless queues of people so listless that motorists had to take special care not to run them down as they crossed the streets.

Yet, until Hoover reported, few people in high places had really cared. The horror of the concentration camps, still being revealed to the world by the film *Nacht und Nevel*, had killed the sympathy even of the humane. On coming out of Belsen, Eisenhower, usually the most equable of men, had vowed he would never again shake hands with a German; Patton had been physically sick. When, a few months later, Patton had tried to restore a sense of proportion by remarking that ordinary members of the Nazi party had not been very different from Republicans or Democrats, there had been such an outcry in America that he had been instantly recalled. If people outside Germany were aware at all of what was happening they felt it was no more than just retribution for the suffering the Germans had inflicted upon others under Hitler.

It is only fair to add that the Allies had acute problems of their own. The French were almost as cold and hungry as the Germans that savage winter and so were the Dutch and the Belgians. The war had destroyed the rice crops of Asia and there was famine in India, South East Asia and Japan. The Americans had large reserves of food, but the dislocation of transport and a series of strikes in the United States made its distribution difficult. In any case the American people were determined that such food as could be sent should go first to the millions of displaced persons and the peoples the Nazis had oppressed. The British felt a special obligation towards the Indians and those in Europe and the Empire who had sustained them in their long struggle. By common consent the Germans were at the back of the queue.

As time went on, mainly for reasons of security, Military Governors did begin to press their superiors at home to send extra supplies to Germany. In the spring of 1946 there had been serious riots in the British zone where crowds of Germans had attacked coal trains and food stores in Hamburg and the Ruhr and taken away as much as they could carry. The British authorities played down the riots, referring to them only as 'disturbances,' but several hundred people had been arrested and there seemed every likelihood that they would recur. Lord Montgomery, in urging his government to send more grain, wisely refrained from appealing to a sympathy which did not exist; instead he went out of his way to reassure the British people that no one was being 'soft' to the Germans, telling an audience at Hastings in one of his last speeches as Military Governor, that the average ration in the British zone could scarcely be considered excessive since it was the same as had been given to the inhabitants of Belsen, who were being deliberately starved to death. He went on to stress the renewed danger of epidemic disease, due to malnutrition, spreading through British troops coming on leave to the British people themselves, who, he feared, might not be in a sufficiently good state after the war to stand up to it.

Supported by public opinion, the British and American governments stoically resisted the appeals of their representatives in Germany. Throughout the war the British had kept a twelve weeks' reserve supply of grain against the possibility of shortage due to the vagaries of the battle of the Atlantic. Although the battle was over, Sir Ben Smith, the British Minister of Food and his successor, Mr John Strachey, resolutely refused to allow these stocks to be reduced. The British people were not hungry – rationing under Lord Woolton had been one of the great success stories of the war – but they were bored to death with their diet and when bread was rationed for the first time in 1946, it seemed the last straw. They clamoured for more variety and a few luxuries and when Mr Strachey arranged for the importation of turkeys, poultry, extra meat, sweets and sugar over Christmas, it seemed eminently reasonable.

The Americans were short of nothing but, as they were already feeding a large part of the world, they saw no reason why they should make things easier for the French and the Russians who, by curtailing their own extravagance and allowing a free exchange of goods between the zones as had been agreed at Potsdam, could have greatly improved things. The Americans insisted, therefore, that each Power should be responsible for its own zone and urged the British to reduce their grain reserve. In this they were powerfully supported by the man who did more than any other individual to awaken the public conscience on both sides of the Atlantic, Victor Gollancz.

Gollancz, himself a Jew of German extraction, had friends among the members of the British Labour Government and, with their official blessing, paid many visits to the British and American zones in the spring and autumn of 1946. As he said in the introduction to his book *In Darkest Germany*, he did so not through any inverted sense of pity for the persecutors of his race, but because he felt that the only hope for the world lay in a general repentance rather than 'self-righteous insistence on the wickedness of others.' In the summer of 1946 he published a pamphlet entitled: *Leaving Them to Their Fate*; *The Ethics of Starvation*, and subsequently carried on an incessant campaign in newspapers, magazines and on the radio to present what he believed to be the case for the just treatment of the Germans.

Apart from the appalling conditions in which he found (and photographed) thousands of Germans, Gollancz was indefatigable in checking his facts. He was able to show that the information on which British ministers were basing their public statements was incorrect. For example, in July, 1946, the Control Commission reported only 1,189 cases of hunger oedema in Hamburg. Gollancz pointed out that these were only the hospital cases. It had been shown already in other parts of the Rhineland that for every case in hospital there were nearly fifty in private homes and even larger numbers which were never reported to doctors, who were themselves very few. *The British Zone Review*, a semi-official publication, said it was impossible to be sure of the number of cases and made a guess at 10,000. The Germans put the figure at 130,000. Gollancz, having made exhaustive inquiries and having balanced British and German estimates, gave the figure of 100,000.[20] Or again, when Mr Hynd stated in the House of Commons in November that the ration had been maintained in the British zone 'apart from local breakdowns', Gollancz was able to contradict him because, with the help of the British Regional Food Officer, he had just established that in Dusseldorf over the previous three weeks only half the amount of flour necessary to meet the ration had been available and in several other towns in the Ruhr, only two thirds; the position in regard to many other rationed foods had been worse.

In the end, without the British public being aware of it, the government did reduce its reserves and just enough wheat was sent to Germany to prevent total collapse of the rationing system, but in retrospect it is difficult to rebut Gollancz's charge that the Allies were starving the Germans not deliberately, in the sense that they wanted them all to die, but wilfully in that they preferred their death to any inconvenience to themselves. To millions of Germans unaware of what was happening outside their own zone, it seemed at the time as if the Allies were bent on liquidating them by a cheaper, slower, but just as effective method as the Nazis had used against the Jews.

Of the 'miracles' that occurred in Germany after the war – and there were several – the first was that so many Germans survived.

20 *In Darkest Germany*, Victor Gollancz, pp. 26–7.

'You had to be clever,' said Georg Schröder, who lived through the occupation with a wife and three children. 'I spent two years doing nothing except scrounge food for my family. I travelled endlessly, sometimes acting on my own behalf and sometimes as an agent for others. I exchanged everything I possessed and a lot more that I acquired, for food.' Schröder, now living in Bonn as the political correspondent of *Die Welt*, one of Axel Springer's more reputable newspapers, managed to have a registered domicile in both the American and French zones. 'I am good with my hands and I made myself every kind of official stamp so that I always had documents to allow me to cross zonal frontiers,' he added.[21]

Sitting in his wide-windowed office overlooking one of Bonn's new luxury hotels, this spare man with fair thinning hair and pale blue eyes whose face showed signs of privation, felt no bitterness towards the Allies. 'A lot of my friends thought that you were out to exterminate us,' he continued, 'but perhaps I understood more of what was going on. The truth was that the State had collapsed and when you suddenly find that there is no State – and I am afraid none of us regarded Military Government as a State – you realise that the only thing that matters is your family. That is why I was unemployed for two whole years.'

Schröder's experience could be multiplied several million times. Few people had the strength to do regular work for more than three or four days a week, the rest they spent foraging and bartering. Ironically, former members of the Nazi party had a certain advantage in that, so many jobs being closed to them, they had the most spare time; even prominent Nazis were only made to clear rubble three days a week. And so for a change the towns went to the country. There was always some extra food in the villages and on the farms for those who could get there and families with relations or friends went regularly to beg or steal what they could on the way. The Germans had always been great hikers and now they hiked *en masse* and with a purpose. A bicycle was often more valuable than a car.

The black market was their widow's cruse. Officially the Allies did not know of its existence; in practice they were its chief suppliers. Since British and American troops had too much of all the necessities of life and the Germans too little, by one means or

21 In conversation with the author.

another the Allied surplus flowed into German hands. Scent, soap, cosmetics, pots and pans, clothes, food and cigarettes were exchanged for cameras, field-glasses, typewriters and jewellery or simply sold for marks which could then be turned into dollars or pounds at the ludicrously over-valued rate of exchange.[22] In the American zone a packet of twenty cigarettes fetched 135 marks – a month's wages for many German workers – a pound of coffee, of which every soldier received 24 lbs. a month, 40 marks.

But P.X. rations were not the only source of supply; many Allied soldiers had looted extensively in the first weeks of the conquest and traded their loot for money or valuables. No doubt such Allied marketeers were a minority, but they ranged from officers of the highest rank to the lowliest clerk or private soldier.

The depredations of two British Air Marshals, who flew their loot out of Germany to an island in the Greek archipelago, were notorious and there is no doubt that the evidence of their activities was suppressed at Cabinet level. The two Americans who stole from Kronberg Castle the crown jewels of the royal family of Hesse valued at three million dollars were caught and sentenced, but it was well known that soldiers and officials would use their leave in Paris or London to buy up goods with the money they had saved – for their living in Germany was cheap – and bring them back to swell the Black Market stocks.

What the Germans did not eat or use, they at once bartered or sold. Any place at which people met, a hospital or school or the street outside a Military Government office, became a market. Even school children became expert traders and, when something special was needed, would be sent by their parents to the great trading centres on the zonal frontiers like Berlin or Kehl, just across the Rhine from Strasbourg. With black market prices what they were, wages were of little use to the Germans; those who worked for the occupation almost always asked to be paid in kind. German businessmen and factory owners were obliged by law to pay out money but, if they wanted results, had to supplement wages by goods of some kind. Since this meant finding goods in quantity, they used black market brokers who scoured the country to amass the quantities needed. In Hamburg, the volume of business these brokers did became as important as that of the official exchanges.

Although they were acting illegally and for their own profit, the

22 The official rates fixed for the occupation were: 40 marks to the £, 10 marks to the $.

Allied forces must have saved millions of lives by their trading. In the first six months of the occupation, American troops sent home several million dollars more than they had been paid, after meeting all their expenses in Germany. A non-smoking corporal of the Women's Army Corps was reported to have made $500 a month from her cigarette ration alone. More than half the total sum which the Allied forces obtained came from the Russian zone where the Russian soldiers, who had not received their pay for months, were suddenly paid in occupational marks. They would give fantastic prices for watches or cameras and their money, too, could be exchanged into dollars or pounds. In all, it was calculated that 250 million dollars' worth of Russian occupational marks were exchanged in this way. When the dollars exchanged for reichmarks are added it is estimated that the American taxpayer alone had to find more than 300 million dollars for the black market operations of his forces.

Of course the black market caused suffering. When money had to be found the prices were fantastic: 100 marks for a 3 lb. loaf of bread whose fixed price was 40 pfennigs, 600 marks for 1 lb. of butter. Throughout 1946 less and less food was being delivered to the authorities by the farmers who sold it direct to Black Market brokers; as a result even the official rations could often not be met. Old people, war pensioners or families whose young were too crippled to move about and barter went cold and hungry.

Yet, in the Allies' defence, it must be said that the temptations were enormous. As Michael Balfour, writing much nearer the event, said: 'A certain power of economic analysis was needed to understand the objections to selling (instead of smoking) one's own cigarette ration.' The Germans wanted the cigarettes which had become the most viable currency, and making a little extra money on the side seemed to most of the victors a minor reward for having won the war. Whether their superiors knew it or not, mess secretaries used the black market quite openly to improve the diet of the troops, just as in many countries to-day foreign embassies change currency at black market rates to alleviate the expenses of their staff.

It is also true that, to a considerable extent, the troops redeemed themselves by personal generosity. Although their orders forbade any member of the armed forces or Control Commission to take any action which might improve the German standard of living, there were not many people who could happily see women and children starving around them. The rations of the British and American troops were so generous that the waste from a single army kitchen would have trebled the ration of any medium sized German town, and although in the first flush of victory there were occasions when food waste was buried or burned in front of Germans hoping to scavenge, they were rare and soon ceased. Over the years probably as much was given away as was traded.

Schröder recalls an occasion when some American soldiers, standing on top of a truck outside his lodgings, jokingly asked him what he thought of democracy. He replied that he had been hungry for too long to think about it. Whereupon they tipped an enormous tin of Frankfurter sausages on to the road at his feet and drove off. He and his family had the best feast they had had for years. Such instances are legion. A British Colonel, sent to requisition a house, saw a child lying in bed. 'That child looks ill,' he said to the mother, 'why don't you send for a doctor?' 'How can I send for a doctor?' the lady replied. 'All the ones round here are in internment camps and I have no means of reaching the others.' The Colonel said nothing, but the next day a regimental doctor visited the child, who had typhoid fever, gave the mother some antibiotics and told her that she would receive medicine and the right kind of food until the child was well. The doctor visited her again and made sure of the child's recovery, but neither he nor the Colonel ever told the mother their names nor did she see them again once the child was well.[23]

No one could conceivably estimate the amount of food and clothing which reached the Germans in this way, but it is rare to meet people of the older generation who have not experienced or known of similar actions, and when one asks how it is that there is so little bitterness towards those who were responsible for the occupation, the answer is invariably, 'Because of the kindness of individuals.' Even in the Russian zone, where the troops had less to eat because none was sent from Russia, innumerable acts of generosity are remembered; it is sad that they were outweighed by excesses and the inhumanity of the system that the communists imposed.

But indiscipline cannot justify a policy. At the end of two years of

23 Told to the author by the mother.

occupation no one could deny that the Allies had fulfilled the terms of their military directives. The leading Nazis had been tried and executed. In the Western zones alone well over one million party members or hangers-on had lost their jobs, their property or both, and tens of thousands more were still languishing in internment camps waiting for charges to be made against them. The average ration was still around a thousand calories a day which, as far as Military Government was concerned, meant that a large part of the population was starving a little more quickly than it had been when the occupation began. The general poverty and misery was greater than had been known in Europe since the end of the Thirty Years' War. More than four million German prisoners of war were still in Allied hands, nearly half of whom, held by the Russians, were never to return. There was scarcely a family that was not mourning its dead or missing a member. In the Western zones alone there were two million cripples. The pre-war surplus of 1,500,000 women had risen to the astronomical figure of 7,279,400. According to German statistics, which were now being sedulously collected, German losses in territory and property amounted to a value of $71,000,000,000 of which $3,000,000,000 were due to dismantling.[24] In other words, Germany had lost about half the natural, manufacturing and mercantile resources it possessed in 1938. No German could have the slightest doubt about the extent of his country's defeat or fail to realise that the entire nation was being made to pay for the crimes of their leaders.

Whether this mass retribution was something of which the Allies could be proud, or was likely to further their long-term objectives of converting the Germans to a democratic way of life, were more open questions. Certainly the Nazis had forfeited any right to normal sympathy; equally certainly the Allies did not hesitate to be severe. Clothed by victory with absolute power, they used it in too many ways which recalled the methods of their predecessors. They arrested wholesale without warrant and imprisoned without trial. They treated the conquered as racial inferiors and while they starved, lived in ostentatious luxury themselves. They exploited the misery of their victims to their own profit and often allowed brutality to go unchecked. They spoke of democracy and initiated certain democratic processes – only to

24 These figures are many times higher than those accepted by the Allies, but the German case is detailed and difficult to refute.

curtail the powers given or contradict the results if they did not suit Allied policy. Most of this can be forgiven them because of the horrors of the war itself and the circumstances in which victory came; but forgiveness does not alter the sobering thought that men and women brought up in a democratic tradition are as easily and as quickly corrupted by absolute power as any others.

CHAPTER IV

Reconstruction

'We found the Germans flat on their backs and somehow had to rouse them to save themselves,' said Sir Gerald Templer. He was still a compelling, if slightly old-fashioned figure with his clipped moustache, bowler hat and rolled umbrella as he walked unrecognised from his London office; it was easy to understand why the official historian had described as 'momentous' his appointment as Director of Civil and Military Government in the British zone twenty-five years earlier.[1] Templer had always been a dynamic leader and, in March, 1945, he was given unique powers; no one else was to hold direct authority over the civil and military branches of the zonal administration.

Until Templer's arrival both soldiers and civilian officials had been obsessed with the sheer logistics of the Occupation. The difficulties of transport alone were a nightmare and, although to the numb and bewildered Germans it seemed as if the Allies cared for no one but themselves, the troops had already performed prodigies of rehabilitation. Yet more was needed. In the first months after defeat few Germans could look more than twenty-four hours ahead or worry about anything other than the next day's food. Templer saw at once that unless he could rouse them to an organised effort, millions more would die before the year was out with disastrous consequences for Europe and the world. Although his instructions allowed him to help rebuild Germany only in so far as this was necessary for military security, he was independent enough to interpret them in the only way that made any sense. Employing all his prestige as a victorious General of immense drive and personal magnetism, he enlisted the services of the army to fight 'The Battle of the Coming Winter' and galvanise the Germans into action.

1 *Civil Affairs and Military Government, N.W. Europe, 1944–6*, F. S. V. Donnison, H.M.S.O., 1961. p. 213.

Coal and transport were the keys to everything. Unless there was coal neither power nor gas stations, railways, food processing plants nor a hundred other essential industries could be got going. A third of the Ruhr coal mines had been seriously damaged and, in June, 1945, production was well below one million tons as against thirty-eight million tons in 1943. Thousands of miners were prisoners of war and thousands more absenting themselves to forage for food. Pit props were the immediate problem. Most of them had previously come from what was now the Russian zone, yet 120,000 tons of pit props were needed to put the mines in working order and 5,000 tons a day to keep them running. Templer asked for and received the help of the British army. Troops were recalled from Belgium and formed into 'forestry' companies to cut trees. When the Germans, who are natural foresters, protested, Templer told them to put first things first. They then set about cutting as many trees as they could not only for props but to provide firewood for the winter.

Next came man-power. Templer had already initiated 'operation barleycorn' by which more than 300,000 prisoners of war were immediately returned to the land; he now launched 'operation coal scuttle' by which some 30,000 prisoners of war were returned to the mines. By the autumn the labour force had risen to nearly 200,000 men, about two-thirds of the minimum required. There was never enough coal to meet the demands made by neighbouring countries who were also desperately short, but at least these measures and the capacity of the German miner to work when hungry, prevented total collapse during that first winter.

Coal was of no use if it could not be moved. In the British zone alone 1,300 railway bridges and 1,500 road bridges were down and in the Ruhr broken bridges blocked the canals every three quarters of a mile. All seven zonal bridges across the Rhine had been destroyed. Templer again appealed to the army; the soldiers, sickened with destruction, performed miracles. Within six months the Rhine was reopened for barges, which meant not only clearing the wreckage from the river but raising the temporary army bridges to a height which allowed barges to pass underneath. When the war ended only six hundred and fifty miles of railway track could be used; by October, 1945, most of the eight thousand miles were functioning, even if much of it was single line. Canals took longer, but steady progress was made with these also and with the Baltic ports. The shortage of petrol kept road traffic to a minimum, but by the end of the year, although several hundred bridges needed repairing, lorries could reach every town in the zone.

Houses were another matter. Not even the most graphic war film can convey the devastation of towns like Cologne, Hamburg, Aachen or Bremen – to say nothing of Berlin; they had to be seen to be believed. And devastation was not the whole story. There had been a shortage of housing in the Ruhr and Rhineland before the war; now the population was being swelled by millions of refugees. Yet in the British zone less than half the houses were undamaged and two-fifths were beyond repair. All the best buildings were taken by the occupying forces themselves. Even if the Allied armies had concentrated upon nothing else, it would have taken them years to clear the rubble and repair what still stood; the work could only be done by the Germans themselves.

Again it was military government which goaded them into action. German housing committees were set up in every district and every available pair of hands was drawn in. Former Nazis were set to clear rubble and every able-bodied man was obliged to do building work of some kind. Training schools were set up to teach women to become carpenters, electricians, painters and plumbers. Millions of bricks were cleaned by hand and millions more fabricated by machines which the Germans invented for processing rubble.

One German firm designed a four-roomed prefabricated house, made from rubble, which could be put up by one skilled man and six assistants in eight days. Even so the position in October, 1945, was so serious that Brigadier J. A. Barraclough, the Military Governor of the North Rhine State, told the President, Dr Lehr, that he would have to evacuate six hundred thousand people into the countryside before the winter began. Dr Lehr asked for a few days' grace and, with the architect who was later to design the Bonn Parliament Buildings, produced plans which earned a trial; within six months he had provided shelter not for 600,000, but for 1,000,000 people.

It was as a result of this vigorous campaign to make the Germans face the appalling task of reconstruction that Templer fell foul of Dr Konrad Adenauer. Adenauer, Lord Mayor of Cologne from

1919 to 1933, had resolutely opposed the Nazis and was arrested and imprisoned more than once. Released finally in November, 1944, he returned to his family home at Röhndorf near Königswinter on the Rhine. Here the Americans found him and reinstated him as Lord Mayor of Cologne before handing the city over to the British.

There was no particular reason why Adenauer should have found the British more difficult to get on with than the Americans. In the years after the First World War he had made friends with General Sir Sidney Clive, the officer commanding the British forces on the Rhine and father-in-law of Sir Christopher Steel who, as political adviser to the Control Commission and future Ambassador to Bonn, was also to play a part in Adenauer's life. Nor did the British officers who took over from the Americans in 1945 realise that Adenauer was finding them harder taskmasters. On the contrary, they respected him. But Adanauer was an experienced politician who had been offered the Chancellorship in the last days of the Weimar Republic and felt that he could teach the Germans the elements of democracy far better than their conquerors. As an ardent Roman Catholic and conservative, he was also suspicious of the British Control Commission because it represented a socialist government.

The spark which ignited the quarrel came from a German. Soon after the British had taken over, a Social Democratic Town Councillor named Görlinger sent a long memorandum to the British Secret Service criticising Adenauer's attitude towards the burning topics of Church Schools and de-Nazification. Probably, although Adenauer's own agents had at once smuggled him a copy of Görlinger's paper, neither Templer nor the majority of his subordinates ever knew of its existence. Yet Adenauer became convinced that his political opponents were intriguing against him and had gained the British ear. As a result he became less and less co-operative. With stony indifference to the desperate coal shortage, Adenauer complained bitterly that Templer's orders about tree felling for household fuel would ruin the green belt he had created around Cologne; he alleged that the British were not giving him the machinery necessary to clear rubble and repair houses.

Templer was not the man to tolerate obstruction. On one of his visits to Cologne in September, 1945, he noticed that less had been done in clearing rubble and repairing buildings than in the towns of the Ruhr where conditions were even worse. He told Barraclough, that the old man who was Lord Mayor of Cologne – Adenauer was nearly seventy – was no good and that he must get rid of him.[2]

Barraclough consulted his colleagues, who disagreed with Templer; so he sent for Adenauer to tell him once more that he must comply with British orders and not only fell trees but make greater efforts to get ahead with reconstruction.[3] Adenauer maintained that he was doing all he could with the resources he possessed – but instead of making even a token effort to comply with British instructions he then did a most provocative thing. He gave an interview to the *News Chronicle*, one of the British newspapers which had consistently printed reports sympathetic to the plight of the Germans, and to a Miss Barbara Page of the Press Association. He not only complained that the Allies 'had no intention of giving house coal to the Germans' for the coming winter, but tactlessly praised a speech made by General de Gaulle in Saarbrucken. De Gaulle, whose representatives were so blatantly exploiting the French zone, had spoken of 'letting bygones be bygones' and of remembering that Germans were a central part of western Europe; but, as Adenauer well knew, de Gaulle was still pressing for the dismemberment of Germany and at that very moment was planning to annex the Saar. His speech was a transparent bid for the Saarlanders' support. Not surprisingly, Barraclough was furious and summoned Adenauer next day to his headquarters in Bunde.

Adenauer's account of the interview differs from Barraclough's. Adenauer describes how, when he entered the room, he was not offered a chair and that when he moved to take one Barraclough said: 'Don't sit down.'[4] Barraclough says that exactly the opposite took place. The first words he spoke – through an interpreter – were 'Won't you sit down?' When Adenauer made no move to do so he assumed that the old man preferred to stand. The interpreter could well have mis-heard, but in any case the point is a minor one. Barraclough proceeded to read Adenauer a letter in which he dismissed him from his post as Lord Mayor for failing in his duty to the people of Cologne. He was to hand over his duties to his deputy, and brother-in-law, Herr Suth, leave Cologne within a week, take

2 In conversation with the author.   3 In conversation with the author.
4 *Adenauer Memoirs*, 1945–53, translated by Beate R. von Oppen, Weidenfeld and Nicolson, London; Henry Regnery, Chicago, 1966, pp. 32–4.

no part whatever in public or political life in the North Rhine Province from then onwards.[5] Adenauer signed the letter as a form of receipt and left the room without a word.

Had Adenauer been an ordinary man of seventy the incident would have been closed then and there. Templer could hardly be blamed for not realising that Adenauer was not only a consummate politician but a man burning to redeem his people with a desire so strong that it was to illuminate the European scene for the next twenty years; for Adenauer was not yet a national figure and outside Germany was hardly known at all. Barraclough was considered by some of his colleagues to be a hard-liner, but was on excellent terms with other Germans, including Dr Lehr, and simply thought he had run into an obdurate old man. Fortunately, however, the Control Commission possessed, in Sir Christopher Steel and one of his political advisers, Lt.-Col. Noel Annan,[6] men who knew German history. Annan, who had been a Cambridge don, pointed out to Steel that Adenauer was already a leading personality among the Christian Democrats, who might well become the strongest party in the Western zones, and that such treatment might turn him into a hero. Steel agreed and between them they got the ban lifted. Steel then sent Annan down to see Adenauer and try to smooth things out.

When Annan arrived at Röhndorf, Adenauer at once said that he could not discuss politics owing to the ban; if he wanted to talk they must drive three miles across the border into the French zone. This they promptly did. They talked for several hours and Annan found Adenauer both charming and entertaining. He quickly came to the conclusion that he would play a leading part in the rebuilding of Germany. Towards the end of the conversation Adenauer asked Annan if he knew what was the greatest mistake the British had ever made in Germany. Half guessing what was coming, Annan said 'No.' The greatest mistake replied Adenauer, was that in 1815, at the Congress of Vienna, Castlereagh had agreed to cede the Rhineland States to Prussia so that they should be a military bulwark against French expansionism. This was one of the causes of Prussian domination over Germany and hence of the lamentable history of

5 This ban was immediately lifted because Adenauer's wife was dangerously ill. He stayed in Cologne and was allowed to visit her, but she died shortly afterwards.
6 Later Provost of King's College, Cambridge, now Lord Annan, Provost of University College, London.

Germany during the last one-hundred-and-fifty years. The old Rhinelander was appearing in his true colours already.

On his return to headquarters, Annan was able to see that Adenauer received a special invitation to make a public appearance at an important Christian Democrat Conference in Bad Godesberg in December. Adenauer accepted, with results which were to be crucial both for Germany and, ultimately, for Britain.

Nevertheless the dismissal left its scar. Adenauer put a good public face upon it and, whenever he met Barraclough in later years, used to tease him by saying that he owed his Chancellorship entirely to the Brigadier; but for whom he would still have been Lord Mayor of Cologne. But although he made friends with men like Lord Pakenham, Sir Brian Robertson and Sir Christopher Steel, he never showed the same warmth towards the British as he did to the Americans or, even more, to the French. And, Karl Marx notwithstanding, Adenauer was another of those individuals who was to change the course of history.

Templer did more than get the Germans off their backs; he began the slow process of reversing Allied punitive policy. By midsummer, 1945, Templer was convinced of the need to rebuild Western Germany, not only because of the danger to the occupying forces of disease and disorder arising from starvation, but because he was one of the first to see how the misery of the Germans could be turned to the advantage of communism and blight the long term political intentions of the Western Allies.

In the Russian zone the Soviet leaders had encouraged the formation of political parties which they were busy grouping into a 'popular front' destined to be controlled by the communists. In the Western zones members of the German Communist Party were already accusing the Western Allies of planning to divide Germany and arguing that the only hope of unity lay in support for the Russians.

The best answer to these wholly logical communist tactics was to revive social and political life in the Western zones and attempt to give them a democratic basis. Even before the Potsdam agreement was published in August, Templer had begun to appoint the nucleus of an administration for each of the zone's four provinces, beginning with rural and urban district councils, and to license trade unions, political parties, theatres and newspapers. After

Potsdam he set up German advisory committees to organise railways, building, the distribution of food, oil and coal, posts and telecommunications. A German zonal economic bureau was established to co-ordinate the committees and supervise industry.

But committees and officials were of little use if the people continued to starve and industry was without raw materials, nor could schools and universities function without books. As an official of the Control Commission remarked, the Germans were a receptive people who had been subjected to a stream of propaganda for years; now that all text books, novels, plays and films produced under the Nazis were being censored, they had nothing to read and little to which to listen. Templer, backed by Montgomery, began to bombard the British Government with requests for translations of British books as well as for food, raw materials and essential machinery with which to get German industry started.

The response was not spectacular, due partly to indifference at home and also to the strain which any gifts to Germany put upon the balance of payments. The trickle of grain increased a little, however, and by the time Templer left in the spring of 1946, £30,000,000 ($75,000,000) worth of other imports had arrived, a drop in the ocean but enough to prevent catastrophe that winter.

Books were an even greater difficulty. There were few translators and fewer books in English dealing with the all important subjects of history, politics and economics which were suitable for German consumption. Owing to an acute shortage of pulp Germans who received licences to publish were not allowed to print more than 5,000 copies of any one work. Both the French and the Russians were in a far happier position. The Russians had unlimited timber for pulp and, because they knew exactly what they wanted to publish and had the services of German communists, had soon printed as many books as all the other Allies put together. The French, believing in the force of their culture, denuded the forests of Bavaria to provide an intellectual fare to compensate for deficiencies in diet. In the British and American zones the literary famine continued for several years.

It was the more remarkable, therefore, that the licensing of newspapers in the British zone produced two of the great romances of the publishing world, both at the hands of the same comparatively junior British officer. Although thirty-five newspapers had appeared in the first year after the war, apart from the British owned *Die Welt*, which attained a circulation of a million copies a day, they were poor things, sometimes a cyclostyled sheet or a four-page printed paper. However, one morning a tall, blue-eyed, fair-haired young German walked into the Hamburg office of Major William Barnetson,[7] one of the licensing officers, and said he wanted to start a magazine. The young man was articulate and persuasive and Barnetson gave him permission to publish a sheet giving details of the Hamburg Radio service which had just been re-started. The sheet, called *Hor Zu* (Listen In), was successful and other licences followed. At the end of ten years Axel Springer owned the largest newspaper empire in Europe. He still looks back with affection on the man who gave him his start.

That same week another young man entered Barnetson's office, this time a recruit to his own staff. A Czech by origin, this tall, dark man with black eyes who spoke perfect German, had risen to the rank of Captain in the British army and won the Military Cross. He showed an interest in scientific books and Barnetson sent him out to see what German scientific books were available and to study the question of copyright. Again the young man did his work well and on this experience Captain Robert Maxwell was to found a publishing empire almost as large as Springer's and even more controversial. However many success stories had their origins in the occupation, few can have emanated from the same Allied official in the same week.

In some ways the Germans under the occupation were like a colony of ants which, having had its hill destroyed, fell victims to different scientific experiments. While the British tried to coax and coerce the main body into producing the wherewithal to rebuild the hill, the other Allies each tried out their own theories of government on the bewildered creatures. The Americans, believing that democracy could best be learned by example rather than precept, held local and provincial elections and established a form of representative administration before anyone in the British zone had been to the polls at all. They sometimes ran into difficulties because the communists, whose party had been declared a democratic organisation at Potsdam, tended to fulfil Russian rather than American directives; but this they dealt with simply by removing the recalcitrants in an

7 Later Sir William Barnetson, Chairman of Reuters and United Newspapers.

undemocratic manner. The Germans after all, were undergoing an experiment which had to be kept on the right lines.

The French were a law unto themselves. For nearly three years they waged a relentless political struggle against all their allies in an attempt to impose not only dismemberment but a degree of disablement upon the Germans which would give France the sort of security of which Frenchmen had always dreamed. Meanwhile they insulated their zone, forbidding Germans to move in or out of it and making it plain that they could work their passage back to independence only by serving the interests of France.

The French were extraordinarily ingenious in devising ways of extracting the maximum out of their zone. In the first few months they simply took away machinery, livestock, art treasures and personal belongings as restitution of what the Germans had taken from them. Once firmly in the saddle, French military government began to revive only those industries which could produce what France needed – coal and steel from the Saar, timber from the Black Forest, chemicals, wood pulp, leather – and forced the Germans to sell a large proportion of what they produced to France at a twenty per cent discount, paying in German marks which the French had captured or printed. What the French did not need themselves they sold on world markets for dollars.

Military government, using German labour, erected two new power lines to export electricity for which the French paid at a reduced rate whereas the Germans had to pay the full price. And throughout the occupation the French not only lived off the land, paying for their food and everything else in occupational marks, but charged the Germans fantastic occupation costs, including a large payment in cash which none of the other Allies extracted. Since occupational marks were not exchangeable into francs, the French taxpayer had no bill to foot at all. The British and Americans were indignant with the Russians for extracting reparations from current German production and in the end refused to allow any more equipment to go to Russia from their zones; but the French, without any fuss and occupying the smallest and poorest territory, extracted proportionately even more than the Russians.[8]

8 Russians defecting to the West reported that the early days of their occupation had been like a gold rush, seventy-thousand officials being assigned to reparations alone in the summer of 1945. In addition 'trophy brigades' had been sent to Germany to collect bicycles, clocks,

In one respect, however, the French were more successful than the other Western Allies. While the politicians were bent on dismemberment and on exploiting their zone for the benefit of France, a group of dedicated French educationalists under M. Raymond Schnittlein and Madame Germaine Giron set about reeducating German youth. Schnittlein, who had been a member of de Gaulle's cabinet in Algiers, had been a professor in Lithuania before the war; Madame Giron had studied at the interpreters' school in Heidelberg. Between them they evolved a policy which aimed at 'breaking the chains of German youth' and bringing them back into the main stream of European culture. In their view a false nationalism, preached during the past century not only by Germans but by many Frenchmen as well, had produced an environment which made it easy for the young to fall prey to aggressive militarism. Young Germans must be reminded first of their own great humanist tradition represented by Goethe, Kant and Beethoven, and then be introduced to the very best in French thought and be made familiar with the French contribution to civilisation.

Helped by a group of students from the École Normale and the Institute of Political Science in Paris, the Directorate of Public Education for the zone concentrated first upon primary schools. Schnittlein demanded and General Koenig agreed that these should be reopened in the autumn of 1945. Buildings were in ruins and at least three quarters of the teachers had been purged, but by setting up teacher training colleges on the French model and recruiting retired teachers, a beginning was made. Next the Directorate tackled text books and by writing, rewriting and translating as well as borrowing from Switzerland, the French managed in the first two years to provide twice as many text books per child as the British and seven times as many as the Americans. From primary the French moved on to secondary schools in which they revised the curriculum and stiffened the examination by which students qualified for university. French became a compulsory second lan-

---

food, trucks, etc., to send to Russia. Eugene Davidson, op. cit. quoting Robert Slusser, ed.: *Soviet Economic Policy in Post-war Germany*, p. 255 n.

The United Nations Department of Economic Affairs ('Economic Survey of Europe since the war') estimated that the Russians had taken approximately 3,000 million dollars' worth of goods from Germany between 1947 and 1950. The Germans, extending the period to 1953, put the figure at more than 10,000 million dollars.

The Germans estimated that the French made a profit from their zone in the region of 2,000 million dollars. Eugene Davidson, op. cit., p. 180 n.

guage and was taught mainly by French men and women. Finally the French revived the universities of Tübingen and Freiburg and resurrected one at Mainz which had existed from 1477 to 1817. 'I want to tell you openly,' said General Koenig in opening it, 'that here you are *chez vous*.'[9] The Germans responded with such alacrity that by the end of a year there were a hundred and fifty-six professors, drawn largely from refugees from eastern Europe, and four thousand five hundred students.

This enlightened effort was made easier because the French had never adopted a policy of non-fraternisation. They might steal or 'persuade' the Germans to sell whatever they coveted, but at least they shared their houses and encouraged as much contact and exchange between French and German youth as possible. Summer courses and summer camps drew hundreds of French boys and girls into the zone and French universities were encouraged to accept German students. The experiment was a success and was gradually extended to adults. Although some Germans protested that they were being stuffed with culture and starved of food, the young Germans felt that they were being treated as individuals and responded enthusiastically, with results which were to have an important influence on the future development of Western Europe.

The Russian experiment was the most complicated. Stalin never wavered in his intention to use the Russian zone as a springboard from which to capture the rest of Germany for communism, but he had to move cautiously. His country was exhausted, the Americans had the atom bomb and he could not afford a confrontation. He had, therefore, to make it appear that he was willing to collaborate with his allies, even if only on his own terms, and at the same time to offer the Germans a sufficient inducement to overcome their dislike both of the Russians and the Soviet system.

His bait was a united Germany. In every speech which Stalin or his mouthpieces made, in every one of the long succession of notes which the Soviet Government sent to its war-time allies on the subject of Germany, the same theme was repeated. Germany, as had been agreed at Potsdam, should be treated as one country and be given centralised 'truly democratic' government with Berlin as its capital. Russia, through the strength of her army and her control over the countries of Eastern Europe, could alone guarantee this unity

9 *The French in Germany*, 1945–9, F. R. Willis, p. 175.

and assure the new Germany of its frontiers. By refusing to accept the Soviet proposals, the Western Allies showed that they wished to keep Germany divided and to exploit it for their own ends in the interests of monopoly capitalism. Let the Germans trust the Russians, therefore, and they would have restored to them a united, independent country from which the only pledge demanded would be one of neutrality in any struggle between East and West.

Although every thinking German knew that a 'truly democratic' government meant, in Russian eyes, one that was controlled by communists, there was much that was tempting in Stalin's offer. Almost to a man the Germans wanted their country to remain undivided, whatever its future frontiers might be, and few of them had any doubt that the Russians would be able to protect them if they accepted Soviet terms. The Americans, on the other hand, were only too plainly in a tearing hurry to get home. Hardly an officer or official with whom the Germans had to deal remained in the same post for more than a few months and, after the victory over Japan, the balance of forces in Europe began moving steadily in Stalin's favour. When Secretary of State Byrnes offered to share the secrets of the atomic bomb with all America's allies, including the Russians, he seemed to be confirming the fear that lurked in every German mind. For if the Americans were not prepared to use atomic weapons how could they stand up to the Soviet Government? And if the Americans were going to leave, then, from the German point of view, there was everything to be said for coming to an understanding with the Russians at once.

The British were tired, insular, full of their own problems and no match for the Russians even if allied to the French, who were a doubtful quantity. The French, unwittingly, were playing the Russian game. By advocating so obstinately the dismemberment of Germany and rejecting every move to treat the country as a whole, they were not only strengthening Stalin's case but allowing him to appear as the champion of unity without the true nature of that unity ever being put to the test.

Seeing, as he thought, the odds running in his favour, Stalin pursued his course relentlessly. He advocated the abolition of the zones and an immediate central German government supported by 'anti-fascist' parties. He demanded an increase in the level of German industry, particularly in the production of steel, and he opposed French demands for the separation of the Ruhr, the Rhineland and the Saar. All of this, he might reasonably expect, would sound like music in German ears and be remembered in the elections which were shortly to be held in all four zones. However, things did not go quite as Stalin planned.

The first shock came in Berlin. Looking ahead to the elections, the Russians began to prepare a 'popular front', through which they hoped to unite the left and so, perhaps, win control even in the western zones. In March, at Russian instigation, Otto Grotewohl, a German communist-sympathiser, who was head of the Social Democratic Party in the city, suggested a fusion of his party with the Communist Party led by Wilhelm Pieck. Several leading Social-Democrats protested and appealed to the Kommandatura to hold a referendum. General Kotikov, the Russian military governor, confident that the Communist Party had a sufficiently tight hold on the city to achieve a successful result, agreed and the date was set for 31st March. But Kotikov had miscalculated. When the polls opened, Social Democrats flocked to the booths and it at once became clear that the communists were going to lose. Within an hour the Red Army closed the polling stations in the Russian sector, alleging 'irregularities,' and Grotewohl issued a hurried instruction to his followers in the other sectors to stay away. He was too late. More than 75 % of the Social Democratic party had already voted and had rejected any kind of working arrangement with the communists by a majority of more than two to one. A new Social Democratic Executive Committee immediately appealed to the Kommandatura for recognition.

Kotikov, angry and humiliated, stalled and immediately arranged for Grotewohl to hold a convention between his rump of Social Democrats and the Communists at which a fusion of the two was announced, the new party being given the name of the Socialist Unity Party, bearing the German initials S.E.D. Grotewohl and Pieck then also appealed to the Kommandatura for recognition. No one had any doubt that the S.E.D. was the Communist Party renamed, but after a long argument both new groups were recognised in the city only. The S.E.D. was not recognised in any of the western zones.

Smarting under this rebuff, the Russians decided to step up their campaign for the elections proper by bringing their differences with their allies officially into the open. Although Roosevelt had accepted $10,000,000,000 as a basis for negotiating the reparations due to Russia, the Foreign Ministers in conference would not adopt it, mainly because the Russians would not allow any examination of the amount they had already taken from their zone. Now their representative in the Economic Division of the Control Council suddenly announced that there could be no question of any exchange of goods between the zones until each had a favourable balance of trade and had paid reparations in full. This was tantamount to an ultimatum to the British and Americans to pay up on behalf of the Germans or say good-bye to any possibility of treating Germany as 'an economic whole'. Clay and Robertson argued with their Soviet opposite members for three weeks at the end of which Clay, on 3rd May, 1946, suspended delivery of all reparations to any zone until a joint import-export policy had been agreed. In other words unless the Russians (and French) honoured Potsdam, Clay in future was going to run his zone as they ran theirs.

Although few people realised it at the time, this was really the beginning of the cold war. The Russian-controlled press, which had been vilifying the West for months, now attacked Clay personally in the jargon that was to become so familiar. He was accused not only of acting illegally, but of being a 'lackey of American big business' defending capitalism against the progressive forces of communism. Russian officials began boycotting the social functions of the Council in which, until then, they had played a full part. For the first time the whole world became aware that the war-time allies were at loggerheads.

It was the Americans who took the next step. At the Foreign Ministers' Conference in July, Byrnes announced that, pending the implementation of the Potsdam Agreement, the United States would merge its own zone with that of any other power. Bevin at once accepted on behalf of Britain and by September the amalgamation of the British and American zones into Bizonia was under way. Molotov was taken by surprise. In one breath he said that Bizonia was in breach of Potsdam and a flagrant attempt to make Germany a colony of American business, in the next he saw it as proof that the Americans, 'disgusted with the bickerings of the European peoples which were not their concern,' were preparing to pull out altogether. However, there was no time to lose. Elections in the American zone had already taken place with the predictable result of a marginal victory for the Christian over the Social Democrats but a disappointing communist vote; preparations now had to be made for those in the British, French and Russian zones which were scheduled for September and October. As the split between the Allies was now an acknowledged fact, the verdict of the Germans was to be given for the first time. Would they support the American view that the Russians had made fulfilment of Potsdam impossible? Or would they accept Molotov's argument that the only future for Germany as a united country lay in his own proposals? Neither Byrnes nor Bevin, both of whom felt that Molotov had made a formidable appeal for German allegiance, were particularly sanguine.

The Russians could scarcely expect to win outright, but if the communists made a reasonable showing in the two western zones and the S.E.D. gained an overwhelming victory in the Russian zone and their sector of Berlin, they could still hope to wear down their opponents by a political war of attrition. The Germans, they felt sure, had only to feel sufficiently uncertain of the future to turn to them for support. First results, however, were not encouraging. In the British zone the Christian Democrats emerged as the strongest party by a narrow majority over the Social Democrats, in the French zone by an overwhelming one. In neither did the communists attain more than a derisory vote.

In their own zone the Russians left nothing to chance. The members of the S.E.D. received every sort of favour and advantage. The leaders were fed with official information and their journals supplied with enough paper to enable them to print much larger issues than their competitors. All pretence of impartiality was abandoned. Christain Democratic leaders who refused to toe the Russian line were forced out of office and their own party news-papers obliged to attack them. Many of their supporters were arrested and it became virtually impossible for the non-communist parties to campaign; yet for propaganda purposes they were obliged to remain in existence.

The rank and file of the S.E.D. were given higher rations, special issues of clothing, paid holidays and travel allowances to enable them to take an active part in electioneering. All the totalitarian organisations, the Free German Trade Union, the Union of German Peasants, the Union of Victims of Fascism, Women's and Youth Movements were roped into the struggle. As polling day drew near the anti-communist parties found that in district after district their list of candidates was disqualified on Russian instructions.

In the urban and parish elections in Saxony, which began on 1st September, a third of the voters had none but S.E.D. candidates to vote for and the disqualifications mounted as the elections progressed. On 8th September, in Thuringia and Prussian Saxony, 40% of the electorate only had one list from which to choose and on 16th September, in Brandenburg and Mecklenburg, the non-communist parties were allowed to present candidates only in a third of the constituencies. In addition, thousands of ballot papers were 'spoiled' on the instructions of the communists who supervised the polling booths.

Even so the result showed an astonishing resistance to the camouflaged communism which the Russians were hoping to have endorsed. The S.E.D. won a large majority of the seats because the Christian Democrats and Liberal Democrats ran separate candidates; but the anti-communist vote was only marginally behind in spite of the disqualifications and ballot-rigging. And when it came to the county councils and five State assemblies, the communist and anti-communist votes were practically equal.

The most dramatic result of all came at the end, on 20th October, in Berlin. Ever since the disastrous referendum in March, General Kotikov, the Russian representative in the Kommandatura, had been nervous of holding elections in Berlin. When his Western colleagues pressed for a date, he stalled, saying that all the most rabid 'fascist' elements remained in the city and he had no proof that the inhabitants were ready for elections. The new government of Berlin must, he said, be composed of 'workmen' and he wanted all who might be described as 'capitalists' banned from being candidates. After endless discussion the whole question was referred to the Control Council.

Marshal Sokolovsky, the Russian representative on the Council, did not share Kotikov's anxiety. He knew that the communists controlled the City Council and had widespread influence among police and officials even in the Western sectors of the city. He thought that, provided the right sort of pressures were exercised, the communists could win. When, in July, the new constitution for Berlin was proposed he voted for it. As a result, elections were announced for 20th October, to be held under the supervision of four-power inspection teams.

Although General Kotikov had been overruled, he did not give up. The inspection teams would only operate on polling day and much could be done to influence or intimidate voters beforehand. First he stopped the small supplies of fresh fruit and vegetables into the Western sectors which had been allowed in from the Soviet zone and organised communist demonstrations in protest. This move was quickly countered by Colonel Howley who threatened to flood the Western sectors with food from the U.S.A.

Next Kotikov tried to influence the electors through their children. Special food parties were given by members of the S.E.D. in schools and extra note books distributed with a note printed on the fly-leaf telling 'the dear children' that the paper was being used for them rather than for propaganda in newspapers because the S.E.D. knew of their great desire to study.

However, the communist newspapers did not go short, and their comment was more virulent than ever. Communist publicity was overwhelming. Red banners straddled the streets, thousands of posters covered the buildings, mass meetings were held at strategic points. On the other hand every conceivable obstacle was put in the way of the non-communist parties. Meetings were suddenly banned, committee members suspended, newspaper editors removed. Copies of speeches were demanded in advance and the speakers often forbidden to make them. A visitor might have thought that only one party existed.

Nevertheless, on 20th October, the inspection teams went into action and the population was able to vote without fear. Between 90% and 95% of the people did so, with spectacular results. The Social Democrats just failed to gain a clear majority over all the other parties, but won 63 seats in the City Council. The Christian Democrats had 29 seats, the Liberal Democrats 12. The Communist Party gained only 26 seats and even in the Russian sector polled only 21% of the votes. In all the twenty boroughs of the city the Social Democrats were returned as the leading party and in several had an absolute majority. In an election which had been held under four-power auspices and upon which the attention of the whole world had been focused, the Russians had suffered a crushing defeat.

The Russians were deeply resentful. They realised at once that, if Germany was to become a bastion for Communism, they would have to impose their creed by force rather than by persuasion.

Those Russian officials like Tulpanov, who had supported Zdanov's idea of spreading communism through popular front movements which included a façade of bourgeois supporters, lost face and influence. In the world beyond Germany Russian attitudes hardened perceptibly. As the farcical election in Poland in January, 1947, demonstrated, opposition to communism began to be ruthlessly suppressed in Eastern Europe. Militancy was encouraged in the large communist parties of France and Italy, in South East Asia and Korea.

In Berlin Kotikov did his utmost to counteract the results of the elections. In defiance of the new constitution, which had been validated at the polls, and without consulting his allies, he issued an order that none of the newly elected officials could take their place in the City Council without the approval of the Kommandatura. Instead of insisting that the constitution be honoured, the Western Powers weakly tried to compromise. Kotikov made the most of his opportunity. Mayor Werner and his communist controller, Maron, remained in office and challenged the credentials of one new official after another. Kotikov supported them. When the new Lord Mayor, a Social Democrat by the name of Dr Ostrowski, announced his intention of assuming office he was told curtly that if he entered the Council building, which was in the Russian sector, he would be thrown out. Eventually he was installed, but as soon as he tried to dismiss communists from their posts and put in members of the victorious parties, he was told by the Russians not to interfere.

Ostrowski did his best but was not strong enough to stand up to Russian pressure. The Russians delved into his private life, discovered that he had recently been divorced, and threatened to expose the details. Ostrowski capitulated and signed a paper saying that he would support the S.E.D. He was promptly disowned by his own party and forced to resign. The Russians then refused to accept his resignation.

The pantomime then took an ugly turn. Ostrowski's resignation was referred to the Control Council and once again the Western representatives, still chasing the 'will-of-the-wisp' of Russian friendship, compromised. They confirmed it only on condition that his successor was given prior approval by the Kommandatura, which was exactly what Kotikov had asked for. As he expected, the man elected was Dr Ernst Reuter, a former Communist who had been to Moscow before the war, become disillusioned and joined the

Social Democrats. Reuter had fled the city when Hitler came to power but returned after the war and had been a successful candidate in the elections. Kotikov vetoed his election as Mayor. Because of the Control Council's ruling the veto had to stand, but rather than surrender to the Russians, the Germans refused to elect anyone else and chose a woman, Frau Louise Schröder, a respected member of the former Reichstag, as Reuter's deputy.

This tiny, grey-haired lady in her late fifties became one of the heroes of post-war Germany. Totally fearless, she began to put Social Democratic policies into force. The Russians countered with thuggery, bringing crowds of Communists in trucks and tanks to the steps of the council offices where they beat up Social Democratic councillors while the police stood idly by. One Social Democratic leader was seriously injured when thugs slammed his car door on his legs as he was getting out and a woman, Frau Leber, whose husband had been executed after the 20th July plot against Hitler, was so badly beaten she had to go to hospital. Frau Schröder remained unintimidated, went regularly to her office and carried on her duties in face of continual Russian obstruction.

In the end neither obstruction nor intimidation could save the Russians from the effects of their defeat. They had failed in their attempt to gain political control of Germany, because of the decision of the Germans themselves. That decision had not been taken through any gratitude to the Western Powers; as Lord Montgomery had said only a few weeks before, feeling against them had never been more bitter than in the summer of 1946. It had been taken because, for the Germans, the choice lay between two forms of oppression and they had come down on the side of the West, since acceptance of Stalin's terms meant becoming a satellite of the Soviet Union. Eighteen months of Soviet rule, exercised through German Communists, had convinced them that this would be the greater evil. The brutality of the Red Army, the ruthless oppression by the secret police, the treatment of refugees from the East and of prisoners of war in Russian hands, the kidnappings and the clear indication that if the whole of Germany fell under Russian domination it would be exploited in the interest of the Soviet Union, had decided them.

Nevertheless, the verdict was not purely negative. Many of the new German leaders had a genuine desire to build a democratic community and organised their parties and campaigns with skill and thoroughness. Although in the Russian zone men like Kaiser, Schreiber, and Koch were banned by the Soviet authorities, they had done their work so well that their parties were forbidden to present candidates. In the West the party leaders, without being too provocative had not hesitated to criticise the Allies or to represent the miseries which the electorate was suffering. They had campaigned with dignity and, with the exception of the communists, without vituperation. Many of them had shown considerable personal courage. Every man and woman who came out openly against communism in the Russian zone or the Russian sector of Berlin risked loss of office, arrest and perhaps deportation. Many suffered all three. Yet others were always ready to take their place. If it was still true that the mass of Germans had little understanding of the working or meaning of democracy, it was undeniable that their leaders had made a most creditable beginning. In this lay the real importance of the vote, for they were soon to be put to an even more rigorous test.

CHAPTER V

The Parting of the Ways

The Russian blockade of Berlin did not begin suddenly. From the moment that Bizonia came into existence on New Year's Day, 1947, the Soviet Government abandoned any serious attempt at collaboration. The Control Council and the Kommandatura continued to meet regularly and a few minor ordinances were passed; but in general there was deadlock. Meanwhile, throughout 1947, the Russians made cautious but deliberate preparations to drive the Western Allies from Berlin and, hopefully, from the whole of Germany. They knew that if they could force the Western Powers out of the city their prestige would stand so high among the Germans that compliance with their wishes would be almost a certainty. Both Schumacher and Adenauer, the foremost of the new German politicians, were still protesting against the idea of a separate West German state and even Clay admitted, in a cable to his Government, that if Berlin fell the rest of Germany would surely follow.

The blockade began with pinpricks. Barriers would suddenly appear on the roads, be maintained for a few hours and then as suddenly disappear. The first of such barriers seen by Robert Murphy, the American political adviser, consisted of a single pole stretched across the road manned by two Mongolian soldiers. He felt certain that the Russians were simply testing the will of the Americans to insist upon their rights and he was convinced that if a military convoy had been sent through, no action would have been taken. But neither he nor Clay could convince their Government.[1] Allied trucks and cars, therefore, stopped at the slightest obstacle and queues many miles long stretched back along the autobahn.

Surprised and pleased at the passivity of the West, the Russians stepped up their obstructions. Locks on canals were closed without notice; trains were diverted into sidings. In the spring of 1948, the Russians demanded identity checks on allied soldiers entering Berlin

1 Robert Murphy, Op. Cit., p. 384.

on military trains. The Western Powers offered to provide lists but refused to allow the Russians to board the trains. Germans, however, were afforded no such protection and were frequently taken from their coaches by Russian soldiers to disappear into the Eastern zone, sometimes for ever. Next, freight trains were held up and barge traffic on the canals stopped. Sokolovsky announced that the Russians were going to hold exercises in the air corridors which would make them unsafe for Western aircraft.

Then, on 20th March, 1948, the Russians made the move for which the Western Powers had long been waiting. Sokolovsky walked out of the Control Council and announced that four-power control was at an end. The only surprise was that Kotikov remained in the Kommandatura for another three months.

During those three months Russian propaganda reached new heights of fantasy. According to the *Tägliche Rundschau*, Marshall Aid, which had been offered to all Europe and was beginning to flow into the Western states, including Germany, was intended to 'impoverish' the Germans; the Russian closure of road and rail services aimed to increase international traffic. Western Germans were being subjected to forced labour and terror and were fleeing in such numbers to the Eastern zone that food supplies were being threatened. (In fact exactly the reverse was happening.) The Russians stated repeatedly that the Western allies were preparing to leave the City and one cartoon showed a parrot, left behind by the Americans saying repeatedly; 'We stay here.' President Truman, 'the provincial Ku Kluxer and later haberdasher from Jackson, Missouri,' was said to vie for laurels 'with the little corporal from Munich.'[2] At the same time the Russians announced they were bringing thousands of tons of extra food and clothing to their own zone to save the Germans from the dire results of ruthless Western capitalism.

This barrage of lies had little effect on the Germans. Too many Western German policemen and civilians were being arrested or kidnapped for anyone to hold illusions about the true nature of Russian intentions. Out of a population of some two-and-a-half-million in the Western sectors of Berlin, only sixty-thousand registered to receive the extra food which the Russians were offering. Ernst Reuter, the Lord Mayor whom the Russians vetoed, told Clay that Berliners were used to deprivation and that he was

2 Eugene Davidson, Op. Cit., p. 186.

certain the people would stand anything rather than surrender to communist rulers. In his opinion the Russians were bluffing.

The Western commanders, however, were apprehensive. According to American and British calculations, if the Russians established a total blockade by land and water, it might be possible to bring enough supplies for the allied forces by air, but there was no hope at all of provisioning the civilian population. General Herbert, the British Military Governor, told General Howley, now his United States opposite number, that a blockade must drive out the Western Powers before the end of the year, and on instructions from his Government began to reduce his garrison and evacuate British women and children. Even Clay, who had become the most determined proponent of air supply, admitted that he did not think the chances of success were worth a snap of the fingers.

Nevertheless, the Western Allies went ahead with their preparations. In April, as the Russian restrictions on road and rail traffic tightened, the Americans and British began flying in supplies for their troops. When a Russian fighter pilot collided with the British transport, killing himself and fifteen others, Sir Brian Robertson threatened to give his transports a fighter escort and Clay backed him up. Sokolovsky, certain that an air-lift could only end in ignominious failure, assured them that no such escorts would be necessary.

Next, the Western Powers announced the long overdue currency reform. Having procrastinated for months in an attempt to get Russian agreement, they went ahead in their own zones. Seventy per cent of all Reichmark accounts in German banks were cancelled and each hundred Reichmarks of the remainder exchanged for six and a half new Deutschmarks. The measure was an instant success. Goods which had been hoarded for years suddenly appeared in the shops and the Black Market lost its sources of supply. The Russians countered with a currency reform of their own and announced that only their notes would be valid in Berlin. The Western Powers agreed on condition that the issue was under Four-Power control. When the Russians refused, the Allies introduced their own currency in their own sectors of the city; it was soon exchanging at the rate of one West mark for four East marks.

The stage was now set. Kotikov had walked out of the Kommandatura on 16th June, and a few days later the Russians imposed a full blockade on the City. Against all the odds an opinion poll showed that half the Berliners believed that they could be kept alive by air. The rest of the world held its breath.

When the air-lift began, on 24th June, 1948, the Western Allies had one small and one large airfield in their sectors of Berlin and the maximum load that anyone believed could be carried was between 3,000 and 4,000 tons a day; when it ended, nearly eleven months later, West Berlin had three airfields capable of taking all loads in all weather, the average daily load had risen to 8,000 tons and the record, reached on 11th April, 1949, stood at 12,849 tons. At the peak, aircraft were landing every thirty seconds and as many as 1,398 flights were made in twenty-four hours. Even fog had been overcome by improvements in radar. Clay himself once landed at the Tempelhof airfield in weather so thick that the pilot dared not move from the runway and had to be guided to the perimeter by a jeep using its headlights.

The air-lift was a prodigious feat of courage and organisation, not only on the part of the British and American air-crews, forty-five of whom lost their lives, but of the thousands of Germans who built the new airfield at Tegel in the French zone, and loaded and unloaded the freight at both ends, sometimes in the face of physical intimidation by the Russians and their followers. The population of Berlin suffered a fourth winter of extreme privation and many thousands died who might have lived had the blockade not reduced their household coal allowances to less than four sacks for the whole winter; yet food rations were marginally increased during the blockade and morale reached a pitch unknown since the surrender.

Nevertheless, the ultimate success of the air-lift in forcing the Russians to raise the blockade, came as a surprise not only to the Western Allies but to the other countries of the world who had been striving, through the United Nations, to prevent the quarrel erupting into a third world war. Certainly the supplies the British and Americans had succeeded in transporting – nearly 1,500,000 tons of food, coal and other necessities – exceeded all expectations. It is also true that Clay saw no reasons why the lift should not go on indefinitely and had secretly prepared a three-year programme to transport even greater quantities. But to most onlookers in most Governments the Russians still appeared to have the whip-hand. The lift was enormously expensive, it cannot have cost less than

£100,000,000 ($2,500,000,000); it made such demands on the British and American air forces that they were incapacitated from any but secondary operations in other spheres; and although it might enable the citizens of Berlin to live at subsistence level, it was no method of keeping industry going and providing work for the population. In other words, if the Russians stuck to their guns, Berlin was doomed.

Nor was there any apparent reason why the Russians should lift the blockade. Their forces were playing a purely passive role. Tanks surrounded the Western sectors but stood motionless; it needed only a few men to hold up trains, motor vehicles and barges. When the Western Powers stopped traffic coming into the Russian zone as a reprisal, only the Germans suffered; the Russians continued to take what they needed.

It was the West, therefore, who tried to break the deadlock. From the moment the Russians declared four-power control at an end and even before the blockade became total, separate dialogues began between the American, British, and Russian Governments. Statements of policy flew back and forth, high officials from London and Washington visited Moscow. Henry Wallace, the American Presidential candidate, who still believed in Russian friendship, wrote an open letter to Stalin suggesting a basis for a German peace treaty. British Trade Ministers, Mr Harold Wilson and Mr Arthur Bottomley, tried to negotiate a long-term trade agreement with the Russians as a gesture of goodwill.

Understandably, the Russians played for time. Stalin gave a conciliatory reply to Mr Wallace and said that it was essential that the American and Russian systems should learn to live together. Having refused for years to hold a Peace Conference about Germany, he now proposed one, suggesting that once it had been concluded all foreign troops should be withdrawn. However, Molotov's arguments in two successive Notes showed that the Russian plan was still a unified Germany with a strong central government of truly 'democratic forces' which the Russians, more openly than before, intimated would take the form of the régimes now being consolidated in Eastern Europe; whatever the allies might think this would certainly not be acceptable to the Western Germans. A year after President Truman had launched his doctrine of 'supporting free peoples who are resisting subjugation' – a complete reversal of Roosevelt's policy of doing nothing to annoy the Russians – he was still saying: 'I like Old Joe. He's a decent fellow but is a prisoner of the Politburo.'[3] It was all very confusing.

Twice Stalin received the Western diplomats and each time agreement appeared to be in sight. He accepted the economic fusion of the Western zones: he registered but did not press his opposition to their political amalgamation. He agreed that, if the East mark became the currency of Berlin, the bank of issue should have four-power supervision and issued instructions to his representatives in Germany to conclude an agreement on these terms. But every time the members of the Control Council met, Sokolovsky found reasons why the instructions could not be carried out and Molotov backed Sokolovsky, a stand which neither would have dared to take in defiance of Stalin's wishes.

Stalin was simply playing a double game. Had he wished he could have ended the blockade in the autumn of 1948 just as easily as six months later. He was still playing for time in the hope that the Allies would crack.

Why then did Stalin back down? Internationally the Russians were stronger than ever. Through the Cominform, founded as an answer to the Marshall Plan, they had finally succeeded in imposing communism on Eastern Europe. Already Maniu, the Prime Minister of Roumania, and Petkov, the leader of the Peasants' Party in Bulgaria, had been arrested; Nagy had been driven from Hungary and his Smallholders' Party destroyed. Following the establishment of the Cominform, Mikolajczyk was driven from Poland, the King of Roumania forced to abdicate and a communist Greek 'Government in Exile' formed.

Early in 1948 pressure was put on Persia to expel the American military mission, a new treaty of 'friendship' was forced upon Finland and finally, communist control was established in Czechoslovakia by a coup which resulted in the death of Jan Masaryk and the reduction of President Benes to the status of a Russian puppet. The Russian stranglehold on Eastern Europe was loosened only by the failure of the puppet Greek Government to make any headway and the refusal of Marshal Tito to bow to Russian dictation. But even Tito had not defected to the West. Elsewhere in the world everything seemed to be going Stalin's way. Although he could not claim credit for the communist victory in China, Mao Tse Tung seemed a loyal communist who could be relied upon to spread the gospel and

3 Eugene Davidson, Op. Cit., p. 204.

eventually extend his power over the whole of South East Asia; already there were rumblings in Korea. Admittedly the strikes fermented by Stalin's followers in Western Europe during the blockade had been ineffective, and the Italian Communist Party had failed to win the general election in Italy; but they had made a good showing and were strong enough in France to make each successive government nervous of joining a Western bloc. Communism was on the march throughout the world and Germany, which the Russians had regarded as the key to final victory, seemed ripe for plucking if only they persevered.

Yet in February of 1949, Stalin hinted to an American journalist that he was prepared to settle the Berlin question and in March and April secret conversations were taking place in the United Nations between the Russians and American delegates. Why?

Fear of a world war, in which only the Americans possessed nuclear weapons, is not a complete answer. The fear was at the back of Stalin's mind and had been uttered in several speeches; but the evidence was overwhelming that war was the last thing the Western Powers wanted. Apart from all the diplomatic approaches, the air-lift itself was proof of a determination to avoid an armed clash at almost any cost. The aircraft came and went without fighter escorts and whenever bolder measures were proposed they were turned down by the Western governments. When Aneurin Bevan proposed in the British cabinet that tanks should be sent down the autobahn, his was a lone voice. Clay suggested sending armoured trains through the barriers and was refused permission.

As a result the air-lift itself was conducted according to a set of unwritten rules, the effects of which were often bizarre. Several times the Russians threatened to hold air exercises in the corridor to shoot down aircraft which strayed outside it, but they never did. Sometimes they seemed to want to make flying safer. When the British complained that a Russian barrage balloon protecting an installation on the border of their sector made landing at Gatow dangerous, the Russians moved it. When, for the same reason, the French blew up a Russian radio mast which had always been allowed to operate from their sector, the Russians made no objection.

In spite of the tension in the City contacts were maintained and traffic flowed between the sectors. Germans went to and fro about their work by tube or bus and American and Russian soldiers still crossed the sector boundaries. If they got drunk or misbehaved they were dealt with as before. Officers and officials ceased to meet socially, but the Military Governors and their deputies would ring each other up or pay each other visits to settle difficulties on the spot. One such telephone call involved Marshal Sokolovsky.

As a counter-measure to the raids and kidnappings of the East German police and N.K.V.D., the Americans had imposed a strict speed limit in their sector. One day two cars, going very fast, refused to stop at the command of a jeep patrol. The jeep driver radioed ahead and within a few minutes an armoured car and some soldiers barred the way. The Russian cars drew up; out of the first stepped a General and three officers, out of the second some Russian soldiers with 'tommy guns'. At the sight of the guns an American G.I. put the muzzle of his sub-machine gun in the General's stomach and kept it there. The telephone wires hummed and an hour later an American officer arrived and identified the Marshal who was at once allowed to proceed. Sokolovsky protested indignantly to Clay, but the episode was passed over.

There were other comical exchanges. Throughout the blockade the Russians continued to build their mammoth war memorial at Pankow. However, some of the material, in particular some bronze wreaths and a giant plaque of Lenin's head, had been manufactured in the Western sectors. The Russians had tried to collect them, but the manufacturer wished to be paid in West marks and refused to deliver until he got them. Kotikov appealed to Howley who let the wreaths go, but said that if the Russians wanted Lenin's head they would have to pay. In the end Kotikov handed over the West marks. On the other hand, when Kotikov threatened to cut the power cables crossing the Western sectors, Howley stormed into his office to tell him that if he did so he would know exactly what retaliation to expect. The Western Powers not only would cut the Russian cables but stop the trains and barges which passed from the East through the Western sectors and into the Russian zone. Kotikov rang up next day to say that the whole matter had been a misunderstanding. It was as if a game were being played which because it was dangerous, must be kept within tacitly accepted rules. But if neither side wanted war and both knew it, why did the Russians not persist? The real reason was that the Germans were making them look foolish.

The Russians had believed that they could force the Western Powers out of Berlin without war by the end of the winter and that,

by doing so, they would convince the Germans that it was better
to accept the position of a satellite than trust in such ineffective
allies. But the Germans came to the opposite conclusion. Their
behaviour, within Berlin and without, showed that they would go
to any lengths and accept any risk rather than succumb to Russian
dictatorship. Under pressure they once again had become a most
formidable people – not militarily but morally.

The Russians tried everything: bribery, cajolery, persuasion and
intimidation. Besides offering to feed the whole city on a scale it
had not known since the war, the Soviet commanders declared an
end to de-Nazification, the release of prisoners of war, the handing
back of such industries as had not been nationalised to their former
owners, increased trade with Eastern Europe and a reduction in
occupation costs.

In answer to the political and economic fusion of the Western
zones, the Russians set up an economic council and, through the
S.E.D. organised a People's Congress to promote their policy of
'One Germany'. Appeals were sent to the Council of Foreign
Ministers and the United Nations; eminent Germans were sent into
the Western zones to play upon the fears of political leaders like
Adenauer and Schumacher, who were loath to see the division of
their country. A plebiscite on the theme 'unity and a just peace,'
was organised throughout Germany, although in the West only the
British allowed voting to take place. Finally a constitution was drawn
up for a People's Republic with a coalition cabinet, two chambers
and a guarantee of personal freedom.

It was in vain. The plebiscite was a failure. All Germans knew
that in the Eastern zones people were forced to vote not once, but
often; in the British zone they did not bother to go to the polls.
Russian promises were not believed. In spite of their guarantee
of extra food, rations in the Russian sector remained so inadequate
that many of those who had registered as citizens in order to receive
food, went back to the Western sectors and asked to be allowed to
eat what was brought in by air.

Instead of succumbing, Berliners became activists. In September a
vast demonstration was organised by Ernst Reuter and Franz
Neumann, the Social Democratic leaders, to protest against the
arrest of some non-communist East German policemen who had
taken refuge in the Western sectors. Kotikov had promised a safe-
conduct and then gone back on his word. The British banned the

gathering but it took place none the less. In twos and threes thousands upon thousands of citizens converged upon the Tiergarten and the Brandenburg Tor until every street within sight was packed with people. They were orderly and listened to the speeches. But when a Russian jeep appeared it was stoned. The Russians fired and killed a man, whereupon the crowd stormed the Brandenburg Tor and tore to shreds the Red Flag which had flown there since the surrender.

The City Council at last decided to defy the Russians. The councillors passed a resolution condemning the blockade as a crime against humanity and dismissed Markgraf, the communist Chief of Police, appointing Herr Stumm in his place. The Russians refused to accept Markgraf's dismissal and organised their usual demonstration which included the invasion of the Council Chamber and the intimidation of the Members. The councillors stood firm. A woman, Jeannette Wolff, who had survived Hitler's concentration camps, was badly beaten up. Unafraid, she rose in her seat, poured scorn on secret police and concentration camps of all kinds and, rounding on the communist members of the Council said: 'I have only one life to lose and this life belongs to freedom. If it should cost my life on your account, gentlemen, and Berlin should remain free, I declare myself ready for death.'[4] The spirit of Frau Wolff carried the day.

Since it was impossible to conduct business in the Russian sector the Council removed itself to West Berlin where, for the first time, Ernst Reuter was able to assume the Mayoralty for which he had been chosen, Herr Stumm also moved his headquarters, to be followed by more than half the city police. Municipal elections, due in November but banned in the Russian sector, were held and overwhelmingly confirmed the Social Democratic majority. Sadly, the majority of East Berliners saw themselves disenfranchised. For the Russian reply to the Council's action was to declare it dissolved and to impose a new Council on their sector headed by Fritz Ebert, the complacent son of a great father, the first President of the Weimar Republic. The government of the city and its police force were now finally divided.

The example of the Council was followed by the citizens. The students of the University of Berlin, which was in the Russian sector, had long been protesting against the authoritarianism of

4 Eugene Davidson, Op. Cit., p. 170.

their communist masters. Now they revolted and, helped by non-communists and unemployed professors, set up a free University in the suburb of Dahlem under the Chancellorship of Edwin Redslob, disciple of Goethe and editor of *Tagesspiegel*, a Western rival of the *Tägliche Rundschau*. Germans who had fought with or against underground movements during the war came forward with plans for sabotaging industry and communications in the Russian zone. One group suggested blowing up the Blue Express from Moscow and commended their plan by remarking that Marshal Sokolovsky might well be on the train at the time. Their offers were refused but, had they been accepted, they could have recruited a formidable underground army. In the end, Stalin saw that his policy was failing and that the Germans could not be bullied into submission. The Western Allies could not hold out in Berlin for ever, but they could certainly continue the air-lift for another year and then not only would Western Germany be in existence but Russian prestige would have suffered calamitously. Already the Eastern zone was becoming a drain on the Soviet Union instead of a source of supply and the Germans were leaving it by thousands a week. Stalin cut his losses.

He seems to have taken the decision to end the blockade on his own. When questioned about Berlin by an American journalist in February, 1949, he answered without mentioning the currency question which, until then, had been one of the chief bones of contention. The State Department noticed the omission and followed it up through the United Nations. When Dr Malik, the Russian representative, confirmed that the omission was not accidental, secret conversations began. Nothing was said to Clay or Robertson, who continued to tell the German press that they knew of no developments which foreshadowed the lifting of the blockade. Then suddenly, on 4th May, the three Western governments informed the Secretary General of the United Nations that they had reached an agreement with the Soviet Union for the lifting of the blockade on 12th May and for holding a conference of Foreign Ministers in Paris on 23rd May to discuss the problem of Germany and the future of Berlin. Clay read the announcement in a newspaper.

So it was, four years after the surrender of the German armies, that the attempt of the victorious Allies jointly to impose a new régime on their defeated enemy collapsed. Immediately an Occupation Statute and Basic Law for the three Western zones was published, foreshadowing the creation of an independent republic. At the same time the Peoples' Congress in the Eastern zone adopted the constitution which the Russians had proposed for all Germany. The Foreign Ministers, therefore, met to consider, not a policy for Germany as a whole, as laid down at Potsdam, but the relationship between two German states being brought into separate existence under the tutelage of their Eastern and Western conquerors. Berlin remained a political island, ruled for a few more years by a Kommandatura which controlled two separate cities living in uneasy competition, until the Russians built a wall to separate them.

Quite as important as the creation of separate states was the effect the air-lift had had upon the Germans. For the first time since the surrender they lifted their heads. The struggle which had taken place over their shattered land had revived in them a sense of their own importance and given to the world a new insight into their character. They had shown great fortitude and endurance and were once again a force in Europe. They sensed that they were needed by both sides; by the Russians as a spear-head to spread communism, by the West as an ally to resist it. By their own efforts they had earned the right to rebuild their country in their own way. In the East this was to be denied them. The Russian zone became a 'Peoples' Democracy', a one-party state ruled by communists backed by Russian bayonets. In the West the Federal Republic had been born.

CHAPTER VI

Knights in Armour

Like the ninety-four thousand 'occupation babies,' fathered by allied soldiers but born out of wedlock, the Federal Republic was an unwanted child, acknowledged by Germans as a product of defeat and cared for only in the belief that, in the near future, it could be re-absorbed into the life of a properly constituted and complete German family.

Its adolescence was precarious. From the outset it was denounced by the Russians as illegitimate and assailed by communists within and without Germany. A rival communist state, The Peoples' Democratic Republic, set up in Eastern Germany, was used as a base for propaganda and subversion and a Fifth Column of communist sympathisers organised within the Federal Republic, whose numbers the Russians put at 100,000.

With the explosion of the first Russian atomic bomb in 1949 and the outbreak of the Korean war the following summer, the Russians again seemed to be on the march; it looked as though their abandonment of the Berlin blockade had been a calculated withdrawal to allow them to assert their supremacy in other parts of the world. The early reverses of the Southern Koreans and their American allies frightened the Germans and made them wonder how long the forces of the United States would stay in Europe and whether, if they did stay, they would be able to protect them. Through 1950 and 1951 the fear that Germany would once again be the main battlefield in a new world war dominated German thinking. It seemed that the Federal Republic might be obliterated even before it had attained full independence or that, because of the danger of war, independence might be indefinitely postponed.

Inevitably, in such a context, conflict raged among the Germans themselves. The new generation of leaders who began to emerge in the West were torn between the desire to remain free of Russian domination and the longing to reunite with the Germans in the

Soviet zone. German communists quickly and aggressively exploited their anguish. At least until the end of the Korean war the Russians remained confident that, if they sustained the pressure, the Western Germans would succumb. German communists reflected this optimism. A detailed programme for the government of a united Germany was drawn up and referred to as if its implementation was entirely a matter of time. Visits and notes were exchanged between German leaders in the Federal and Peoples' Republics and a torrent of speeches and propaganda descended upon the whole people through radio and press.

That the Federal Republic had a promising beginning, in spite of this menacing political climate, was due almost entirely to two men, each powerful enough to control one of the two great political parties which had emerged from the period of Allied occupation, Kurt Schumacher, leader of the Social Democrats, and Konrad Adenauer, chairman of the Christian Democratic Union.

They had some things in common. Both had considerable political experience in the Weimar Republic, both had opposed Hitler and ended up in prison or a concentration camp. Both were men of authoritarian character who believed in asserting their leadership within party and state, subject to the verdict of the polls. On the one hand Schumacher was a Protestant and a Prussian who had been brought up in Kulm (Chelmno), a small town on the Vistula which had been an outpost against the Slavs since the days of the mediæval Teutonic knights, whereas Adenauer was a Rhinelander and a Roman Catholic, with a greater affinity to Latin rather than to Teutonic culture. Schumacher was a man of passionate convictions who clung to a rigid dogma; Adenauer was cold and cunning, flexible in the means he adopted to achieve clearly defined ends. In a different era the clash between them might have resounded through history as loudly as that between Gladstone and Disraeli; even as it was, it elevated the political adolescence of the Federal Republic to the highest level.

In the beginning Kurt Schumacher was by far the better known. Tall and slim, with striking rather than handsome looks, he had grown up with three attractive sisters and a mother who all adored him. His father, a small business man, seems to have been correct but unimaginative and to have played little part in his development. Living in East Prussia (now and after 1918, Poland) where the Jewish community was very much part of the German colony, he had many Jewish friends as a boy and retained a liking for Jews throughout his life.

Although Schumacher always loved his mother and remained close to one of his sisters, he soon developed intellectual interests which they could not share and by the time he entered the university was already interested in social democracy. The First World War came when he was nineteen and Schumacher, an ardent patriot who saw it as part of the great struggle between German culture and Slav barbarism, at once volunteered. Afraid that the fighting would be over before he had taken any part, he transferred from the artillery to the infantry, was sent to the Eastern front and within a few weeks was so badly wounded that his right arm had to be amputated. At the age of twenty Schumacher became a cripple.

Schumacher met this disability with courage, but the effort strengthened that part of his nature which set him apart from other men. He became once more a dedicated student, moving to Berlin in 1917, where his studies led him in to a 'marriage' with politics which obsessed him for the rest of his life. He did not become anti-social. He loved food, wine and political talk and had at least one serious love-affair; but he never proposed to any woman and his family and friends soon accepted the fact that he would never marry. To obtain his doctorate he wrote a thesis on the place of the worker in bourgeois society; long before it was finished he had become an active member of the Social Democratic Party.

The revolution of 1918 and the German surrender brought the second dramatic change in Schumacher's life. Western Prussia became a part of Poland and his family lost their home and property. From then onwards Schumacher had to make his own way. In Berlin he had already made a mark as a militant young socialist and in 1920, at the instigation of some of the social democratic leaders, he was made assistant editor of the *Schwäbische Tagwacht*, the socialist newspaper produced by Wilhelm Keil, the leader of the party in Stuttgart, the capital of Württemberg. This was the beginning of his political career.

Schumacher was not content with editing the newspaper. He had a powerful pen and was a compelling speaker and soon became leader of the Social Democratic youth organisation in Stuttgart. Having gained a foothold in the party, he never looked back. He attracted a group of young men around him who became known as

'The Young Turks' and ceaselessly attacked not only his 'bourgeois' opponents, but the older leaders of his party who, in order to preserve the Republic, were forced into coalitions which, in Schumacher's view, diluted their socialism.

It is difficult to categorise his socialism. He accepted much of Marx's interpretation of history, particularly of the class struggle; but although anti-clerical, there was a strong streak of Protestantism in his make-up and he remained throughout his life a bitter enemy of communism. Lenin's teaching he thought a mixture of 'lies, cunning and stupidity.'[1] He was an admirer of Ferdinand Lassalle, who had founded his party under Bismarck and claimed to be free of dogma. Yet a passionate belief in the class struggle coloured all Schumacher's thinking and he was intolerant and impatient of those who disagreed with him. Some of his contemporaries described him as a 'militant social democratic nationalist bent on revolutionary reformism.'

Schumacher was elected to the Württemberg state legislature in 1924 and by 1932 had won the leadership of the state party, ousting his former benefactor, Wilhelm Keil. Meanwhile he had also been elected to the Reichstag and became a member of the national executive of the party. In the Reichstag he became a national figure. Schumacher had opposed the Nazis the moment Hitler appeared on the scene in the 1920s; now he attacked them virulently. Nazism he said 'was an appeal to the swine in man.' Goebbels he described to his face as a 'presumptuous dwarf too big for his breeches,' and he promised that when the Social Democrats had achieved power, an event he believed imminent, they would send the National Socialist leaders 'not to the gallows but to the padded cells where they belonged.'[2]

Yet even Schumacher recoiled from fighting the Nazis in the streets. He had been instrumental, with other militants, in founding the Iron Front, a combination of socialist and trade-union organisations which held mass demonstrations against both communism and national socialism. Like de Gaulle in France a decade later, he used to go to meetings surrounded by gangs of socialist thugs who did not hesitate to use violence on interrupters; he sanctioned the carrying of arms. But as the election of 1932 approached and the intimidation employed by the Nazis threatened his whole cause, he

1 *Kurt Schumacher*, Lewis Edinger, Stanford University Press, 1965, p. 40.
2 Lewis Edinger, Op. Cit., p. 42.

held back. When Von Papen took over the government of Prussia he acquiesced, along with other social democratic leaders, although two days before he had publicly declared he would never do so. The Iron Front was waiting to be called to arms for election day, but he never sent it into action. There is no doubt that his intransigence in later life stemmed partly from his sense of failure at this critical moment.

Schumacher expected no mercy from the men he had reviled and warned his friends that he faced a long imprisonment. He was arrested on 8th July, 1933, and sent to a concentration camp, where his guards had been given definite instructions 'to break the man.' As he entered the gates he was beaten, and later one of the guards advised him to hang himself because he did not think he could take what was coming.

But Schumacher was unbreakable. He never submitted, never condoned. Although he was subjected to the full range of camp brutality, sometimes being given senseless work that would have driven other men insane such as filling a bucket with stones from the compound, emptying it and filling it again, he never signed anything or accepted any post of responsibility which might have signified collaboration. He became emaciated and fellow prisoners thought he would die. But after two years of deliberate torture he still had the strength to go on hunger strike. The mystery is why the Nazis did not let him die. Perhaps they hesitated to kill a war veteran or perhaps someone in a high place secretly admired him. They sent him to Dachau which, by comparison with the camps he had been inhabiting, was surprisingly mild in its treatment of such prisoners as escaped the gas ovens.

There, for the next eight years, Schumacher remained. He continued to stand aloof, although he often showed kindness to individual prisoners, especially Jews. He usually talked only to those he considered his intellectual equals. Yet by his total incorruptibility in a world in which moral values were systematically undermined, he won the admiration even of the 'Kapos', ex-convicts and time servers who, by collaborating with the S.S., really ran the camp. It was they, the librarians and the hospital orderlies, who saved him from the gas ovens and saved his life. They gave him food and drugs, took his name off the fatal lists and at one moment persuaded the S.S. to send him to Munich for an operation on his eyes.

In March, 1943, a minor Nazi official obtained his release. If anything his resistance to the régime had stiffened, but his brother-in-law, named Trinkwater, gave a guarantee of his good behaviour. Schumacher went to live with him and his sister Lotte in Hanover. There he worked in a factory, strictly observing the terms of his probation and refusing all political contact. He was arrested again after the July attempt on Hitler's life in 1944 and sent for a few weeks to Neuengemme. It was here, his inner fire still burning, that he began to take up the threads of his political life and organise underground the nucleus of a new Social Democratic Party. When the Western Allies arrived he was once more ready for action.

The ordeal through which Schumacher had passed had refined the steel in his nature without softening any part of it. He was, perhaps, even less tolerant of subordinates or opponents than before and his authoritarianism was tinged with an understandable self-righteousness. Gaunt in appearance, wracked with pain and crippled in health, he could not hide his contempt for those who had in any way collaborated with Hitler's régime. He believed himself destined to lead Germany back into the path of democratic socialism and his one fear, in the last months of the war when the Trinkwaters were bombed from their home, was that he might not live to fulfil his ambition.

It never occurred to him that any other party could assume the responsibility of building the new Germany which, he proclaimed, must be based on the trinity of 'Peace, Freedom and Socialism.' By their record in the Weimar Republic and their opposition to Hitler the Social Democrats alone, he believed, deserved the confidence of the German people. He was as antagonistic to 'capitalist oppression,' which in his eyes had reached its zenith under Hitler, as to communist dictatorship. As his biographer wrote, 'Either German democracy must be a socialist democracy or it would not be a democracy; either socialism was democratic or it was not socialism; there was "no dictatorship of the proletariat, only a dictatorship over the proletariat".'[3]

Schumacher's hopes were nearly blighted even before he had been able to reconstitute his own local party in Hanover, for he suddenly found himself battling against other members of his party. The Soviet government encouraged the formation of political parties long before any of its Western allies and, by May, 1945, Otto Grotewohl and a group of former Social Democrats who had been

3 ibid., p. 83.

members of the Reichstag, had set up a central committee which immediately began to speak in the name of the party as a whole. In June, by which time nearly half a million members had been enrolled in the Soviet zone, the committee issued a manifesto calling for an early fusion with the Communist Party.

Although the Russians put pressure on Grotewohl, there is no doubt that he thought it the right thing to do. He had been encouraged by the goodwill the Russians had extended towards noncommunist parties; he thought that the German communists had become more co-operative; he genuinely believed that divisions among socialists had been largely responsible for the downfall of the Weimar Republic and that a fusion would prevent such a thing happening again. Grotewohl's name was respected and a large number of social democrats throughout Germany shared his view. The central committee, operating in Berlin, was looked upon as the natural centre for a party which could hope to win control in the country as a whole only if it had Russian as well as Western support.

Schumacher saw the danger. If Grotewohl succeeded he would automatically become leader and the party inevitably fall under communist control. He acted at once and with great energy. Although political activity in Hanover was officially forbidden, he formed a personal staff of devoted adherents and summoned from London members of the committee in exile which included Erich Ollenhauer, eventually his successor. With the help of this group, which became known as the 'Bureau of Dr Schumacher,' he then got into touch with the leaders of the embryo branches of the party which were forming in the Western Zones. In August these groups authorised him to summon a conference at Hanover to discuss Grotewohl's proposals. With the invitations he sent out a pamphlet setting out his views on the future of the party, stressing in particular its relations with the occupying authorities, the 'bourgeois' parties and the communists. He also invited the Berlin central committee to attend.

The conference met in October. Grotewohl urged it to accept the manifesto and expand the central committee into a provisional national executive. Schumacher countered by arguing that any such move would be illegal until the Occupying Powers permitted interzonal organisation. He succeeded in persuading the delegates to accept the central committee only as the party's provisional organisation in the Soviet Zone and the 'Bureau of Dr Schumacher' as its counterpart in the Western Zone. Grotewohl had lost the first round; Schumacher was already in the stronger position.

Schumacher followed up his success by travelling round the Western Zones, visiting the leaders of all the party branches which had been formed and strengthening their resolve against a merger with the communists. By now the behaviour of the Russians in Berlin and the treatment meted out to the Germans who had been driven from their homes in the east, was widely known. Fear of Russian domination detracted from the appeal of united socialist action. In January, 1946, the Social Democratic leaders in the British and American zones voted formally to support Schumacher against Grotewohl, and when, in February, Schumacher flew to Berlin in a British aircraft to confront the central committee, he openly denounced their plan for a merger and gave his support to those members of the party who were standing out against it. The result was the Berlin referendum in March, when an overwhelming majority of social democrats repudiated Grotewohl.

Schumacher by now was not only the best known politician in Germany but internationally recognised as the most formidable German opponent of totalitarian rule. Already the Russians were comparing him to Hitler; his followers and many Allied officials were claiming that by preventing the absorption of the Social Democrats into the party of Socialist Unity, he had forestalled a peaceful take-over of the whole country by the communists. In May, at the first post-war national congress of the Social Democrats representing more than six hundred thousand members, he was elected chairman without opposition. The road seemed open for him to assume the leadership of that part of his country which was free from Russian control.

The party of which Schumacher found himself the head differed greatly from the highly centralised organisation of which he had been an executive some fourteen years earlier. It had been reconstructed from the bottom up, first in districts and then in the separate Länder. As there had been no national committee these provincial parties were autonomous, the officials being chosen and paid not by a national executive, which did not exist, but by local parties. Most of the leaders were elderly men who had played a part in the Weimar republic and lain low under Hitler. Their interests were mainly local and, as the relief of the general misery was so obviously the primary concern, they were willing to collaborate with any other party, including the communists, to get things done.

This loosely federal structure, in which the provincial parties had far more independence than in the days of Weimar, was not at all what Schumacher wanted. He believed in a strong central government and was determined that it should operate on un-diluted socialist principles. But in asserting his authority he suffered from two handicaps which arose directly from defeat and occupation. The seizure of the eastern provinces of Germany by the Poles and Russians had robbed the party of those areas where, in pre-Hitler days, it had attained its greatest numerical strength. Although Schumacher believed that the millions who had been driven out of their homelands and become refugees would eventu-ally return to the fold, there was no doubt that for the moment they were too preoccupied with keeping body and soul together to take any interest in politics at all.

Secondly, he had lost the automatic support of the Trade Union Movement. Although the British in particular encouraged and helped Schumacher, they had also encouraged Hans Böckler, the emerging Trade Union leader, in his determination not to affiliate with any political party. Sensible though this was, it not only deprived the Social Democrats of a source of funds but meant that trade-unionists joined the party only as individuals; a surprisingly large number joined other parties and insisted that the unions remained politically neutral.

Schumacher dealt with this fluid situation by exerting his per-sonal magnetism and using his Bureau as if it were already the party executive. Among local party leaders, most of whom were self-educated, no one could match him in intellectual capacity or force of expression. He did not flout the federal constitution of the party, but persuaded the various regional committees to accept his policies and endorse his actions. Meanwhile, the Bureau made it their business to isolate recalcitrant members of the old guard and put in positions of trust men on whom they could rely. Men like Keil Severing and Rossmann, former Reichstag deputies who had passively accepted Hitler's rule, were quickly discredited. Paul Löbe, the former Social Democratic President of the Reichstag, was publicly censured and forced to resign for trucking with Grotewohl. Others were more gently eased from office; they simply failed to get re-elected to their posts in face of the 'Bureau's' candidates. Within a year of becoming chairman, Schumacher was in undisputed control. Although the party machinery formally circumscribed his powers, he was never over-ruled and himself made every major decision on national policy. In the beginning of 1947, on the eve of the final merger between the American and British zones, Schumacher was poised to take charge of the first provincial postwar German administration. Only a new and untried political alliance, led by a man already in his seventies, stood in his way.

Konrad Adenauer's childhood had been altogether more austere than Schumacher's. Born in Cologne in January, 1876, he was brought up in the days of Bismarck's triumph. But the splendour of the age scarcely percolated to the level of the small house in the Balduinstrasse. As secretary to the district court of Cologne, Konrad's father earned barely enough to feed his large family; his mother, the daughter of a bank clerk, had no dowry. Konrad's parents had to let the two best floors of their house to make ends meet. Until he was seventeen Konrad shared a room with his two brothers and a bed with one of them; his sisters slept in another room. While at school the boys used to give private lessons to help swell Frau Adenauer's housekeeping money and, but for the help of the Catholic Students Association, Konrad would not have been able to go to university. Even so, while working for his degree at Freiburg and later at Bonn, his pocket money amounted to only £4 ($10) a month.

The young Adenauer never thought of himself as an intellectual but worked hard and in 1901, at the age of twenty-four, took his final law examinations. He passed, but not with sufficient distinction to encourage him to apply for admission to the Bar; instead he became a clerk in the State Prosecutor's office. Two years later he entered the chambers of one of Cologne's foremost barristers and there, as a junior, began to make his reputation in court. This was the beginning of Adenauer's career. Through his leader, Justizrat[4] Kausen, Adenauer was introduced not only into Cologne society but into politics, for Kausen was head of the local Catholic Centre Party. Then for the first time Adenauer fell in love, fortunately with a girl both of whose parents came from old and distinguished Cologne families, the Weyers and the Wallrafs. In 1904, at the age

4 An honorary title accorded to distinguished lawyers.

of twenty-eight, Adenauer married Emma Weyer and went to live in a suburb of Cologne.

His marriage shaped his career. Although it was through Kausen that he got his first municipal job (by suggesting himself when an important post fell vacant), a Wallraf was Lord Mayor and this undoubtedly helped him. By 1909, aged thirty-five, he was Chief Clerk. As Lord Mayor Wallraf was often away in Berlin, Adenauer frequently had to deputise for him. A glutton for work, he virtually took charge of the administration. When war broke out in 1914, he asked that the Food Department be transferred to him and, by skilful handling of the farmers, soon made Cologne the best provisioned city in Germany.

There was no question of such a prominent civil servant being drafted into the army and Adenauer's career now seemed secure. He built himself a house to cater for his growing family and worked ferociously to preserve his city from the effects of the war. Then misfortune struck him. In October, 1916, his wife died. She had been ill for a long time and he had seen it coming, but the shock changed him. He no longer took his children for walks in the woods on Sunday – he was an ardent botanist, and knew the name of almost every plant that grew – he gave up his hobby of invention. In his spare time Adenauer had always invented things – a streamlined motor car, a new kind of hairpin and, during the war, a new sort of sausage containing soya flour and special maize bread. None had been successful commercially but each had been part of the children's life and a source of their jokes. Now the fun ceased and although Adenauer never allowed himself to show his grief, his house became sombre.

A few months later he himself was nearly killed. His driver fell asleep and his car crashed into a train. Adenauer was terribly injured. His cheek, nose and jaw were broken, his legs damaged and, worst of all, his sight endangered. Although he crawled out of the wreckage and, covered in blood, walked to the hospital alone, he was there for four months. When he came out he was hardly recognisable. His injuries had given his face a tigerish, mongol look, his vision was blurred and he suffered from chronic headaches. It seemed that he might have to give up his work just when his ambition was about to be fulfilled. For while he was convalescing in the Black Forest, Max Wallraf was appointed a minister in the Federal Government and the Lord Mayoralty fell vacant. Adenauer was the obvious successor, but no one was sure whether he was well enough to take it on.

Two City Councillors visited him to try and find out. For two hours they talked about everything, the war, the city of Cologne, his colleagues, the weather; then Adenauer cut them short. 'Gentlemen,' he said, 'it is only outwardly that my head isn't quite right.' His visitors burst out laughing and offered him the post of Lord Mayor. On 18th October, 1917, Adenauer was installed with great pomp in the 'Hansa-Saal' of the city hall. He was forty-one.

Two years later Adenauer remarried. In 1919, he took his second wife, Gussi Zinser, a girl eighteen years younger than he, the daughter of a professor who was a close friend and neighbour. By her he had a second family and they remained devoted until her death in 1949.

Like Schumacher, who was then studying for his degree in Berlin and learning to use his left arm, Adenauer had shown immense fortitude in face of adversity. He, too, was capable of the strictest self-discipline but, being cast in a less heroic mould, conserved his energy. Where Schumacher was passionate and excitable, Adenauer was controlled and unruffled. For the next sixteen years he remained Lord Mayor of Cologne and shepherded his city through the revolution of 1918, the years of inflation and unemployment, until the final clash with the National Socialists in 1933.

In the course of those years Adenauer had become a well-known political figure. In 1920, he had been nominated President of the State Council of Prussia, a curious appointment in view of his much publicised desire to hive-off the Rhenish counties and form a new Province of the Rhineland; in 1926 he was pressed by the centre parties to let his name go forward for the Chancellorship but refused because he could see no evidence that a centre coalition would survive. It was a prescient decision for, had he accepted, he would almost certainly have failed and joined the queue of discredited politicians soon to be overwhelmed and obliterated by the Nazis. Perhaps because of this political involvement, in 1929 he was re-elected Lord Mayor by only one vote, a margin he was to enjoy on an even more important occasion. Slender though it was, this majority kept him in office until Hitler was appointed Reich Chancellor.

During the revolution of 1918, a German officer in charge of the repatriation of troops streaming through Cologne from France and

Belgium, described Adenauer as 'the bravest man' he had ever met; fourteen years later he was to show the same sort of courage in an even more violent upheaval. Like most Germans, Adenauer under-estimated the Nazis and thought the party's electoral gains ephemeral. When Hitler came to power he spoke out boldly against him and twice defied his government.

Hitler had announced an election for 5th March, 1933, and came to Cologne for a mass meeting on 19th February. Adenauer considered that as Lord Mayor, he must remain impartial and neither went to meet the new Chancellor nor arranged to see him. The citizens of Cologne, however, felt differently. Although the National Socialists had previously had little following in the city, swastika flags blossomed in every street. Adenauer had already issued instructions that they should not be flown from municipal buildings and, when storm troopers put them up on the bridge over the Rhine which was municipal property, he had them taken down. Hitler was furious and from that moment Adenauer began to be treated as a leper by most of his former colleagues and subordinates.

As the municipal elections were to be held a week later, some of his few remaining friends urged him to leave the country or at least take a holiday. Adenauer refused. On polling day, 12th March, he attended a memorial ceremony to the dead of the First World War and was warned that the storm troopers planned to kill him by throwing him out of a window in the Town Hall once the elections were over. This was not the first warning he had received, but when he appealed to the Chief of Police, who had sworn the day before that he and his force would protect him 'to the last man', he was told that the police could do nothing without orders from Berlin.

Next day the Cologne newspapers came out with headlines announcing first that the Lord Mayor had fled the city, secondly that, as a result of the elections, he had been dismissed from office without a pension. All sorts of accusations were made against him. Adenauer had, in fact, gone to Berlin to protest to Göring, the Minister of the Interior responsible for the conduct of the elections, against the open intimidation which he had witnessed in Cologne and his own summary dismissal. Göring replied by quoting some of the charges being made against him, in particular that he had absconded with millions of marks from the Cologne treasury. Adenauer dismissed these with contempt and the interview ended. For a few weeks, Adenauer lived alone in the official residence of the

President of the Prussian State Council, but when he defied the Government again by refusing to sign a decree dissolving the Prussian parliament he became a fugitive.

Adenauer's detractors, and in particular Rudolf Augstein,[5] the proprietor of *Der Spiegel*, the successful post-war imitation of the American Magazine *Time*, implied that Adenauer survived the next decade because, within a week of his dismissal, he made his 'obeisance' to the Nazis in a letter to Wilhelm Frick, the Minister of the Interior, in return for which he received a pension and compensation for the requisitioning of his two houses in Cologne. Adenauer later admitted that he wrote to Frick about his pension but the letter has never been produced and the report was inaccurate since Adenauer did not receive any payment until 1936 and even then not from Frick but from the reigning Lord Mayor of Cologne. Nevertheless, Adenauer's survival under the Nazis does require some explanation.

Remembering the ruthlessness with which Hitler pursued his enemies – and there can be no doubt that Adenauer was one of them – it is remarkable that until July, 1944, so prominent a man was allowed to live in comparative comfort and obscurity while many of his friends and former colleagues were murdered or forced to flee the country. There were times when Adenauer had to hide. He spent the first year of Nazi power in a monastery presided over by one of his school-mates and on three occasions he was arrested. During the Rohm purge in 1934, the Gestapo picked him up and threatened him with torture if he did not confess his part in the 'plot'. He was arrested again in July, 1944, and thrown into a concentration transit camp, from the hospital of which he escaped in time to avoid being sent to the gas ovens. His escape became known and his wife was arrested and she revealed his hiding place when her children were threatened.

But although Adenauer had suffered, he was never imprisoned for long and for most of the decade lived undisturbed. An American business friend lent him ten thousand marks and this and the compensation for his Cologne property enabled him to buy some land and build a house in Röhndorf, a village in the Siebengebirge not far from Bonn, where he lived with his family. His three sons were called into the army and he looked after their wives and children.

5 *Konrad Adenauer*, Rudolf Augstein, Trs. Walter Wallich, Secker & Warburg, London, 1964, pp. 11–12.

It was there, in Röhndorf, that the Americans found him at the end of the war.

There must have been thousands of other families the head of which was known to be opposed to the régime, who sustained a sort of twilight existence, keeping out of trouble and hoping for better days; but it was none the less remarkable that a man of Adenauer's courage, with a long and honourable political record, should have been content to remain passive while his country was led inexorably to its doom.

The truth is that Adenauer was not cast in a heroic mould. He was a patriot and a Catholic with an ingrained respect for authority which even the hideous brutality of the Nazis could not eradicate. He could easily have gone abroad and often advised others to do so, but although he knew he was in danger he preferred to stay. Yet where Schumacher courted martyrdom, Adenauer sought survival. When he was approached by Gördeler, Lord Mayor of Leipzig and one of the leaders of the movement against Hitler, he refused to have anything to do with him. He despised revolution and to plot even against the Nazi state was to him unethical. His duty was to endure. By avoiding any political entanglement whatsoever and using his undoubted prestige to persuade others to help him in moments of danger, he emerged in 1945, emaciated but sane, as cool and calculating as he had always been and ready at the age of seventy to take up the tasks he had declined twenty years earlier.

CHAPTER VII

The Duel

Adenauer was only half-joking when he thanked Brigadier Barra-clough for enabling him to become Chancellor; his dismissal in Cologne was the beginning of a wholly new political career. Suddenly he had become young again. His energy was immense, he was amu-sing and biting with his friends, gay with his children and seemed able to absorb effortlessly not only the problems of his city, but of Germany as a whole. Almost overnight he had developed an uncanny political instinct. Long before any other German politician, he had become convinced that the centre of gravity for the New Germany must be on the Rhine rather than in Berlin. This, of course, suited his own inclination, but his reasoning was sound. With Germany's frontiers pushed back so far to the west, Berlin was an outpost rather than a centre; the arsenal of Germany's recovery must be the Ruhr, its main artery the Rhine. Even if the Russians had not been in occupation of the eastern third of the country, the capital must be Frankfurt, Cologne or some other Rhineland city. While waiting for the ban on his political activities to be lifted, therefore, he made two crucial decisions. He would found a new political party and its working base should be the British Zone.

The new party's political philosophy should be his own. For some time he had been convinced that the only hope of establishing democracy in Germany lay in reasserting Christian values. Catholics and Protestants must work together; Christian ethics must replace the materialism of Marx and Hitler; the power of the state be limited by the 'dignity and inalienable rights of the individual.' In practice this meant that economic power must never be con-centrated in the hands of a few people, whether they represented the state or giant industrial combines, and that 'the acquisition of moderate property by all those who genuinely and sincerely create wealth and value is to be encouraged.' In other words, Adenauer was planning a mixed economy, based on private enterprise but controlled in the interests of minorities and the individual citizen.

Adenauer was not alone in his thinking; groups of Christians had been forming up and down the country to debate the same general idea, but they seemed to be in favour of a 'movement' rather than a party. Although not in the chair, Adenauer was able to change this in the first big Christian political gathering held in Bad Godesberg in December, 1945. It was an extraordinary meeting to which men and women from every part of Germany somehow managed to come, hitch-hiking, bicycling, walking, many in rags and all of them hungry. This was the first time that most of the delegates had seen or heard Adenauer, and he made a considerable impression, speaking strongly in favour of the new party and outlining its policies as he saw them. The conference not only endorsed his views but decided that the party should be called the Christian Democratic Union. A further meeting, in Herf Westphalia was called by Heinrich Holzapfel, leader of the Westphalian group; but there was no agenda and no one except Adenauer seems to have realised that the first issue would be the choice of a chairman for the British Zonal Executive who, most probably, would become the leader of the party as a whole. There were several other prominent candidates besides Holzapfel, including Schlange-Schöningen from Hamburg and Andreas Hermes from Berlin; but the chair had been left vacant because no one felt entitled to take it. Adenauer had no such inhibitions. Remarking with a smile that, as he was seventy, he presumed that everyone would accord him the right of seniority, he sat down and opened the meeting. Not a voice was raised and at the end he was unanimously elected chairman of the Executive Committee. Three weeks later he became chairman of the whole Zonal party, with Holzapfel as his deputy; the others faded away.

Within three months Adenauer had transformed himself from being an outcast to a contender for the leadership; but he had one more political battle to win before he could be sure of the victory. In Berlin, Dr Jacob Kaiser, a man better known than Adenauer, had been elected leader of the Christian Democratic Union for the Eastern Zone. In spite of the forced merger of the Social Democrats and the Communists, Kaiser clung to the belief that the Russians would allow some sort of democratic system to function and urged the party to make Berlin its headquarters. It was the only way, he argued, of preventing a party split and the only hope of preserving a united Germany. In the hope of attracting disgruntled social democrats, he announced a programme of 'Christian Socialism' which included the nationalisation of heavy industry and a large measure of workers' participation in industry as a whole. But although Kaiser's thinking is still evident in Germany to-day and his plans were later temporarily adopted by the C.D.U. in the Ruhr as 'The Ahlen Programme', Adenauer was too quick for him. At a meeting in Stuttgart, he persuaded the delegates to merge the Berlin C.D.U. with the other zonal branches and to lay it down that neither Berlin nor any other city in the Eastern Zone should become the party's headquarters, even if the Russians withdrew.

Kaiser continued to struggle, making the re-unification of Germany his theme; but at a meeting of all four zonal parties held at Bad Konigstein in February, 1947, Adenauer finally won the day. It was decided that under no circumstances must the party be exposed to Soviet interference and that it was better to work for German unity through the merger of the three Western Zones than through Berlin. Having failed to do their bidding, Kaiser was himself dismissed by the Russians at the end of the year. By then the struggle between Adenauer and Schumacher was in full swing.

The great duel began dramatically. In the spring of 1946, Sir Sholto Douglas, the British Military Governor, invited the two main political parties to send two delegates to the new Advisory Council he was setting up for the British zone. At first Adenauer said he would not go as he did not think the Council would be able to do anything useful; but he relented and took with him Dr Otto Paul, an industrialist from Osnabruck. Schumacher, who had recently returned from a visit to London, had with him Heinrich Kopf, a Social Democrat, then Administrative President of Hanover province. During the conference Kopf took Paul aside and suggested that the two of them get their leaders together so as to try and form a common German front in dealing with the Allies. Adenauer and Schumacher had never met.

That same day they had their first conversation at a small table in the corner of the hall in which the conference was being held. Schumacher, speaking animatedly in a voice that all could hear, began by expounding his favourite theme of the 'total responsibility of the Allies for the plight of Germany' and inveighed against dismantling. Adenauer pointed out, rather dryly, that his own party had said the same thing in rather different words at its recent conference. Schumacher nodded and then went on to say that he was ready to co-operate but on one condition; Adenauer and his 'young party' must recognise the claim of the Social Democrats to leadership since the S.D.P. was the largest party and had the best prospects for the future. Adenauer replied coldly that he did not share Schumacher's opinion and thought the decision about the leadership should be left to the elections which had already been announced for the autumn. There the conversation ended.

Although the two men were to meet and correspond frequently in the years to come, all hope of close collaboration vanished at that first meeting. Schumacher differed from Adenauer not only in his passionate belief that the only remedy for Germany's ills lay in socialism but in his attitude towards the Allies. Convinced in his own mind that the Social Democrats alone had withstood Hitler, he expected everyone to admit that the future of Germany lay with them and them alone. He was as intolerant of the attempts of the Western Allies to tell Germans how to become democrats as of the Russian imperiousness. He saw German social-democracy as the inheritor and guardian of the liberal tradition not only in Germany but in Western Europe as a whole and could see no good reason why power should not be handed over to him immediately. In his view a socialist Germany was the only safeguard against both Russian expansion and the revival of capitalism. Attempts by the Russians or the West to harness Germany to their cause were equally obnoxious.

Adenauer was no less German, but infinitely more adroit. He, too, was irritated by the 'moralising' of the Anglo-Saxons, but he was aware of the deep distrust in which they held the Germans and, in particular, of their fear of Prussian domination which Schumacher represented in a new but scarcely less arrogant form. Adenauer had also formed a far clearer view of the intentions of the Russians than Schumacher and regarded the latter's belief that democratic socialism could be a bulwark against communism as naïve in the extreme. Schumacher's conception of a highly centralised socialist German state, asserting its total independence from East and West alike, seemed a dangerous fantasy which would only lead to communist infiltration and eventually Russian domination.

Although therefore, Adenauer was to work unremittingly for the reassumption of sovereignty by elected German representatives, he realised the necessity of working with rather than against the Allies. In the last resort he had already made up his mind where the best hope for his country lay.

Some Germans argue to-day that the struggle between Adenauer and Schumacher was the making of modern German democracy. In the past Germans had always striven to avoid head-on clashes; hence their longing for an authority which would put an end to argument and friction and assert 'unity'.[1] Whether this is a correct diagnosis or not, there was no doubt about the intensity of the battle which now began. At every stage in the evolution of the German State, Schumacher took one view, Adenauer another. They hardly ever compromised and, although Schumacher's successors were of an altogether different character, they so far followed his example that, with one short interval, the Federal Republic has always had one major party in power and the other in opposition. In British eyes at least, this is no bad constitutional practice.

The first open evidence of antagonism appeared in the zonal Advisory Council. Critical though Adenauer was of the efforts of the Western Powers to rule Germany, he decided that it was better to attend and offer advice than stay away. Schumacher was contemptuous, seldom appeared, and in speeches and writing continued to denounce all the conquerors as fools or villains. Their first public disagreement came in July, three months after their initial meeting. At the Foreign Ministers' Conference in Paris, which ended in its usual deadlock, the Russians had abandoned their qualified support of the French demand for the separation of the Ruhr and Rhineland, and came out for a united 'democratic' Germany. The British, who were by now equally set against any further dismemberment, countered with a practical move. Adenauer and Schumacher were summoned to Berlin and told that the British government had decided to create a new 'Land' in their zone, to be called North Rhine-Westphalia. An A.D.C. traced its boundaries on a map and the two German leaders were asked if they agreed with the idea. Schumacher said 'No'; Adenauer 'Yes'. The conference ended.

1 See in particular *Society & Democracy in Germany*, Ralf. Dahrendorf, Weidenfeld & Nicolson, London, 1968; Doubleday, New York, 1969.

Adenauer would have liked a larger province fitting more closely his old conception of a west German federation; but as this was impractical he welcomed the measure not only because it made it more difficult to detach the Ruhr, but because he suspected that the addition of Westphalia would strengthen his party rather than Schumacher's. Schumacher resented an Allied *diktat* which, for the same reason, he thought would weaken his party, and therefore, in his view, make the reunification of Germany more difficult. Adenauer's hopes were soon fulfilled. Already the local and State elections held in the United States zone had shown that, except in Hesse, the Christian Democratic Union were the largest party and in Bavaria their allies, the Christian Social Union, held an overwhelming majority. Now, in the autumn of 1946, came the local elections in the French and British Zones confirming the view Adenauer had earlier expressed to Schumacher. In North Rhine-Westphalia the Christian Democrats won nearly a thousand more seats than their opponents and in the French zone polled an even greater number of votes than in Bavaria. Adenauer was not yet a national leader, but there was no question that the party he represented was already the largest in West Germany. The British authorities recognised the results by changing the composition of the Parliament they had nominated for the new North Rhine-Westphalian province, giving a clear lead to the representatives of the C.D.U. Adenauer was now beating Schumacher on his home ground.

From the beginning of 1947, the area of the gladiatorial struggle widened, first from the British zone into Bizonia and then gradually to the frontiers of the West German Federal Republic; but the issues were broadly the same. Internally Schumacher fought for the nationalisation of the basic industries and an economy 'planned' centrally according to socialist principles; Adenauer wanted a market economy controlled so as to prevent too narrow a concentration of power. In relation to the Occupying Powers, Schumacher struggled to avoid being committed to the West or the East (a cliché which in his view was nonsensical), Adenauer more and more came to the conclusion that only by co-operation with the West could any degree of independence be attained.

The battle over nationalisation began in the reconstructed but nominated Parliament of North Rhine-Westphalia in 1946. Schumacher made it the touchstone of his authority and the gauge by which he judged each new stage in the emancipation of his country. When provincial elections were finally held in the British and French zones in the spring of 1947 the C.D.U. emerged as the strongest party overall; but in several provinces the Socialists had won most seats and even where they were second, Schumacher tried to make it a condition of joining a coalition that a Socialist should hold the economic ministry. In most cases he succeeded and when, in the summer, the new Economic Council for the Bi-zone was set up, he demanded that its financial and economic directors should both be socialists. This was refused by the other parties and he at once ordered the Social Democrats to go into opposition.

Further rebuffs were to come. He felt badly let down when in July, 1947, Mr Mayhew, the Labour Under-Secretary at the British Foreign Office, said that although his government was in favour of nationalisation of the German coal mines, it was a question that must be decided by Germans after a general election. He was even more indignant when, three months later, the nationalisation of the basic industries in Schleswig-Holstein, where there was a socialist majority, was disallowed by the zonal authorities on the grounds that such legislation was a national and not a provincial matter.

Schumacher was obsessed by the fear of repeating the mistakes made by his party leaders under the Weimar Republic when social-democracy had been crushed between 'authoritarian' foreign capitalism and communism. The Americans who had made loans which were misused, withdrew their support just when it was most needed by Brüning. As a result Schumacher not only suspected Marshall Aid in the post-war era, but denounced the currency reform in the spring of 1948 because it favoured the 'bourgeois' party. The rich were getting richer, the poor poorer. He, the Tribune of the Workers, was convinced that when the people grasped what was happening they would sweep him into office to build a new Germany, free from 'the irresponsible power of the capitalists and cardinals.' Even when the powers of the Economic Council were extended in February, 1948, so that it became an embryo German government under Allied tutelage, he forced his followers to remain in opposition, denouncing the coalition parties as exploiters and monopoly profiteers.

All this was grist to Adenauer's mill. He did not believe that the mass of the German people cared about socialism or even democracy. They wanted food, houses and work and would vote for whoever seemed to offer the best chance of providing them. And since the Western Allies had provided almost all the help they had received so far – little though it may have seemed – they were unlikely to sympathise with a man who was always denouncing their benefactors.

Schumacher's opposition in the Economic Council enabled Adenauer to appoint business men, bankers and economists to the key posts, giving them invaluable experience and the chance to channel Marshall Aid, when it began to flow, as much into industry as to social services. Like Schumacher, he was eager to meet the test of a general election in which he and his party would now be judged not only on their theories, but on the two years of practical administration with which Schumacher had provided them.

The first climax to the great debate came with the preparations for a constitution for the three Western Zones to which the French at last reluctantly agreed in the spring and summer of 1948. The Russians had left the Control Council and the Kommandatura and begun the blockade of Berlin. Egged on by Holland, Belgium and Luxembourg, who were dependent on a revival of German industry for their own recovery, the Western Powers abandoned any further attempt at four-power collaboration and announced, through the mouth of the British Military Governor, Sir Brian Robertson, the formation of a 'provisional' West German State. Robertson, addressing the deputies of the North Rhine-Westphalia Parliament, stressed that the ultimate object of both Bizonia and the new state was the 'real unity' of a Germany with an independent freely elected government. 'For the time being,' he said, 'we must accept as a fact that an Iron Curtain splits Germany.' 'Come forward,' he went on, 'determined to make the best of the larger part of your country which is on the right side of the Iron Curtain. The rest will come in time.' He finished by exhorting the deputies not to be frightened of being called 'collaborators'. 'We all form part of Europe . . . it may be very important to be a good party man. It is much more important to be a good German. If you fail you may wake up one day to find that your party no longer needs your support because it no longer exists . . .'[2]

It was, as the speaker admitted, a strange speech for a conqueror to be making after three years of punitive occupation, but then they

2 *Konrad Adenauer*, Paul Weymar. The Authorised Biography, trs. Peter de Mendelsohn, André Deutsch, London, 1957, p. 231.

were living in strange times. It was received with mixed feelings by the audience. Adenauer, dressed in mourning – for his wife had just died – listened impassively. Schumacher, not being a deputy, was not there. But although Adenauer might be more in sympathy with the Allied plan than his rival, not even he could publicly regard the proposed new State as anything more than a temporary expedient, necessary only until the Allies ceased quarrelling among themselves and permitted Germany to rise again as a whole. For Germans still were not ready to accept the permanent division of their country. However, neither Schumacher nor Adenauer was in a position to refuse the Allied plan.

In July, the three Western Military Governors summoned the Presidents of the eleven West German States to Frankfurt and presented them with three documents. The first authorised the Presidents to summon a Constituent Assembly to prepare a constitution 'of a federal type best adapted to the eventual re-establishment of German unity.' The second asked the Presidents to consider changes in the State boundaries; the third outlined the rights and duties of the Occupying Powers once the federation came into being and intimated that these would later be incorporated in an Occupation Statute. These documents were the outcome of the recommendations of the London Conference of the six which had also stipulated that the industries of the Ruhr should be put under an international authority and that Germany should continue to be demilitarised.

First reactions in Germany were unfavourable. The executive of the C.D.U. published a declaration stating that the London recommendations were an 'insufficient basis for peace and liberty.' Far from seeing themselves as 'beneficiaries' of the quarrel between the Allies, the executive was so disturbed by the proposals that they asked for a further attempt to hold a conference with the Russians in which the Germans themselves could be represented. As far as Adenauer was concerned, this was window-dressing. No one knew better than he the futility of further talks with the Russians. But he realised what a shock the dawning truth would be for the German people and he at once sent a telegram to Schumacher suggesting that they make a common stand over the proposals. Schumacher was very ill but although he agreed with many of Adenauer's fears, particularly of a recrudescence of violent nationalism if the Allied plan went through, he refused to make any joint declaration.

However, on 10th August, at a meeting in Coblenz, the eleven State Presidents did what Adenauer and Schumacher had failed to do and announced that they were unwilling to draft anything as formal as a constitution, but would devise instead a Basic Law applicable at first to the Western Zones but capable of being extended over the whole of Germany as soon as opportunity arose. Nor did they wish to convene an elected 'Constituent Assembly', for this would clothe the Basic Law with too much authority; they agreed, however, to convoke a Parliamentary Council, consisting of delegates from the State parliaments on the basis of one delegate for every three million inhabitants. The Allies acquiesced and Adenauer was chosen to be President with the Social Democrat, Professor Carlo Schmid, as Chairman of the Steering Committee in which most of the work would be done. The socialists were pleased with this arrangement because they looked upon Schmid, a genial German with a French mother, as one of the wittiest and most persuasive speakers and a brilliant negotiator. However, it was Schumacher from his sick-bed who really directed socialist policy in the Parliamentary Council, and with startling results.

The argument within the Council was still centred upon the basic difference in outlook of the Social and Christian Democrats. Schumacher, more confident than ever that he would win the general election which must follow, wanted a strong Presidency, a federal civil service and over-riding financial powers for the Federal Government. Only with these powers would he be able to carry through his measures of nationalisation and direct a planned economy. The Christian Democrats wanted sufficient powers for the separate States to give them a genuine autonomy, and this meant a weaker Presidency and a weaker central government. The Western Allies favoured the Christian Democratic view, the French in particular demanding the loosest possible type of federation, without a federal civil service.

The Parliamentary Council worked fast and well – far faster than the Allied Control Council in framing the Occupation Statute. Adenauer kept in touch with the Military Governors who, from time to time, expressed views on the points under discussion. On the whole he and Schmid got on well and, as the latter's colleagues had expected, Schmid succeeded in persuading the standing committees to accept most of his party's suggestions. When the final draft of the Basic Law was presented to the Allies on 11th February, 1949, it provided for the strong central authority which Schumacher desired. On 2nd March, the Allies rejected it, demanding more clearly defined powers for the Federal and State governments and in particular greater financial autonomy for the States.

Now came the crunch. Adenauer was in favour of accepting the Allied amendments. Speed seemed vital. The Western Allies had already adopted the Ruhr statute and no German could sit on the International Ruhr Authority, which would control the most important German industries, until the Federal Government had been set up. In his view the Basic Law was less important in itself than the way in which it was operated. Changes were bound to come. He felt the same about the Occupation Statute which had at last, on 10th April, been delivered by the Western governments and which not only reserved foreign policy to the Allies but in certain emergencies – meaning a Russian threat – allowed them to suspend the constitution and resume power.

Schumacher, however, was adamant. He instructed Carlo Schmid to tell the Military Governors that his party must reject their demands and that he, Schumacher, would give his reasons at the Social Democratic conference which was to be held on 19th April. At the conference Schumacher, who had sufficiently recovered from his amputation to take part, delivered what was virtually an ultimatum. The Social Democrats would assent to the Basic Law only if Germany's freedom to make political decisions was absolute – a side swipe at the Occupation Statute – and the financial and legal powers of the Federal Government were sufficient to make it independent of the States. 'You can only be a German patriot,' he thundered, 'and not a patriot of eleven German States. That is the whole difference between the Social-Democratic Party and the C.D.U.'

To Adenauer's consternation, the Allies immediately gave way. There was no question of their altering the Occupation Statute, which was due for revision within eighteen months in any case; but on most of the other points they withdrew their objections. On 8th May, the Basic Law, drafted mainly by Carlo Schmid, was voted by the Parliamentary Council. On 12th May, it was approved by the Allied Control Council. On 23rd May, having been ratified by the parliaments of all the States except Bavaria, it was promulgated by Adenauer on behalf of the Parliamentary Council as 'The Basic Law of the Federal Republic of Germany to give a new order to political life for the transitional period.'

The promulgation came just in time. The blockade of Berlin had ended and that same day the Foreign Ministers' Conference met in Paris to consider a new version of the Russian proposals for the government of a united Germany. Had there been no Basic Law, progress in the Western Zones might have been held up for months while the Western Allies again probed Russian intentions and tried to secure guarantees for free elections in the Soviet zone. As it was, Ernest Bevin was able to counter Andrei Vyshinsky's proposals by suggesting that the Occupation Statute and Basic Law guaranteeing human rights and free elections be extended to the whole of Germany. The conference dragged on through June and reached the same deadlock as its predecessors. The Russians gained none of their objectives and Western Germany began to assume positive constitutional shape.

Nevertheless, for all the praise Adenauer bestowed upon his colleagues in the Parliamentary Council, it seemed that he had suffered a mortifying humiliation. Schumacher had triumphed, not only over the C.D.U. but over all the Allies. His 'No' to any further compromise over the Basic Law had apparently stampeded the Western governments into making concessions and the Russians into lifting the blockade.

The Press resounded with Schumacher's praise. It was Schumacher who 'determines the destiny of Western Germany,' Schumacher who had emerged as the statesman. It seemed at last as if his expectations must be fulfilled and that, as champion of prostrate Germany against its oppressors, he was bound to win the general election which had already been announced for 14th October. Adenauer, on the other hand, appeared to have been too conciliatory, too anxious to shelter behind American protection to assert true independence. Opinion polls predicted an overwhelming Social Democratic victory and hailed Schumacher as post-war Germany's first Chancellor. Schumacher was contemptuous; Adenauer, however, remained strangely unperturbed. It was not for another two months that the country was to understand why.

The Parliamentary Council fulfilled two further functions. It determined the electoral law under which the general election would be held and chose the future capital for the West German republic. The electoral law was a hybrid; half the deputies were to be chosen in constituencies by a simple majority vote, half from the party lists under proportional representation. More important, no party which did not win at least three seats outright or poll five per cent of the valid votes would share in the allocation of proportional representational seats. This regulation virtually ruled out splinter parties.

The choice of the Federal Capital provided some small compensation for Adenauer. Bonn, a small provincial town in the Rhineland near Cologne and his own village of Röhndorf, was preferred to Frankfurt by a narrow majority. The stage for the general election was now set. Adenauer, having thanked its members for their work, dissolved the Parliamentary Council.

Adenauer had some difficulty in organising his party for the election. In the first place he was officially only leader of the branch in North Rhine-Westphalia – one among several prominent Christian Democrats in the Western zone; secondly he had failed, after long negotiations, to merge the remnants of the old Centre Party into the C.D.U. which could not, therefore, fight as one all-embracing Christian party. However, he was far more confident than circumstances seemed to warrant. Schumacher's attacks upon him as well as his Presidency of the Parliamentary Council had so singled him out, that he was able to act as a national leader almost from the start.

He appointed Dr Alois Zimmer, a Minister of the Rhine Palatinate government, as national election agent and told him that his job was to win power and keep it for at least eight years. He then invited Dr Ludwig Erhard, Professor of Economics at Munich university, who had recently become director of the bi-zonal economic committee, not only to expound his theories of a Social Market Economy at party meetings but to join the C.D.U. and lead its economic team. This was a master stroke. Erhard's name was already linked with the currency reform which had brought about such an astounding resurgence of economic life, and his proposals to curb prices to stimulate private enterprise by allowing foreign competition rather than rigid controls seemed to promise an extension of the success he had already achieved. Schumacher might scathingly describe him as 'the fat propaganda balloon of private enterprise, filled with the putrid gases of decaying liberation,' but the mass of the people already thought of him as something of a wizard.

Schumacher, meanwhile, was harping on all his old themes – dismantling, independence from the Allies, nationalisation of heavy industry and a planned economy – and exploiting for all it was worth his 'triumph' in the Parliamentary Council. He would have been wiser to play this down.

For Adenauer had known for some time what had really happened during those April days of deadlock and was quietly waiting for the right moment to expose his rival. He chose the first mass meeting of the election campaign at Heidelberg on 22nd July, when the Press of the world were present. There he explained that Schumacher's heroic 'No' to further compromise on the Basic Law had not been taken in lonely isolation but in collusion with the British. For the letter from the three Western Foreign Ministers, authorising the Military Governors to make the concessions which Schumacher was demanding, had been in their hands for ten days before they acted upon it and its contents had been leaked to Schumacher by a high-ranking British officer, apparently on the instructions, or at least with the connivance of, the British Labour government. Before he took his stand, therefore, Schumacher knew that the Military Governors would give way; whereas Adenauer had to take at its face value their uncompromising rejection of the first draft.

Schumacher's fury at Adenauer's exposure only made matters worse, for Adenauer then revealed his source – another British officer who was indignant over the help the British government was giving clandestinely to the Social Democrats. According to Adenauer a Foreign Office spokesman was obliged to confirm the story. The People's Tribune, the emerging statesman, began to look like a trickster after all. Nevertheless, right up to polling day, Schumacher remained a hot favourite.

The result of the elections was a shock from which Schumacher never really recovered. The Christian Democrats won eight more seats than the Socialists and with the Free Democrats and the small German Party could govern through the same coalition that had worked so successfully in the Bi-zonal Economic Council. Even if the Social Democrats concluded an alliance with the ten communist deputies, which Schumacher would have been reluctant to do, they could not command a majority. The new Germany, therefore, was not to be launched as the model Socialist state of which Schumacher had so confidently dreamed. The Presidential powers and the strength of Federal Government for which he had fought and for which he deserved the credit, were to be employed by his rival to further policies which Schumacher feared would be disastrous for democracy, for Germany and the world.

CHAPTER VIII

Pyrrhic Victory

Within a week of polling day, Adenauer invited the leaders of the Christian Democratic Union to an unofficial meeting at his house in Röhndorf at which three vital decisions were made. The state of the parties made a coalition inevitable. With whom should it be formed? Schumacher had let it be known that in principle he was in favour of joining a 'grand coalition' with the Christian Democratic Union, but on one condition: the Ministry of Economic Affairs must be given to a Social Democrat.

Among Adenauer's guests that day were many who were already members of just such a coalition in their own Province and who wished to co-operate with Schumacher. Adenauer, however, took the line that Erhard's Social Market Economy had been the main plank in the C.D.U.'s electoral platform and that to accept Schumacher's condition would be to emasculate the policy they had been elected to fulfil. After a long discussion, in which it became evident that many of Adenauer's colleagues greatly feared Schumacher in opposition, Adenauer adjourned the meeting and suggested supper. He plied his guests with the best Rhine wines and, when the meeting resumed, rose and said: 'Now, if we start from the assumption that the future government will be formed jointly by the C.D.U., Free Democrats and the German Party,' – and he paused – 'all that remains for us to do here is to decide on the distribution of offices.'[1]

Someone proposed Adenauer for Chancellor. After a slight pause, Adenauer remarked that he had consulted his doctor who had no objection and went straight on to suggest Professor Heuss, a Free Democrat, for President. Within a few minutes these vital questions were settled, subject to confirmation by Parliament when it met.

A month later, on 17th September, the first freely elected deputies to a German parliament since 1933 were sworn in by the

1 Paul Weymar, Op. Cit., p. 282.

Speaker, Dr Erich Kohler. As his first act in the new chamber, the Speaker then put to the vote President Heuss's nomination of Adenauer as Chancellor of the Federal Republic. When the ballot papers were counted Adenauer received the exact number of two-hundred 'ayes' to give him the absolute majority he needed. 'Since I was determined to accept the appointment,' he said later to his son, 'I should have felt it sheer hypocrisy not to have voted for myself.'[2] Three days later he presented his cabinet of thirteen to the House. Erhard became Minister of Economic Affairs.

Schumacher regarded the formation of Adenauer's government as a catastrophe. 'A unique opportunity to deprive the remnants of big business cliques in Germany of their power,' had passed, he said. He attributed his defeat to an unholy alliance between the Western Powers and reactionary capitalism which was once more paving the way for an authoritarian régime in Germany. Nevertheless, Schumacher never gave up. Once his condition for a coalition had been refused, he unhesitatingly took his party into opposition, convinced that Adenauer would soon prove so incompetent and so obviously a puppet of the Americans that the people would turn against him.

Even before Parliament met Schumacher had gone out of his way to stress the uncompromising stand he was making by forcing his party to nominate him as their candidate for the presidency in opposition to Theodor Heuss. Several of the leading members, both of the S.P.D. and the C.D.U., wanted a moderate socialist such as Wilhelm Kaisen, the Minister-President of the City-State of Bremen, to become President so as to mollify the antagonism between the two major parties. But neither Adenauer nor Schumacher would agree to this. When the special convention met on 12th September, to elect the Federal President, Schumacher duly stood and was duly defeated.

In Parliament, Schumacher was flamboyant, denunciatory and contradictory. He attacked indiscriminately all those who seemed to him to be preventing the emergence of the new united socialist Germany. The C.D.U. was dominated by Roman Catholics and harboured 'tried friends and path-makers of the Third Reich who have fought all their lives against democracy.'[3] Because it favoured federalism and close links with Western Europe it was not only

2 *Ibid*, p. 292.   3 Lewis Edinger, Op. Cit., p. 151.

preventing German re-unification but 'serving alien interests at the expense of its own working class'. He held the Western Allies as guilty as the Germans for the rise of Hitler because of their supine acquiescence in the 1930's; he now attacked them for 'interference' in German politics, for 'moralising property acquisition,' and for dividing Germany through their quarrel with the Russians. 'Many Germans do not realise,' he had said in 1945, 'that the world is well able to survive without a united Germany.'[4] He now saw American and British insistence on the close integration of the Federal Republic with Western Europe as proof that the conquerors wanted to keep the two halves of Germany apart.

In the same breath Schumacher attacked the Russians and their stooges, the German communists, those 'sheep in wolves' clothing' who were nothing but 'co-operating members of the Russian state party.'[5] The Russians were preventing free elections in the Soviet Zone because they knew that it would end their rule and result in the overwhelming victory of the Social Democrats. He bitterly opposed the annexation of the eastern territories by Poland and Russia and the expulsion of the German population. He encouraged an underground movement in the Soviet zone through a specially created Eastern Bureau of the S.P.D. which was later held responsible by the Russians for the uprising in 1953. Yet he never for one moment acknowledged that, by antagonising both East and West, he made the prospect of reunification more remote than ever and the rise of his own party to power more difficult.

Above all Schumacher attacked Adenauer. Although Schumacher often proclaimed his willingness to co-operate with the Chancellor, the only issues of any importance on which they ever spoke with the same voices were dismantling – which both described as insane – and the Co-determination Law through which the trade unions would obtain a voice in the conduct of German heavy industry – which both supported. In all else Adenauer was the archenemy of socialism, democracy, and of true German interests. Schumacher despised Adenauer as a man who had demonstrated his love for Germany neither on the battlefield nor in a concentration camp. He demanded 'more shame and less arrogance.'[6] in such a 'fellow traveller' of the Nazis. He accused him of being a 'collaborator' of the Western Allies, of representing those 'discredited reactionary elements' who had betrayed Germany to Hitler.

4 *Ibid*, p. 133.   5 *Ibid*, p. 158.   6 *Ibid*, p. 220.

When Adenauer failed to consult him on government policy – an expectation that was unreasonable in view of his unrelenting hostility – he alleged that Adenauer 'had already outdone the authoritarian state of Wilhelm II' and was leading Germany back to fascism.

Soon Schumacher's hatred of Adenauer became an obsession. They met fairly regularly and wrote each other innumerable letters; but neither in conversation nor in writing did either make any concessions. They simply restated their views and registered their differences. Grudgingly Schumacher came to admit Adenauer's political skill, but the more European Adenauer became in his outlook the more Schumacher looked upon him as a traitor. 'We cannot regard as a friend of the German people anyone whose political actions deny or hinder German unity,' he said in one of his first speeches in parliament, and he was clearly referring, not only to the Allies, but to Adenauer as well. Yet the terms on which he demanded reunification were acceptable neither to the Russians nor the West and remained an utopian dream.

A major clash came as soon as parliament assembled. In the interval between the elections and the summoning of the Bundestag, Adenauer had negotiated what was known as the Petersberg Agreement[7] with the Allied High Commissioners. Under the Occupation Statute the Allies retained wide powers over the German government, particularly in relation to demilitarisation, reparations, dismantling and foreign affairs. There was no Foreign Minister in Adenauer's cabinet and in so far as Germany was allowed any independent initiative abroad, Adenauer had to assume the responsibility himself. In addition the statute setting up an International Authority for the Ruhr had been passed by the Allies without German consent and now had to be accepted or rejected by the new German government.

Adenauer negotiated the agreement himself and obtained many concessions. Although reparations and dismantling were to continue, both were largely reduced. The ban on the production of synthetic oil and rubber was removed and eleven plants in the steel industry were taken off the dismantling lists. The Federal Republic was to be allowed consular and commercial representation abroad and to build ships large enough for competitive coastal trade.

7 The Petersberg is a vast hotel on the hills overlooking the Rhine near Bonn which the High Commissioners used as their headquarters.

Adenauer also agreed, 'unreservedly' to join the Military Security Board which was to ensure that no overt or covert rearmament took place, for in spite of the arming of the German People's Police in the Eastern zone, he was still unalterably opposed to the formation of any German military units under German command. Most of this was pure gain and all of it acceptable to a large majority of the new German deputies; his struggle with Schumacher came over the proposed German membership of the International Authority for the Ruhr and of the Council of Europe.

The Council of Europe had just been formed and was then regarded as the first tentative step to Western European Union. The High Commissioners intimated that, if Germany would like to join as an associate member with the prospect of full membership in the near future, the application would be considered. But this encouraging gesture was bedevilled by the question of the Saar. For the Saar had already applied for membership and not only the opposition but Adenauer himself felt that if the Saar were admitted then it would legalise its status as a French satellite and make a German application impossible. Adenauer wrestled both with Robert Schuman, who had become the French Foreign Secretary, and with the High Commissioners and extracted an undertaking that the Saar's membership would only be regarded as temporary and be subject to a confirmation at a peace treaty. On that understanding he was prepared to sponsor a German application.

The Ruhr Authority was an even thornier proposition. It was to include the Benelux countries as well as France, Britain and America and although Germany was to be a full member, she would be subject to decisions taken by a majority vote. From the Allied point of view this was part of the price Germany had to pay for her aggression. The Ruhr was the industrial arsenal not only of Germany, but of Western Europe as a whole. Countries like Holland and Belgium were dependent upon its production for their prosperity and had a right to have some say in the way production was planned. France had always insisted on international control for reasons of security.

Adenauer took a slightly different view. He had always believed that the Ruhr and the Rhineland belonged to Western Europe rather than to the East and he was convinced that, as his government grew in authority and the plans for Western European Union developed, all three statutes governing the Allied occupation, the

Ruhr and the Saar would soon be overtaken by events and merged in wider voluntary organisations. On the understanding that no further 'edicts' such as the Ruhr Statute would be imposed by the Allies, he was prepared to recommend it to the Bundestag.

Schumacher was furious. He resented the Allies retaining any control over German policy and especially over the core of German industrial life. He regarded the Ruhr Authority as a capitalist plot and brushed off any suggestion that the countries of Western Europe had reason to fear a revival of German industry by saying that socialism was the only safeguard. For him any step which anchored the Federal Republic to Western Europe only made re-unification more difficult. Although he had refused to make common cause with Adenauer in his dealings with the Allies, he was indignant that Adenauer had negotiated the agreement without consulting him.

The debate in the Bundestag was violent. The Social Democrats accused Adenauer of being authoritarian and of treating the Basic Law like a scrap of paper. They demanded the total cessation of dismantling and objected to membership of the Ruhr Authority because they wished to avoid sharing responsibilities for its decisions. Adenauer pointed out that the Ruhr Authority existed and was at work and that unless Germany was represented she would lose all chance of influencing its decisions. If the agreement were rejected all concessions would be withdrawn and dismantling would go on to the end. The socialists were not prepared to listen. A left-wing deputy cried out: 'Are you still a German? Do you speak as a German Chancellor?' 'Chancellor of the Allies,' interjected Dr Schumacher, and the debate dissolved in uproar.[8] Schumacher refused to withdraw and was suspended for twenty days: only after three interviews with Adenauer did he send a letter of apology. The particular incident was closed, but the parliamentary battle had only just begun.

Adenauer had been right in thinking that external pressures would quickly render the Occupation and Ruhr Statutes obsolete. The first move came from France. Anxious to formalise its annexation of the Saar before it could become the subject of a wider European debate in which the Germans could take part, the French government negotiated a series of conventions with the government of the Saar in the winter of 1949/50, the effect of which was to give

8 Paul Weymar, Op. Cit., p. 326.

France a fifty-year lease on the Saar mines and virtually detach a million Germans from the Federal Republic. Adenauer got wind of these conventions and begged Robert Schuman, the French Foreign Secretary, who, as an Alsatian, had a closer interest in good Franco-German relations than some of his compatriots, to postpone their publication. But although Schuman agreed with Adenauer that Franco-German understanding must be the basis of a new Europe, he was unable to carry his government. On 4th March, 1950, the conventions were signed.

Adenauer saw the whole framework of Western Europe, which he had been patiently constructing, threatened with collapse. Although the Saar conventions were allegedly subject to ratification at a peace treaty, many Germans were becoming doubtful whether such a treaty would ever be signed. He himself felt that the terms of the conventions were so explicit they must prejudice all future discussion. There was a very real danger that even his own supporters would lose all faith in the intentions of the Western Allies towards Germany. He, therefore, told the High Commissioners that it was impossible for him to apply for membership of the Council of Europe and doubted whether, even if an invitation from the Council were received, he could carry it in Parliament. He then went much further and in an interview with Mr Kingsbury-Smith, an American journalist, proposed a complete union of France and Germany. It was a gesture almost as dramatic as Winston Churchill's offer to France in 1940, but it had much greater effect. For it gave Schuman the impetus he needed to launch a plan he had been preparing for some time.

On 9th May, 1950, Schuman announced, on behalf of the French government, a proposal that the entire production of French and German coal and steel should be amalgamated under a High Authority, which other Western European nations could join, so as to form the basis of a Western European Federation. This proposal, which exploded in the world's chancelleries like a minor atom bomb, was communicated to Adenauer while he was holding a cabinet meeting. He saw at once that it transformed the entire situation. If the High Authority came into existence it would supersede not only the Ruhr Authority but the Saar conventions as well and virtually put an end to Allied occupation. He accepted at once.

Now it was Schumacher's turn to be in difficulties. He had already attacked Adenauer savagely over his compliance with the Saar's application to join the Council of Europe and, when the invitations came from the Council at the end of March, had carried his party in opposing German acceptance. But in doing so he had run foul of every other Western European socialist party. If he were now to oppose the first great gesture to come from the French, he could be accused of an intransigence which could only result in placing Germany in a position of dangerous isolation. But Schumacher was deaf to all but his own ideas.

Although Ulbricht, the East German leader, had just recognised the Oder Neisse boundary with Poland, to which Schumacher was unalterably opposed, he still considered any step towards a European Federation fatal to German reunification and, both in Parliament and in the Provincial elections which took place in the summer, opposed not only joining the Council of Europe but also the Schuman plan.

He lost all three battles. The elections went against him, Parliament accepted the invitation from the Council of Europe and, in spite of Schumacher, the S.P.D. sent delegates to it in August. Within less than a year a treaty embodying the Schuman Plan had been signed with France and four other Western European countries. Adenauer seemed to be winning all along the line. Yet something had already happened which was to lead to his first great failure and within a few months set the pendulum swinging back towards his rival.

CHAPTER IX

Riposte

No conflict could seem farther removed physically from Western Germany than that which began on 25th June, 1950, when North Korean troops crossed the thirty-eighth parallel and invaded South Korea. Yet because the North Koreans were using Russian arms and had the political backing of the Soviet Union and Mao's New China, the West Germans were thrown into a state of near panic. What was happening in Korea seemed to them only too likely to happen in Europe.

Trouble in Korea had been smouldering for some time. After Hitler's war, North Korea had been occupied by the Russians, South Korea by the Americans. Negotiations for free elections covering the whole country broke down but elections under United Nations auspices were held in South Korea in 1948. Afterwards the two halves of the country were each granted independence and both the Russians and Americans withdrew their troops. However, the communist government of North Korea had never accepted the division of their country and, by infiltrating guerrillas and exploiting a numerous Fifth Column, had continually threatened the security of Syngman Rhee's government. Then suddenly the North Koreans announced their intention of 'liberating' South Korea, crossed the frontier and occupied most of the country within three months.

Not altogether illogically the West Germans suddenly saw themselves as a second South Korea. The Russians were known to have thirty divisions in Eastern Europe and the East German armed police was believed to number between 100,000 and 150,000 men. The West Germans were defenceless and had no guarantee that their allies would resist an invasion if carried out by the East Germans alone. Ulbricht claimed to have an organised Fifth Column in the West German zones a hundred-thousand strong and had already issued instructions that all vehicles belonging to its members should be thoroughly tested and ready for immediate use when the East German 'police' marched in. The Americans were becoming heavily involved in what looked like a protracted Korean war, and it seemed only too likely that they would want to cut their commitments in Europe and perhaps withdraw their forces altogether.

'The Federal Republic was in a very dangerous situation indeed,' wrote Adenauer later. 'The forces of the Western Allies in Germany were not strong enough, so far as I could judge . . . if the Russian Zone army (i.e. 'The People's Police') were to attack with tanks, as had happened in Korea . . . the population of Western Germany would stay neutral . . . first and foremost for psychological reasons, because the advancing troops would be Germans. But the people would also stay neutral because events in Korea had taken away much of their faith in the United States . . .'[1] The United States, he added, would not use nuclear weapons against an attack from the Soviet zone, even if it were supported by Soviet tanks. However, Adenauer was at his best in a crisis and he at once saw a way of using the panic to further his strategic plan.

The question of German rearmament had been aired in the foreign press for several months. With what looked like total cynicism, America and Britain suddenly had stood their policy towards their defeated enemy on its head. Whereas a year before the United States Secretary for Defence had vigorously denied that there was any question of Germany being rearmed and Ernest Bevin had welcomed enthusiastically the creation of a Military Security Board to prevent that very thing, now Allied statesmen were talking openly about the desirability of the Germans 'sharing the responsibility for their own defence' and even reproaching them for hesitating to do so.

However, German public opinion was almost unanimously against rearmament. In the aftermath of defeat people had come to loathe the whole profession of arms and to regard a uniform as a badge of shame. Only a year or so previously Franz Joseph Strauss of the Christian Socialist Union in Bavaria had said: 'Anyone who again picks up a gun – his hand should drop off.' Now, suddenly, he was talking of 'expunging the Soviet Union from the map.' The somersault was too great for the electorate. In an interview which

1 *Adenauer Memoirs. 1945-53*, p. 273.

appeared in the *Cleveland Plain Dealer* in December, 1949, Adenauer tried to quell anxiety by stating categorically that he was opposed to a German army and would not allow Germans to serve as mercenaries in foreign forces. The only circumstances in which he could even consider such a question would be in reply to a request for a German contingent to serve in an army belonging to a European Federation.

Now in the autumn of 1950 this hint took on a new significance. The Council of Europe had met in August, with Germany as an associate member. Winston Churchill, then leader of the British Opposition, had carried a motion calling for the formation of a European army. This Adenauer welcomed first because he saw that such an army might become the foundation of a genuine European Federation, but also because by offering to make a contribution he might extract the last concessions from the Western Powers and establish full German sovereignty.

Accordingly, after the meeting of the Council of Europe, he sent two memoranda to the High Commissioners, one offering a German contingent if a European army were formed, the other asking that the state of war between Germany and the Allies, which still officially existed, should be terminated and that the 'Occupation' should be transformed into an alliance for mutual defence. The High Commissioners agreed to forward these memoranda to the Foreign Ministers' Conference shortly to be held in New York.

But however statesmanlike Adenauer's approach may have been, it was not popular in Germany. Opinion polls showed that nearly half the German population was against any form of rearmament and considered it preferable to try and unite with the East as a neutral country. As the months went by this passive attitude increased in strength. Schumacher was quick to exploit it.

Adenauer had consulted Schumacher before sending his memoranda to the High Commissioners in the hope that they could form a common front, at least in this emergency. But although Schumacher was not opposed to rearmament, he took a different view. He agreed that Germany must be treated on a basis of absolute equality in any military co-operation and that, while the German units were being trained and equipped, the Western Allies must greatly increase their own forces and be seen to guarantee Germany's defence. But Schumacher rejected the idea of a European

Army and insisted that a German army must be German, that it must be democratised and taken out of the hands of the old military caste.

Schumacher's ideas were impractical and in some ways surprising. He had frequent talks with German generals and not only showed a grasp of military matters, but plainly enjoyed discussing them. He must, therefore, have been aware that the one thing the Allies, and particularly the French, would not tolerate was a new German army with a German High Command. He must also have known that the training of a new officer cadre, taken mainly from the ranks, would jeopardise the effectiveness of any German contribution just when it was most needed.

Schumacher's motives were plain even if his thinking was muddled. Whereas the Social Democrats had lost ground in the provincial elections in the early summer, they made considerable gains in the autumn, due mainly, he thought, to Adenauer's rearmament proposals. The sudden rise of a new party representing the refugees from the East strengthened his conviction that Adenauer's policy of integration with the West was also unpopular. Since, in spite of economic recovery, unemployment remained high and wages, salaries and pensions had hardly increased whereas the new bourgeois 'entrepreneurs' were making fortunes, he saw the tide turning in his favour. He therefore not only attacked every move towards the building of Western Europe but continually demanded new elections so as to allow the German people to decide their future now that circumstances were so radically different from those in which they had voted in 1949.[2]

Adenauer refused to be rattled. Whatever opinion polls might show, he made it clear that so long as he could command a majority in parliament he would continue to govern. The Western Allies had been receptive to his memoranda and by the spring of 1951, the international situation had become more stable. The Americans had restored the frontiers in Korea to the thirty-eighth parallel and American rearmament, designed not only for Korea but the cold

2 Although De Gaulle was not an ally of Schumacher, it is interesting to remember that he was, at that moment, in a very similar position in France. His *Rassemblement du Peuple Français* had swept the country in the municipal elections and De Gaulle was vociferously demanding a general election. His objectives also were similar. Like Schumacher he was bitterly opposed to the idea of a European Defence Community and wanted the French army to be French. He would not, however, have supported Schumacher's demand for a German army under a German General Staff.

war, was proceeding at a tremendous pace. The panic of the West Germans began to subside.

Slowly Adenauer made headway. At the end of September, 1950, the Council of the North Atlantic Treaty Organisation proposed the creation of a mixed force for the defence of Europe under a Supreme Commander (who was bound to be American) and envisaged the possibility of a German contribution. The Council also declared that it was going to increase its forces in Europe, end the state of war with Germany, amend the Occupation Statute so that Allied forces remained to defend rather than control Germany, and remove many of the restrictions on German production and legislation. The Federal Republic and the Provinces were to be allowed armed mobile police and a German Ministry of Foreign Affairs was to be established. So far so good.

However these communiqués had been issued largely on the insistence of the Americans and against the wishes of the British and, even more, the French who were reluctant to see a revival of German arms in any form. Now, seeing the way the wind was blowing, the French took the initiative themselves. In October, M. Pleven, the French Prime Minister, published a plan for a European army which had the support of his government. Like the Schuman Plan, it was based upon the assumption that Western Europe would unite. There was to be a European Minister of Defence, responsible to a European Defence Council, a European budget and an army to which the various member states would contribute units on the understanding that they would be integrated at the lowest possible level. Germany would be invited to make a contribution but, to avoid reviving mistrust, there was to be no German national army or Minister of Defence.

Adenauer welcomed the plan, although it bristled with practical difficulties. It was hard to see how companies of different nationalities could fit into a battalion, or battalions into a division, but he felt that the gesture from France was so important that it must not be rejected. Inside and outside Parliament he appealed to the West Germans to accept it and make a contribution to their own defence.

Schumacher stigmatised the Pleven Plan as a device to force Germany to defend French interests and demanded that before a single German unit was formed the Western Allies increase their forces to a point which guaranteed the security of the Federal

Republic, to which Berlin should at once be added as the twelfth Province. A debate began which raged in the capitals of Europe for the next four years.

Adenauer had already had one defection from his cabinet. Gustav Heinemann, Minister of the Interior and President of the Synod of Protestant Churches in Germany, had already resigned in protest against rearmament. Since God, he said, had twice dashed the weapons from the hands of the German people, they should not reach for them a third time.[3] Heinemann was supported by Pastor Niemöller, whose resistance under Hitler had made him the best-known churchman in the country. This defection, therefore, was serious. Heinemann joined the Social Democrats and, with Niemöller, supported Schumacher who now also began to receive support from a powerful but hitherto unwelcome quarter.

Neither the Russians nor the German communists had watched the growth of Western Europe with equanimity; the prospect of German rearmament filled them with genuine alarm. Both saw their plans for the penetration of Western Germany evaporating and both feared that, under the American nuclear umbrella, a European army might one day be used to drive the communists from power in the Eastern Zone and hold the general elections under United Nations' auspices which they knew would put an end to their rule. From the autumn of 1950, therefore, the East Germans and the Soviet government revived the campaign for German unity which they had lost with the failure of the Berlin blockade. By playing upon German fears of war and appealing to German nationalism they hoped to prevent, or at worst delay, the whole complex of agreements which Adenauer was negotiating with the Western Allies.

Ulbricht's opening salvo took the form of a purge within his own ranks. In September, 1950, six prominent members of the inner ring of the S.E.D. were dismissed along with some six hundred leading party officials and perhaps as many as three hundred thousand ordinary party workers. This eliminated almost all leaders who had spent the war in the West as well as most former Social Democrats.

Next came the first of a long series of notes from the Soviet government to the Western Allies protesting against the decisions of the N.A.T.O. Council. This was followed by a meeting in

3 Paul Weymar, Op. Cit., p. 364.

Prague of the Eastern European satellites which was attended by Molotov.

The Prague meeting echoed the Russian note, denounced the re-armament of Germany, called for a Four-Power meeting to implement Potsdam and create a 'peace-loving Germany' through a peace treaty. The only new suggestion was that an All-German Constituent Assembly, with equal representation from East and West, should be convened to frame a constitution. In November, Grotewohl took up the idea of the Constituent Assembly and a few days later the Russians demanded a Four-Power conference.

There was still a large minority in both Britain and America which hankered after agreement with the Russians and felt that any approach ought to be seriously examined. Nevertheless, Acheson and Bevin were undoubtedly speaking for the majority when they pointed out that it was East and not West Germany that had been rearmed and that equal representation for 17,000,000 Germans in the People's Republic was out of all proportion to the 47,000,000 Germans in the West. They also asked pointedly how the East German representatives would be elected, since free elections in the zone had never been held. Both Adenauer and, at this stage, Schumacher, dismissed Grotewohl's suggestion as a delaying tactic; but the Russians and their German colleagues persevered.

At Grotewohl's instigation, the Assembly of the Peoples' Republic sent an invitation to the Federal Parliament to hold a joint session on the questions of a constitution and a peace treaty. In his speech Grotewohl spoke of 'free and secret' elections; but it soon transpired that this meant elections held on the farcical lines of those conducted in the Eastern Zone the previous October. Next the Russians persuaded the Western Powers to hold a 'preparatory conference' for a Four-Power meeting; but after four months' wrangling in the *Palais Rose* in Paris no basis for such a meeting could be agreed.

In September, Grotewohl again returned to the charge, this time offering the same electoral conditions throughout all four zones, free movement between them for all Germans, a free press and freedom for all political parties to conduct their campaigns. He was plainly under extreme pressure from his masters to devise some formula which would halt the progress of Western Europe. But as Schumacher at once pointed out, Grotewohl's offers were worthless unless backed by the Soviet Union and the Soviet authorities remained silent. Both he and Adenauer demanded United Nations supervision of all elections.

Nevertheless the Communist offensive was making ground. The World Peace Council, led by eminent international Communists like Professors Joliot-Curie and Bernal, held conference after conference and collected millions of 'votes' in favour of a German peace treaty as proposed by the Russians. It was not without effect. In Germany, Church leaders began pleading for at least an examination of Grotewohl's proposals as offering the only hope of liberation for the oppressed people of the Eastern zone. In June, both houses of the American Congress passed resolutions which, while carrying an implied criticism of the Russian government, reaffirmed American friendship with the Russian peoples. All those well-meaning people in the Western world who shrank from the reality of the struggle for power, began once more to take Russian advances at their face value and to evade or deny the experience of the past decade.

Adenauer remained utterly unmoved. The more threatening the Soviet offensive, the more resolutely he pressed on with Western Union. All through the winter he had been wrestling with the governments of the Western Allies or the High Commissioners to try to hurry the negotiations for what had become known as 'the German treaty' which was to replace the Occupation Statute, and the treaty setting up the European Defence Community. Twice he had been to London, in December at the invitation of Sir Winston Churchill, once again Prime Minister of Britain after the October elections, and two months later at the funeral of King George VI.

On both occasions he had tried to remove the fears still entertained of a resurgence of German militarism. After his talks with Churchill he reluctantly accepted that Britain would join neither the Coal and Steel Community nor the Defence Community. Churchill, who had raised Adenauer's hopes by organising the conference at The Hague four years before, had been unable to persuade Eden, or indeed more than a small minority of his colleagues, to share his European vision. Although he assured Adenauer of Britain's backing for a European Defence Community he had lapsed into the attitude of the previous Labour government, trying to bolster a nebulous Commonwealth with an Atlantic alliance but without political ties in Europe.

Despairing of Britain, Adenauer urged the three Foreign Ministers whom he met at the King's funeral to hasten the formation of a European Defence Community without her. He had just survived a vote of confidence by a majority of only forty-eight, about half his usual strength, and been forced to accept motions from the opposition which demanded greater concessions than the Allies could possibly grant. He pointed out that if the negotiations went on much longer he might well lose his majority altogether and that then the Foreign Ministers would have to deal with Schumacher.

The Allies seemed unable to make up their minds. The British and Americans were asking for innumerable but inexact restrictions on the arms that Germany might make; the French objected to an armed police force and, ironically in view of what was to come, wanted guarantees that Germany would never back out of the European Defence Community once the treaty had been signed. Adenauer patiently insisted that, if the Allies were not prepared to trust his signature, there was no point in concluding the treaties at all. He forced the Allies to face the alternative – a neutral Germany under constant pressure from East and West, with the East holding the trump card of reunification. Gradually the Allies thawed.

In April, 1951, the treaty establishing the European Coal and Steel Community was signed. In May the Federal Republic was accepted as a regular member of the Council of Europe. In June, Adenauer was able to appoint diplomatic representatives in Washington, London and Paris. Between June and October the Americans, British and French ended the state of war with Germany and in November they agreed to grant full sovereignty to the Federal Republic as soon as it entered a European Defence Community. But here lay the danger. In spite of Schumacher's contemptuous rejection of all communist approaches, he was still utterly opposed to any form of European Army. The nearer the creation of that army came, the wider grew the gulf between himself and Adenauer.

Sensing that a crisis was at hand, the Soviet Government intensified its propaganda at the beginning of 1952. First Grotewohl wrote to all the Allied governments demanding the speedy conclusion of a peace treaty with a united Germany. Then, on 9th March, the Soviet Union sent yet another note suggesting that Belgium and Holland as well as Poland and Czechoslovakia should take part in a peace conference, that foreign troops should be immediately withdrawn from Germany and that the Germans be allowed to rearm to a level which enabled them to defend their own neutrality. The

Western Powers and the Federal Republic replied at the beginning of April, welcoming the new Russian initiative for the reunification of Germany but making the usual reservations about free elections and East German representation.

Up to this point Schumacher and the Social Democrats had been in broad agreement with Adenauer. Schumacher had consistently rejected any idea of German neutrality, but for some reason, perhaps because he saw Western Europe taking definite shape, he now began to have doubts. When on 8th April, the Soviet Union again replied refusing United Nations supervision but suggesting that the four occupying powers themselves ensure free elections, Schumacher completely changed his ground. In a letter to Adenauer, sent on 22nd April, he urged him to demand a four-power conference to make a final test of Soviet intentions. If no agreement resulted, he added, at least the world would see that the Federal Republic had let slip no reasonable chance of reuniting Germany and freeing Europe.

Adenauer was taken aback. He pointed out to Schumacher that there was nothing new in the last Russian note, that the Western Powers had often tried to arrange free elections throughout Germany but had always been balked by the Soviet government and that, as Schumacher had himself said, any Russian interpretation of neutrality could only be one that never conflicted with Russian interests. Schumacher was adamant in his turn. He called for the postponement of the treaties and reiterated his demand for a conference to test good faith. He received powerful support from leading members of the Labour Party, now in opposition in Britain, from Congressmen in America and from members of socialist and centre parties as well as the Communists in France. It looked once again as though Adenauer's hopes might founder.

Adenauer redoubled his efforts. He knew the French were wavering and that, unless he struck at once, another and almost certainly fatal delay in the signing of the defence treaty would follow. In May, 1952, he had further talks with the High Commissioners. He persuaded them to make certain amendments and by the end of the month both treaties were ready. He then made careful preparations for their signature by himself and the Allied Foreign Ministers.

However, at the last moment, Edouard Herriot had expressed 'great anxiety' and begged the Allies not to press the French to sign. Whereupon the French government demanded yet another formal guarantee from Britain and America against the possibility of a German withdrawal from the European Defence Community. Adenauer wisely countered by asking that, if ratification of the Community was too long delayed in any country, the German Treaty, granting the Federal Republic full sovereignty, should come into force independently. In a mood of near exasperation, the guarantees were given.

On the morning of 26th May, the German Treaty between the Western Allies and the Federal Republic was signed in Bonn. That afternoon, Adenauer and the Foreign Ministers of Britain, Holland and Belgium flew to Paris to join their colleagues from Luxembourg and Italy. The next day The Six signed the treaty setting up the European Defence Community, and Eden – on behalf of Britain – signed a guarantee that if any of the partners in the Community were attacked, Britain would come to their assistance. It seemed as if Western Union had truly been born.

But as Adenauer knew, a grim struggle for ratification lay ahead. A stream of notes and protests came from the entire communist world accusing the Federal Republic of surrendering to American Imperialism, strengthening the hand of those Germans who believed the treaties were provocative and would engender retaliation. Although ratification came swiftly in the Benelux countries and Italy, opposition grew in the two key countries of France and Germany.

Schumacher had become almost hysterical. 'Anyone who accepted this treaty,' he said, 'had no right to call himself a German.' With his entire party he boycotted all the ceremonies attending the treaty's conclusion. He now embarked upon a campaign of procrastination. Charge and counter charge were laid before the Supreme Court at Karlsruhe, questioning the constitutional validity of the treaties. President Heuss added to the confusion by himself asking the Court's advice whether, if the Bundestag ratified the treaties, he was empowered under the Basic Law to sign them. It was to be another year before Adenauer could get his third reading and final ratification.

By then Schumacher was dead. Although he asserted that he had entirely recovered from the stroke he had suffered the previous December, and from April onwards was as active as ever, broadcasting, campaigning, leading the fight in the Chamber, he carried the marks of death in his face. It came on 29th August, 1952.

Adenauer, who was on holiday in Switzerland, was genuinely shocked at the news. Schumacher had been a great opponent who, by focusing his opposition on Adenauer himself, forcing him to state and re-state his arguments to the Bundestag, and the country, had greatly enhanced Adenauer's prestige. Adenauer recognised this and knew also that no successor had Schumacher's capacity to sustain an argument at such a high level. 'Despite many differences,' he said in the message he sent to Germany, 'We were united in a common goal, to do everything possible for the benefit and well-being of our people.'[4]

Yet Schumacher's ghost was almost as pervasive as his presence. While he had lived his inconsistencies had made it comparatively easy for Adenauer to meet his arguments. Schumacher's main charge, that Adenauer cared more for Western Europe than for a united Germany was undoubtedly true. All through the negotiations for the European Defence Community, Adenauer had himself stressed that the foundation of a Western European Federation was of infinitely greater importance than the treaty revising the Occupation Statute. 'Do not forget,' he is reported as saying to François-Poncet just before the vote on the Defence Community in the French chamber in 1954, 'that I am the only German Chancellor who has preferred the unity of Europe to the unity of his own country.' But this charge was only a reproach if it could be shown that German unity could have been attained on any but Russian terms. And here, Schumacher had been wholly unconvincing.

His complaint that the rejection of Stalin's proposals in the spring and summer of 1952 threw away the last chance of finding out whether the Russians would allow genuinely free elections in the People's Republic was not only wishful thinking, but contrary to every view Schumacher had previously expressed. The price Stalin demanded for elections supervised by the Four Powers was strict German neutrality. Germany must enter no coalition or military alliance which could be interpreted as directed against any power which had fought against Hitler. She could possess a national army, but only to defend a position of political impotence. Even a trade treaty, let alone an agreement like the Schuman Plan, could be interpreted as hostile by the Soviet Union and banned. It was for just these reasons that Schumacher had always refused to accept any imposed neutrality at all.

4 Weymar, Op. Cit., p. 479.

Indeed it was merciful that Schumacher did not live to see Adenauer's overwhelming triumph in the federal elections of 1953 and to read the eulogies that cascaded upon him. Adenauer was described as the greatest German since Bismarck, as divinely inspired, as the architect and saviour not only of the Federal Republic but of Western Europe and the Western World. The American magazine *Time* voted him 'the man of the year.' Yet Adenauer's work was only half done and he was never to be able to complete it. The truth behind Schumacher's charge was to haunt him to the end of his life.

For Adenauer had always claimed that the reunification of Germany could only come when Western Europe had been welded together in a political federation which would permanently exclude any possibility of further Russian penetration. Schumacher, on the other hand, had always warned that the Western Powers were using Germany for their own ends, that militarily and economically they were binding Germany to themselves before she was in a position to make up her own mind and that Adenauer, by collaborating with them, was mortgaging the future without any guarantee that it would develop as he wished. And the Chancellor was soon to discover that there was more truth in Schumacher's fears than he had ever allowed.

Although Adenauer had never admitted it, Britain's tragic refusal to join any European organisation had been a fatal blow to his plans. He failed to see that, without the British, the French would always be too much afraid of German domination to make any federation work. Months had gone by and still no French Prime Minister had dared to bring the European Defence Community to the Chamber for ratification. Even Schuman was showing signs of nervousness as the powerful new German army and air force went through its rigorous training across the Rhine. When reviewing the guard of honour on one of his frequent visits to Bonn, he noticed that the German soldiers were wearing American-type boots with rubber soles and heels. 'Good God,' he exclaimed in the hearing of the B.B.C. correspondent, 'next time we shan't hear them coming!'[5]

Meanwhile the French war in Indo-China had been going badly and in 1954 insurrection broke out in Algeria. The French were having second thoughts, not only about the Defence Community

5 Douglas Stuart, A Very Sheltered Life, Collins, 1970, p. 59.

but the North Atlantic Treaty as well. They wished to be free to withdraw their troops from Europe and use them in the Empire as they pleased. From the wilderness de Gaulle was thundering against supra-national institutions and insisting that the French army must remain French.

Western Europe was at a standstill. A year after the Bundestag had ratified the treaties for which Adenauer had worked so hard, no German units had been formed. West Germany was still in limbo, without full sovereignty and without any federal organisation to take its place. When at last, on 30th August, 1954, Mendès-France brought the Defence Treaty to the French Chamber, it was rejected. In spite of all the assurances of German good faith that the French demanded, in the end it was France's word, not Germany's, which could not be trusted. Adenauer's hopes lay in ruins.

Adenauer put a bold face on failure. During the summer the British and Americans had agreed that, whether the Defence Community were ratified by France or not, Germany should be accorded full sovereignty and allowed to rearm as a full member of the North Atlantic Treaty. Now Eden and Dulles acted. Making hurried trips to Europe they obtained agreement to their plan from the Benelux countries and Italy. Mendès-France proposed in the Council of Europe that Germany be admitted to N.A.T.O. Adenauer, on behalf of Germany, renounced any intention of building atomic, chemical or biological weapons or long range guided missiles and accepted membership not only of N.A.T.O. but of the Brussels Treaty, which included Britain and was to be enlarged into Western European Union. An agency of Western European Union would determine the size of the German army and supervise the manufacture of weapons. This time ratification followed swiftly, although by a narrow majority in the French parliament, and on 5th May, 1955, the Federal Republic became a fully sovereign state. Only in Berlin did the wartime Allies remain as Occupying Powers.

And so, after ten years, the Allied occupation of Western Germany ended. A majority of Germans were once more free to run their own country. Allied troops remained in the Federal Republic only at the invitation of the German government and on negotiated terms. For this liberation Adenauer deserved the gratitude of his countrymen. Yet it had taken a form he feared and, as if sensing his disappointment, his own people began to lose faith in him.

In private conversation Adenauer deplored the fact that the Germans were once again to have their own army. He believed, rightly, that it would revive French fears, encourage chauvinism, and weaken the hand of that brilliant group of French Europeans who had done so much to get Western Europe started. He feared that one day such a German army might fall into the hands of German nationalists. 'Make use of the time while I am still alive,' he had begged Spaak and Bech, the Foreign Ministers of Belgium and Luxembourg in a conversation overheard by a reporter of *Der Spiegel*, 'I do not know what my successors will do once they are left to their own devices, unless they are set on a clearly defined path and tethered to Europe.'[6]

There was more time than he thought and he underrated his successors. But his doubts were genuine and for the next eight years, while he remained in power, he tried to find a pillar, other than a Western European Federation, to which he could tether his country while he exorcised the twin demons of nationalism and socialism. But Adenauer had lost his touch and instead of pointing the way, he allowed himself to be led into paths that were fatal to his dreams. 'If only Schumacher were alive . . .' he would sometimes lament, when the complexities of Western Europe seemed over-whelming. But it was not Schumacher, but an even more formidable and seductive figure with whom he soon had to deal. De Gaulle was waiting in the wings.

6 *Konrad Adenauer*, Rudolf Augstein, p. 35.

CHAPTER X

The Miracle Workers

'The miracle' began in the most brutal fashion. What is now spoken of in West Germany as the 'currency reform' was, in fact, one of the harshest acts of confiscation ever imposed upon a people by their conquerors. Yet it saved Western Germany. The reichmark had ceased to have any value. Theoretically wages and prices were fixed as they had been under the Nazis, but no one, except an official dispensing what little was available of the food or fuel ration, would accept marks in exchange for goods. Everything else, clothes, shoes, medicines, pots and pans, a service like the mending of a chair or the chopping of wood, had to be paid for in kind, and only those with land or a factory backed by secret stores of raw materials like cotton, cloth or leather, could command these things in any quantity. Scrounging, acting as middleman in the barter system, or as purveyors to the black market, was the coveted occupation. Apathy was so great that production three years after the surrender was still only half what it had been in 1938 and life, not only in Germany but in the neighbouring countries of Holland and Belgium which had always depended upon Germany as their industrial arsenal and market, seemed condemned to a continuing and desperate struggle for existence.

All through 1946 and 1947, conversations about currency reform had been taking place between the four occupying powers. They were agreed that no real economic recovery in Germany could begin without it, but as the original instructions to all the military governors had stipulated that recovery was not their business there was no real sense of urgency. However, Clay's economic experts, Joseph Dodge, Gerhardt Colm and Raymond Goldsmith, having consulted economists in countries which had experienced drastic currency reforms, including Russia and Czechoslovakia, wrote a report in the spring of 1946 which foreshadowed what was to come.

At first the Russians seemed to agree, but then they demanded that two sets of plates for printing the new currency should be made, one to be kept in Russian hands. Remembering the millions of occupational marks which the Russians had printed and for which the American taxpayer eventually had to pay, since the American government had guaranteed to redeem occupational marks, the Americans made the counter-suggestion that all new currency should be printed in Berlin under four power control. This the Russians refused and the conversations languished.

In 1947, Mr Dodge was recalled to America and Mr Jack Bennett, another Treasury official, took his place. It was he, working with Mr Eric Coates on the British side, who was really responsible for what came to be known as 'Operation Bird Dog'. Meanwhile many German experts were consulted, including Ludwig Erhard, then Chairman of the Economic Council of the Western Zones. Shocked by the severity of the Allied proposals, they produced a Plan which would have carried through the reform in milder phases. However, the Allies persevered.

Towards the end of 1947, persistent rumours that the Russians intended to revalue the reichmark and to force their own new currency on the whole of Germany kept circulating in Berlin. The Americans, therefore, printed their new deutschmark in the denominations planned in the Dodge-Colm-Goldsmith Report and shipped them secretly to Germany so as to be ready to issue them immediately if the Russians moved.

On 15th June, when it had become absolutely clear that the Russians were going to attempt to drive out the Western Allies by blockade, the British and Americans announced the reform of the currency in the Western Zones. Overnight everyone's money became worth only one tenth of what it had been the day before. This applied to bank and other savings deposits as well as loans and mortgages, for obviously debts had to be scaled down at the same rate as the money with which they could be repaid. So that people with little money should not find themselves destitute, a minor exception was made in regard to cash. Everyone could exchange forty of their old reichmarks for forty of the new deutschmarks and two months later another twenty marks at the one for one ratio. This, it was calculated, would meet immediate needs while balances were worked out and wages and prices found new levels. Businesses were allowed sixty deutschmarks for each employee on the same one for one terms. State, local and public authorities were given an allowance equal to a month's revenue. The rest of their funds, however invested, were cancelled outright.

This was economic savagery of a kind that could never have been attempted in less desperate circumstances. It meant that twelve million individual savings accounts – all those of 500 RM or less – were wiped out; that municipalities and public utilities such as the railways lost their reserves entirely. People who had lent money on mortgage had lost their security, for they could not know the true value of the tenth they would receive back. And worse was to come. When the final calculations were made of the money required to get the wheels of the German economy moving, the Allied authorities decided that the ten to one ratio was too high and cancelled a further $3\frac{1}{2}\%$ of the old currency to make the final rate 6.5 DM for every 100 RM. No wonder Erhard and his colleagues had been apprehensive.

But they were wrong. The truth was that, because the old reichmark was generally considered worthless, the loss of small savings was not really felt. The money had only existed on paper and the owners had not thought it worthwhile to draw it out. They scarcely missed what they had mentally written off. On the other hand – and this is where the Western Allies had made a brilliant psychological judgment – the German people immediately believed in the new money. The reduction in the number of marks in circulation was so drastic that everyone seems automatically to have assumed that the new notes must be worth what was printed on them. It was a conjuring trick, but its very boldness made it a success.

As if by magic the goods appeared in the shops – or what passed for shops. Shoes and clothes, pots and pans, were lined up along the sills of ruined windows; old and new furniture was laid out in cellars or under tarpaulin roofs or along the pavements. Binoculars and cameras, typewriters, adding machines and a medley of 'surplus army equipment' were shown to special clients in back rooms. They were bought without any questions being asked as to the means by which they had been acquired. Medicines, which chemists had assured the authorities they were 'utterly unable' to supply the day before, became immediately available for those with prescriptions and with the money to pay; in cases of obvious need they were now supplied free. The black market, which had dominated German life for so long, shrank to a trickle of goods smuggled across the zonal frontiers from the east.

Small though the supply of new cash was, the entire population of Western Germany went on a buying spree. Those with larger savings spent them – 600,000,000 DM in the first four months of the new currency. The spree went in identifiable waves. First there was the food wave, when people found that deutschmarks would actually buy bread or a bottle of schnapps. All over Western Germany the day-dreams of the hungry came true in a short but glorious binge. Then came a household equipment wave, blankets, pillows, pots and pans, radios, table cloths, blossomed through the half-ruined rooms of dingy basements in which whole families lived. Finally there was the clothes wave – first new shoes, then a coat and at last a little colour as men and women once again took an interest in their appearance.

When they had spent all they had, although often technically destitute, they found that they were really in exactly the same position as the rest of the population. Since all debts had been reduced to a tenth of their value, practically no one could live off income from a mortgage or interest on an investment. All had to work or, if they could not work, to eke out an existence on the dole or a pension; but this was no different from the life they had been used to since the surrender. The currency reform was the final leveller; the hardships it inflicted were only minor additions to a misery that had been general for three years; the opportunities it offered, on the other hand, were open to all who had property or even just energy or an idea.

The spree was just a beginning. The real 'miracle' began with the policies proposed by Erhard and seized upon by thousands of entrepreneurs as soon as the Federal Republic came into being. Erhard believed in private enterprise and the forces of competition with almost religious fervour. In a country where most people were still hungry, living in ruins and often in rags, the continuation of some form of rationing to ensure 'fair shares' seemed inevitable, particularly to the occupying authorities. Erhard took a different view. If individuals were given the chance, he believed they would relieve the general want far more quickly than any state-controlled apparatus, however well-intentioned. Where almost everything was lacking, there was unlimited opportunity for enterprise of every conceivable kind, large and small.

Erhard also believed that by encouraging competition from abroad he could keep prices down and prevent the public being exploited more effectively than by rationing. No doubt some would make large fortunes and spend vulgarly and conspicuously, but the quantity of luxuries they would consume would be infinitesimal compared to the desperately needed goods and services they would produce, provided there were sufficient incentives for them to re-invest their profits. And if discrepancies in wealth became intoler-able, they could in the end always be corrected by taxation.

This was the philosophy which Erhard had imbibed from Professors Walter Eucken and Wilhelm Röpke at Freiburg University in the early thirties and which he presented as the *Sozialemark-twirtschaft* – the Social Market Economy – to the C.D.U. party conference in the summer of 1948. First as director of the bi-zonal economic council and then as Minister for Economic Affairs in the newly constituted Federal Republic, he put it into practice.

As a condition of the currency reform, he bullied the Allies into accepting drastic reductions in taxation from the levels they had imposed in 1946. The Americans in particular protested that it was unfair to their own taxpayers for the Germans to lighten their burdens just when the United States was giving them millions of dollars under Marshall Aid. Erhard persuaded them that if they agreed to exempt from taxation income which was saved and in-vested, they would pay much less in Marshall Aid in the long run.

At the same time, flying in the face of the same opinions, he abolished the rationing of a large number of goods, including some foodstuffs. Although prices rose, they were never as high as they had been on the black market.

Finally, and again in the teeth of Allied objections that their taxpayers were financing unnecessary imports, Erhard abolished import duties on a number of consumer goods to make sure that, if German producers tried to take advantage of the general shortage, they would be undercut by competition from foreign countries.

Erhard's policies worked, literally, like magic. From the sale of stocks which the owners had illegally hoarded against just such a day, high profits were made which became tax-free the moment they were ploughed back into a business or saved in one of the many saving schemes. New enterprises mushroomed. Gross investment rose from a trickle before 1948 (what there was was mainly sup-plied by the Allies) to an annual total of more than 30 billion deutsch-marks in the first five years. Three-quarters of this came from private sources and more than half from cash generated by businesses themselves.

Finance Minister Schäffer's budgets reinforced Erhard's schemes. Nearly half of all Federal revenues came from turnover and sales taxes which hit rich and poor alike; and although income tax in 1948 was reasonably progressive, the exemptions were so many that a very large number of Germans kept most of what they earned. Overtime was virtually free of tax – a huge incentive in a country where so much still needed doing; personal income tax was reduced four times in five years (in 1953 by as much as 15%). Every conceivable type of saving including life insurance was deductible and expense allowances for those engaged in any form of business were so generous that people in the higher income brackets could not only live off their firms but buy a lot of luxuries as well.

As for companies, all of them were allowed to revalue their assets arbitrarily at the time of the currency reform, which meant writing up their assets and writing off large amounts each year and so generating extra cash. Special depreciation allowances were granted for capital expenditure on repairing war damage, for new houses, or forms of new plant including office equipment. Undistributed profits escaped tax altogether and what was distributed was treated as earned income.

Deutschmark millionaires began to blossom in their hundreds on every industrial tree. To-day there is a whole German literature on the men who began in a back room and are now multi-millionaires or the managers of multi-million enterprises. Some of the new millionaires started with virtually nothing; Wilhelm Becker, the largest motor car dealer in the Ruhr, who won the sole agency for Rolls-Royce, was the son of a peasant; Willie Schlieker, who became a steel magnate and shipbuilder, was the son of a docker who went through years of unemployment between the wars. As the last of twelve children, Becker had come under the legal protection of the House of Hohenzollern and the Roman Catholic church and received a better than average education; Schlieker, a clever boy, had won a technical diploma from school.

Becker developed his passion for cars in the army and, having learned how to repair almost anything on wheels, started a much needed second-hand car business by scrounging one old car and making it go; within ten years 'Auto Becker' had a turnover of

£100,000 ($250,000) a year and the richest list of clients in Germany; its owner had bought a villa in Oberkassel and a fleet of cars of his own. Schlieker's career was more chequered. Having won his diploma, he joined Speer's organisation and rose to be head of the steel division. After the surrender he performed much the same function for the Russians. But communism did not attract him and he fled into the British zone, fell foul of de-Nazification and had to start all over again. However, by using his old contacts and importing American coal and steel during the shortage, he soon built up a business which was said to have been worth £100 m. ($250 m.). Then, to the relief of the older ship-building families in Hamburg, he over-stretched himself and went bankrupt.

But although there are hundreds of successful men with similar backgrounds, the majority of the eighteen thousand West Germans who, in 1965, owned property worth more than a million deutschmarks came from middle class families.

The young man who, in 1945, was seen wheeling a barrow-load of old machinery through the streets of his home town of Furth, just outside Nuremberg, to set up shop as a radio mechanic, had been salesman for his father's radio shop before the war and had learned more of his trade as a radio operator in the German Air Force. With the machinery, which had been hidden in a defunct laundry, Max Grundig and eight other men began repairing radio sets – then almost the only means of mass communication – and, more ingeniously, designing and constructing tool kits, known as the 'Heinzlemann', with which people could make their own receivers. To-day Grundig owns twenty-two major factories with more than seventy subsidiaries spread out across the globe, employs twenty-seven thousand people, has an annual turnover of more than £100 m. ($250 m.) and produces nearly four million units a year. His television factory is the largest in Germany, his radio factory the largest in Europe and his sound-track factory the largest in the world.

Grundig is the archetype of the self-made, self-financed modern German industrialist. This short, dark, thick-set man in his early sixties literally lives for his business. Until 1971, when he founded a trust through which his employees and the public could acquire some of the equity, he himself owned all the Grundig shares and had financed the expansion of his business almost entirely through profits ploughed back tax-free. He is an autocrat with strong paternal instincts. Many of his employees live in houses built by the firm, bought or rented on special terms; special trains pass through the factory grounds to take hundreds more to their homes in the country round Nuremberg. The factory club, run by the employees, provides good, cheap meals and every kind of social amenity. A promotion and publicity department not only tells the world about Grundig but keeps the employees informed about the progress of the business through a whole range of brochures, films, specially recorded tapes and closed-circuit television.

Grundig's office is low-ceilinged and long, with wide windows filling the whole of one wall looking into the courtyard of the administrative block which has a garden in the middle. The furniture is modern, and expensive abstract pictures hang on the walls; yet nothing is lavish. To save time, visitors are flown by helicopter from Furth to the factory on the other side of Nuremberg, past the medieval castle which has been so faithfully rebuilt; but they eat plain canteen food in severely clean dining-rooms. And although photographs of Grundig, his wife and sons, adorn the walls and figure prominently in the promotion literature, there is no question of his founding a dynasty. Under the new trust, the direction of the firm will pass, on Grundig's death or retirement, to the men who have built it up with him; his sons must take their chance.

In the beginning it was much the same with Axel Springer. The licence to print the radio magazine *Hor Zu* (Listen In) was given to him jointly with his father because the latter owned a small printing works in which Axel had served his apprenticeship before the war. But whereas the father had been content with producing the *Altona News*, the son had ambitions. Springer did not know Grundig in those days, but as the 'Heinzelmann' sold in its thousands and tens of thousands, so the circulation of *Hor Zu* grew. To-day it is one of the triumphs of modern journalism, a magazine which is a housewife's Bible, a family journal, a picture record rather like the old *Berlin Illustrierte* and a programme catalogue all in one, with a circulation of nearly 4,500,000 copies a week.

With the money that *Hor Zu* earned, Springer started other papers. Since Hamburg was his base a *Hamburger Abendblatt* (*Hamburg Evening News*) was a natural beginning. Then came *Kristall*, an illustrated magazine with intellectual pretensions, followed by *Bild* (*Picture*), the first German tabloid and the only daily newspaper in the Republic to achieve a mass circulation of more than four

million copies a day. Continuing to balance profit with respecta-
bility, Springer bought the declining *Die Welt* (*The World*) from the
British Occupation Authorites and turned it into a high-class conservative paper. Like many such papers, it has never earned a
profit, but is more widely read than its rivals such as the *Kölnische
Rundschau* or *Süddeutsche Zeitung* which do not circulate far outside
their own province. In 1960 Springer turned his attention to Berlin,
which he regarded as a symbol of the Free World in its struggle with
the communists, and bought what remained of the famous Ullstein
publishing house, including the *Berliner Morgenpost*, and at once
produced Berlin editions of *Die Welt* and *Bild*. Partly as a challenge,
he then proceeded to build a new twenty-story office block on the
edge of what soon turned out to be the infamous Wall, which he
now 'shares' with Ulbricht, the East German communist leader.

Almost all Springer's publications were a success. At one time a
reporter of *Der Spiegel* estimated that two out of three families in
West Germany got all their information and literary entertainment
from the Springer publishing house. This was a less damaging
exaggeration than the allegation that Springer was trying to establish a newspaper monopoly. In fact, the whole German provincial
press, including five independent newspapers in Berlin, was thriving
and radio and television were spreading faster than in any other
European country. But because Springer was a dedicated disciple
of Erhard's and an outspoken supporter of Adenauer's government,
he became the chief target for left-wing criticism. When, in 1966,
the Grand Coalition absorbed the Social Democrats into the
government and emasculated constitutional opposition, this criticism, led by Rudolf Augstein the proprieter of *Der Spiegel*, grew in
virulence and volume until, with the outbreak of student unrest in
1968, it developed into a hysterical demand for the expropriation
of the entire Springer empire.

Springer stood up boldly to the onslaught. He inclined his head to
the recommendations of a parliamentary committee sufficiently to
sell two of his popular weekly magazines, but otherwise maintained
his papers and his policies. He stood unashamedly for a democratic
system, a free market economy, reconciliation with the Jews and a
united Germany. His hatred of totalitarian régimes received constant stimulus, for from the windows of his sumptuous flat, which
runs the whole length of the top floor of his Berlin office, he looked
out over Ulbricht's city; at all hours, both he and his employees

could watch the ceaseless patrols along the wall which kept the East Germans in.

One day the whole office crowded to the windows. From the buildings facing them beyond the wall, a man had appeared in working clothes, carrying a ladder and walking straight towards the danger zone in which anyone can be shot without warning. The man never paused and, while everyone else held their breath, expecting each second to hear the rattle of machine-gun fire, he walked slowly to the wall, placed his ladder up against it and, without turning his head, climbed up, stood on the wall to pull the ladder up after him, and then climbed down on the other side. No one had stirred. Not a word of explanation was allowed to appear in the press for fear his secret might be betrayed.

A German editor has explained the outcry against Springer as the result of 'pent-up feelings of aggression' which calls for medical rather than constitutional treatment. Perhaps the absence of such treatment accounted for the charge of hypocrisy levelled against him for his dealings with the Jews. There were tens of thousands of Germans who share Springer's sense of shame over the concentration camps; few have been lucky enough to do as much to atone. Springer paid more than one visit to Israel, has founded a library there and took the view that Germany must at all costs support the Jewish State. This may have been embarrassing for a German government, but it was scarcely a matter for personal reproach.

Most of the larger stones which have been hurled at Springer came from another Hamburg house, the office of *Der Spiegel*. As Hans Habe, the novelist, wrote in a spirited defence of Springer, it was difficult to repress a smile when Rudolf Augstein attacked Springer for allowing his political views to colour his newspapers. Augstein stands on the political left, as the millions of readers of *Der Spiegel* are instantly aware, and Augstein to-day is every bit as ardent a supporter of Willy Brandt as Springer was of Adenauer. Augstein has bought out three partners, changed his editors and used his magazine to publish his own articles, letters and speeches as unashamedly as a McCormick or a Beaverbrook. In doing so he undoubtedly served the cause of German democracy and became at one and the same time one of the men most feared in Germany and a multi-millionaire.

Augstein was one of those who began not with property but with an idea. He was born in Hanover in 1923 of respectable Catholic parents and while still at school distinguished himself by writing a brilliant essay on the impossibility of defeating Britain. No doubt because of his age the authorities chose to ignore it and he duly joined the infantry and found himself on the eastern front where he not only survived but became a company commander. After the surrender he escaped capture by arming himself with a khaki uniform and an old bicycle and, pretending to be a Canadian soldier taking local leave, rode to his sister's house in Offenbach where he lay low for several months.

At the end of 1945 he went back to Hanover and there made friends with the British press-control officer, a Major Chaloner who, with the help of two former German refugees on his staff, was trying to launch a magazine in the style of the American *Time* and *Newsweek*. Augstein became one of the founders of *Diese Woche* (*This Week*). But *Diese Woche* soon ran into trouble. It was outspokenly critical of the Occupation, made fun of members of the Control Commission and was in danger of having its supply of paper withdrawn when the British suddenly decided to hand it over entirely to the Germans. Augstein, a photographer named Stempka and a journalist named Barsch, received the licence. In January, 1947, the magazine reappeared with a new title, *Der Spiegel* (*The Mirror*), and by the end of the year had achieved a circulation of a hundred thousand copies. Augstein was launched and the battle with Springer, and with a succession of industrialists and politicians, was about to begin.

In many ways Augstein and Springer were well matched. Springer, tall and fair, had large ideas whether in politics or newspapers; Augstein, dark and so small that his staff called him 'the little man', had a passion for detail. Springer enjoyed the good things of life, shot grouse in Scotland, partridges in Spain, had several houses and a private aeroplane whereas Augstein insisted, so long as his staff would let him, on riding to his office in Hamburg on a bicycle, dressed in an old shirt and shorts. Both men considered themselves moralists, but where Springer was urbane, Augstein had all the self-righteousness of the Socialist intellectual. 'When that man smells a rose, it stinks,' remarked a German aphorist, and *Der Spiegel* has become notorious, not only for exposing public scandals but for hounding private individuals, raking up details of their private lives with a disregard for privacy and sometimes accuracy which has resulted in actions in the courts. In spite of his high-mindedness, Augstein did not hesitate to publish conversations accidentally overheard. Yet by his fearlessness in attacking public men and institutions, whether it was millionaires who avoided taxation, the excessive power of the banks or the evasions of politicians, he undoubtedly inspired and sustained a critical sense among a people who traditionally have nurtured an exaggerated respect for authority. At one time during his long struggle to obtain control over his publishing house, Augstein is said to have asked Springer to join him; Springer allegedly refused, not on personal grounds, but because the proprietor of the sensational *Bild* did not consider *Der Spiegel* sufficiently serious. Fleet Street in its heyday has seen no livelier duel.

The fortunes made in communications were new and flamboyant but they did not lie at the heart of 'the miracle'. Heavy industry has for long been West Germany's greatest asset and manufacture its people's greatest skill; most of the families which dominate the Ruhr to-day not only had something to begin with but had had it for a long time. In spite of ruin, degradation and often imprisonment, the bearers of names like Krupp, Thyssen, Flick, Haniel, Werhahn, Röchling or Siemens, who formed the plutocracy under both the Kaiser and Hitler, are still household words in coal, steel and engineering.

Those who saw the twisted mass of metal, which was all that was left of the Krupp works in Essen in 1945, could scarcely believe that anything would ever be made on that site again. But while Alfried Krupp served his sentence as a war criminal – he was released in January, 1951, on the orders of Mr McCloy, the American High Commissioner, after six years in prison – the 20,000 employees who remained on his books cleared the rubble and kept going whatever machinery had not been sent away as reparations or destroyed as being capable of war production. When Alfried came out he at once made it plain that he intended, not only to resume control of his concerns, but to expand them.

Under the leadership of Berthold Beitz, a young man without knowledge of iron or steel whom Alfried selected to become the overlord of his business, the entire structure was recast. 'Children not Cannon,' became the slogan and Krupp representatives spread out across the world winning large contracts for every kind of engineering product other than weapons of war. As he built his second empire Alfried took possession once more of the monstrous Villa Hugel which the Allied Control Commission had confiscated for its own use. But Beitz, like Schlieker, over-reached himself and, to meet a crisis in liquidity, the Government was obliged to provide a guarantee as a condition of which it appointed a consortium to take over the firm. Arndt von Bohlen und Halbach, Alfried's son, renounced his inheritance for a 'pension' of some £250,000 ($625,000) a year.

When Fritz Thyssen was asked by an obsequious client whether he should be addressed as *'Herr Generaldirektor'*, he replied, 'No, I have a *Herr Generaldirektor*.' Fritz, who backed Hitler and Ludendorff in 1923, ended the war in a concentration camp and died soon afterwards. Within a few years his widow, Amelie, his daughter Anita, who married a Hungarian Count, and his nephews were presiding over one of the largest steel empires in the world with not one but several *Generaldirektors*. Once again, it was a case of those who possessed even ruins making good, provided they were prepared to reinvest. The Werhahns, an old Neuss family into which Adenauer's daughter married, are another example of the pre-war entrepreneur making the most of post-war opportunities. To-day they own, through holding companies, a controlling interest in fifty large businesses as various as steel, food stores, dairies, breweries, printing works and coal mines, of one of which Adenauer's son, Konrad, became chairman.

Friedrich Flick was an exception in the constellation of the Ruhr, in that his father was a peasant. Like the Werhahns, Flick had never been concerned with only one industry. From the smallest beginnings, he became a financial pioneer in the Weimar Republic, buying one factory or firm after another, reorganising it and then selling, until, under Hitler, he reached a commanding position, particularly in the armaments industry. Flick served five years in Landsberg gaol after the surrender and when he came out was forced to sell his remaining coal and part of his steel interests. But this was a blessing in disguise. He invested what he had left in expanding industries like chemicals, paper and motor cars, re-entered steel and was soon in control of a larger empire than before. When he died in July, 1972, he was perhaps the richest man in Europe.

The Flicks and the Werhahns, like Thyssen and Krupp and most other large-scale proprietors, were greatly dependent on their 'overlords' or 'managers' for the success of their enterprises. The cult of the manager in Germany goes back to the beginning of the industrial revolution. In those days 'managers' were not so much men who had risen up through an industry as 'men of confidence', someone the pioneer industrialist could trust implicitly like a family lawyer, the 'factor' who looked after his estate, a caretaker or even the tutor to his children.

In 1816, Wilhelm Lueg was tutor to the Jacobi children when his employer, for only a slightly increased wage, made him 'manager' of a small foundry which he and his friends, Haniel and Huyssen, had bought from a member of the Krupp family in Essen. By the end of the century Wilhelm's son Carl, who had succeeded his father as manager to the firm of Jacobi Haniel and Huyssen, was himself one of the richest men in Germany and his brother and sister had married into the Jacobi and Haniel families. The Luegs had become part of the establishment. In their turn the Luegs and their partners chose a new manager, a geologist named Reusch, who in his turn founded a new dynasty of managers; Hermann Reusch became one of the most active and controversial figures in the Ruhr under the Federal Republic.

The 'Managers' who helped make 'the miracle' had several things in common with their predecessors. They had to be men in whom the reigning Thyssen, Krupp, Flick or Haniel had complete trust; they had to possess immense energy and a general rather than a specialist competence; they usually had to leave the limelight to the proprietor and work in obscurity. To-day names like Kerschbaum, Dunbier, Overbeck, Muller or Heyne are known in industrial circles, but their bearers will pass through the doors of many hotels or restaurants unrecognised and their photographs seldom appear in the newspapers. Yet each has been appointed General Director or 'overlord' of groups of companies employing tens of thousands of people with turnovers of billions of pounds, and each sits on so many boards that at least a quarter of their working time is spent in formal meetings. Their salaries range from £30,000 to £50,000 ($75-000 – 125,000) a year but they may earn as much again from bonuses and outside directorships[1] and, since each keeps nearly half his income, they would have to be profligate to a degree to avoid amassing some capital.

1 These extra emoluments are sometimes retained by the firm.

But however impressive their power, most managers remain employees; if their business falters or they lose the confidence of their principal share-holders, they can be dismissed. Although Fritz Aurel Goergen had resurrected the Phoenix-Rheinrohr steel combine into a gigantic and successful concern for the Thyssen family, when he decided to let his own wife, rather than the widow Amelie Thyssen, christen one of the company ships, he suddenly found himself without a job. Goergen, a rough diamond, had fallen foul not only of widow Amelie but of her real 'man of confidence', Professor Ellscheid, a lawyer who had successfully steered the Thyssen fortunes through the shoals of de-Nazification during the Occupation.

Goergen seemed to have learned his lesson when, having been awarded massive damages by the courts for wrongful dismissal he was summoned to do for the famous Henschel steel and locomotive works what he had done for Phoenix-Rheinrohr. Again he was successful, within a few years turning a business which was losing heavily into a group worth many millions; but this time, instead of remaining a mere 'manager' he was able to acquire more than half the equity for himself. But Goergen was unpopular and perhaps unlucky. In 1964, the police raided the Henschel works, took away all the files and subsequently accused the firm of having overcharged the Minister of Defence for spare parts. A few days later, during a dinner in honour of Chancellor Erhard, Goergen was arrested. Rumours of a swindle involving 'billions' immediately spread but after an inquiry which reflected little credit on the government, the amount in question was reduced to less than £50,000 ($125,000). Although Goergen was released, he was obliged to sell his shares for much less than they were worth and retired, a frustrated millionaire, to Switzerland.

Goergen was exceptional in his ability, ruthlessness and brashness, but he was a prototype manager of the kind badly needed by the Federal Republic in those tumultuous early years when so much of industry needed restructuring. Where he eventually failed, men like Hans-Gunther Sohl, who finally reintegrated the Thyssen interests, Christian Kracht, who overseered the Springer Empire, Wilhelm Zangen and Egon Overbeck who successively ruled Mannesmann, the third of the great steel groups, succeeded. Heinrich Nordhoff who, having been appointed by the British to manage the half-ruined Volkswagen works, smote his masters with almost biblical fervour by producing the world's most competitive motor car. While owner-managers like Neckermann, whose mail-order business is the largest in Europe, or Franz Burda, the great printer of Offenburg who believes that British and American magazines are failing because of the poor quality of their print and pictures, stuck closely to their own last, these 'overlords' re-fashioned their undertakings into groups which were large enough to make the best use of modern administrative and mechanical technology and so become the basis of the twentieth-century international company. In spite of some scandals and crashes, they were the ideal complement to the entrepreneurs who took the risk of employing them.

The prophet Erhard had found his charioteers in the entre-preneurs and managers, but for all their energy and enterprise the Grundigs and Flicks, Goergens and Nordhoffs were not the archi-tects of 'the miracle'. These came from a less glamorous source. Bankers are not often seen as heroes, perhaps because they are apt to make as much money out of disaster as of triumph; yet the role of the banks in the German recovery was not only dynamic but often courageous and also sympathetic.

Under the Occupation, the German banks were affected by the Allied fear of large cartels, which Erhard shared. The old central banks were dissolved and several new provincial banks created, allegedly to act in competition. But if only to safeguard their depositors, the limits within which banks can compete are circum-scribed and unless they agree broadly on credit policy they can soon produce economic chaos. Nobody was surprised, therefore, when after independence, the provincial banks were merged into the Deutsche, Commerz and Dresdner Banks of to-day, to which must now be added the bank belonging to the Federation of German Trade Unions. Savings banks, which handle not only the small savings of the German people but their contributions to health and life insurance, have always been locally based and remain so.

The banks, along with cinemas and restaurants, were the first to open in those chaotic days after the surrender and although many of their accounts were wiped out by confiscation, ruin or later the currency reform, they never ceased to function nor lost the confidence of their clients. The black market in its heyday greatly reduced their business, but it was remarkable that an apparently destitute people somehow managed to maintain insurance and mortgage premiums and, by living through barter, to save cash. The flow of deposits never wholly dried up.

By custom the German banks play a larger role in the economy of their country than do their British or American counterparts because they acquire large holdings in private and public enterprises and are also used as nominees by millions of small shareholders whom they represent at annual general meetings. Bankers, therefore, appear on the boards of a very large number of industrial companies and act as midwives, managerial consultants and sometimes as overseers to a degree that would be unthinkable in London, New York or Paris.

The banks had a dual role in 'the miracle'. They had to increase the supply of cash and credit sufficiently to allow production and investment to rise without the total quantity of money outrunning the goods and services available, and they had to select those to whom they would grant credit. They did both brilliantly. It is impossible to draw an exact line between old and new money but if, as one American economist has calculated, all short-term credit granted in the early years of the new currency was new money, then it ran into many billions of deutschmarks and it was a considerable feat to have created it without causing inflation. Prices rose, but after six months remained remarkably stable. In spite of the demand – and there were always more people wanting to borrow than the banks would accommodate – they kept the supply of money comparatively tight.

German bankers sometimes claim that they lend more adventurously than others, perhaps because their industrial shareholdings offer them a greater reward; what is certain is that after their country's defeat they were forced to lend, if they were to lend at all, on the flimsiest collateral or none. In thousands of cases only the first of the banker's three 'C's' – character, collateral, capacity – could be assessed; the rest had to be taken for granted. Yet they had comparatively few failures.

It was, perhaps, less deliberate but equally important that banking policy also promoted exports. Western Germany, having lost the provinces which formerly supplied it with food and raw materials, had to export to feed its swollen population. By keeping money tight the banks not only forced businesses to plough back their profits but set a limit to the amount the Germans themselves could buy. Once they had satisfied the home market, manufacturers had to look abroad for sales if they were to make the fullest use of their capacity.

Soon, therefore, West German salesmen spread out across a world which had been virtually closed to them for five years, only to find that the peoples they visited were starved of almost everything they had to offer. They also discovered that, as Germans, they possessed two great advantages. Their country was forbidden to manufacture arms, so they could concentrate on everything else, and every industrial country was crying out for the capital goods which the Federal Republic was peculiarly fitted to supply. The results were phenomenal. As Erhard said when opening the Industrial Exhibition in Berlin ten years later: 'Who would have dreamed in the summer of 1951, when Germany's balance of payments was plunging into the red and she had to beg for special help from her partners in the newly formed European payments Union, that within a year she would have repaid her deficit and be moving into the black?'[2] In 1947, the Federal Republic could pay for less than 40% of its imports; in 1952 she was breaking even and by 1954 had reserves of gold and foreign exchange worth DM 11 billion. Within five years of being the most down-and-out country in the Western world, supported by doles from her conquerors, Western Germany had become Europe's major creditor. She has remained so ever since.

The bankers who bore such a large share of this achievement were shadowy figures to the German public. Robert Pferdmenges, for many years head of Oppenheim, one of the few private banks in Germany, who could boast of Friedrich Engels as a great-uncle and was imprisoned by the S.S., was an old friend of Adenauer's and had helped him escape from prison. He became the nearest thing to an *eminence grise* that Germany has known since the war. Pferdmenges would sometimes appear at Christian Democrat party meetings and invariably threw his weight behind the Chancellor. He was believed by many to have been responsible for many of Adenauer's most crucial decisions, particularly in regard to the trade unions; but he shunned publicity and could walk unrecognised through the streets of his home-town of Cologne.

Carl Blessing, von Salomon's fellow internee who became chairman of the Bundesbank and one of Germany's ablest inter-

2 *The Economics of Success*, Ludwig Erhard, Translated by J. A. Arengo-Jones & J. S. Thomson. Thames and Hudson, London; Van Nostrand, Reinhold, New York, 1963.

national negotiators, sometimes acted as a go-between for his friend Erhard in his dealings with Adenauer, but otherwise kept strictly to finance. Rudolf Münemann, who developed the idea of revolving credits (through which money on short call could be used many times over), and rose to be head of the Trade and Industry Bank of Frankfurt, became better known abroad than in his own country; for it was he who was chosen by *Fortune* magazine to share with Pferdmenges the honour of being one of the two financial geniuses of 'the miracle'.

But one banker, who was neither shy nor retiring, was pre-eminent. Chancellors come and go, but for twenty years Hermann Joseph Abs sat at the pinnacle of German economic power, not only as chairman of the Deutsche Bank, but with so many other chairmanships and directorships that in 1965 a special law was passed, nicknamed the 'Abs Law', limiting the number of such posts that any one individual could hold. It has been said that Abs looks like a cross between an English bishop and a country gentleman; thickset without being heavy, dark with slightly wavy hair, wearing a neat moustache, he conveys the impression of always being slightly amused at life and, in spite of his multifarious interests, of having time to spare.

Abs was born in Bonn in 1901 of a Roman Catholic family and was destined for the law, but the inflation after the First World War impoverished his parents and he turned to banking, spending his first seven years abroad in London, Paris, Amsterdam and New York. Returning to Germany in 1930, he entered the private bank of Delbruck Schikler and Co., and was soon offered a junior partnership. However, Abs's ability had already been noticed elsewhere and soon afterwards he was invited to become a director of the Deutsch Bank. As this was one of the central banks it involved an association with people committed to the support of Hitler's government some of whom wore brown or black uniforms in the office.

Abs is refreshingly open about his role under the Nazis. 'No one who is alive can claim to have belonged to the resistance against Hitler,' he says and leaves it at that.

In fact, as a Catholic with many Anglo-Saxon connections, he would have found the party uncongenial in any case. Fortunately, as head of the foreign department, he was able to negotiate for the bank without too frequent contact with party officials. Nevertheless Abs became chairman of more than one company which was furthering the war effort and, following the surrender, was arrested by the British and spent three months in prison in Hamburg. After his release and without a job, he spent his time writing a series of memoranda on the rebuilding of the German economy which he presented to the British Military Government. The memoranda were often highly critical, one of them ending with the observation that if the Allies were determined to turn Germany's economic clock back a hundred years, as seemed evident, then they must face the fact that they would be unable to find work or bread for sixty million people. The British were impressed and when the vitally important Reconstruction Finance Corporation was set up to administer the Counterpart Funds arising from Marshall Aid, they chose Abs to be its head. His foot was once more on the ladder.

Within a few years Abs had achieved the commanding position which he still held in the early seventies, in spite of his official retirement from the bank. (He was still chairman of the German Railways, the Lufthansa and the Institute of Bankers.) A story has it that when he joined the board of the newly constituted Deutsche Bank, he suggested at its first meeting that the chairmanship should be held in rotation, selection being by alphabetical order. When a colleague asked him how soon the rotation would begin Abs replied: 'That, of course, is in the hands of God. We must all die sometime.' Although, no doubt, this story is apocryphal, it illustrated Abs's brand of humour and his supreme self-confidence. When journalists wrote that a nod or a frown from Abs could make or mar a firm or a man, they were not far wrong. His power stemmed not only from his chairmanships but from his relationship with Adenauer, less intimate than that of Pferdmenges but close; with successive Ministers of Finance; and from his personal knowledge of the leading personalities in German industry.

The Deutsch Bank is the largest of the Big Four and owns stocks in a vast network of industrial companies running into several billions of deutschmarks. It also controls many trusts and institutions which invest the peoples' savings as well as acting as nominee for nearly a million small investors. When a German company gets into difficulties, therefore, more often than not it is a banker, who is probably also a director, who steps in to reorganise it; and when important companies are concerned, more often than not it has been Abs who has been involved. To give just one example: when the great firm of Krupp faced bankruptcy, it was Abs who was appointed to reorganise it and Abs who, with great foresight, drew in the Trade Union Bank and found a seat on the board for Walter Hesselbach, the chairman of that bank, and Otto Brenner, the head of the steel-workers' union.

But although Abs accepted many appointments at their hands, he had a disdain for politicians unless they had a business background. Adenauer he respected and it was he and Pferdmenges rather than Erhard who supplied the Chancellor with such economic understanding as he possessed. Adenauer responded by using Abs on many international negotiations, particularly when they involved the British or Americans. It was Abs who led the German delegation to the London conference at which Germany's pre-war indebtedness was settled – a prerequisite for entry into N.A.T.O.

But Abs had little time for Erhard. 'It is not what he did but what he left undone that was important,' he is fond of saying, meaning that Erhard had so little practical knowledge that the bankers could run the economy much as they pleased. This was both an exaggeration and a mistake. Abs never understood Erhard's role as a prophet nor appreciated the extent to which his political courage in defying the Allies and his persuasiveness in reconciling the German people to the inequalities of the early years of recovery, made the exercise of his own financial power possible. Had Abs shown more political understanding he might well have been Chancellor, for when the quarrel between Erhard and Adenauer was at its height, Heinrich Lübke, the President, favoured him above Erhard as Adenauer's successor; but the Christian Democrats rejected him as decisively as he himself had previously rejected proposals that he should become Foreign Secretary. 'They think of me for the post,' he is said to have remarked, 'only because I speak fluent French, Spanish, English and Dutch – as well as German.'

Yet Abs was essentially humane and there is no question that the work he most enjoyed as a banker was the rehabilitation of those who had lost everything but had the skill and courage to start again. He still delights in telling how one hundred men from the firm of Zeiss, in Jena, escaped from the Russian zone and arrived in Bizonia. The Americans and British immediately approached them and tried to persuade them to emigrate. All but one refused. The rest had nothing but their skill, but they wished to employ it in the Federal Republic. Abs and his colleagues estimated that a capital sum of 1.2 million deutschmarks per man was necessary to get them going and lent them DM 120,000,000 straight away. Zeiss became a flourishing firm employing five thousand people and making lenses and photographic equipment equal to that which they produced before the war. They successfully disputed with the men they left behind the right to put the world-famous name on their products.[3]

Dozens of similar examples could be cited. The great complex of buildings, proudly bearing the name of Pittler, which dominates the small town of Langen, south of Frankfurt, is another of Abs's foster children. Before the war Pittler's machine-tools were already world-famous and in 1939 the firm celebrated its fiftieth anniversary at its Leipzig headquarters. However, Hitler's rearmament programme was already affecting development and in 1941 the firm was virtually taken over by the banks, Abs becoming chairman of the supervisory board and Dr Hans Pilder, of the Dresdner Bank, the Vice-Chairman. Under their leadership and at the insistence of Speer's ministry, the firm developed five satellite factories, one of them in France, and eventually employed seven thousand people.

For a few weeks after the surrender Leipzig was occupied, and the factory partly dismantled, by the Americans. But, as the unbelieving employees gradually learned, the Americans were there only temporarily. However, before the Russians took over, the Americans invited all senior executives and engineers to come into their zone, promising them compensation for all the belongings they must leave behind. Many refused, partly because the Americans changed their minds so often and would give no written guarantee, but also in the hope that the Russians would prove more amenable than they had been led to expect. In June, 1945, a party of eighteen Pittler engineers and executives with their families embarked in a fleet of American army lorries and were eventually deposited in the rural district of Usingen, in Taunus, where they were billeted in villages. Among them was a Dr Wilhelm Fehse, a senior engineer.

As the villages were already full of evacuees from the Ruhr, the newcomers were not particularly welcome, the less so since the American army on the Rhine had heard nothing of the evacuation and provided neither clothes, rations nor compensation. Fehse and

3 In the 1970s Zeiss ran into financial difficulties due largely to the effects of successive devaluations on their exports, but this does not detract from their, or Abs's original achievement.

his friends were destitute and he still describes with emotion how grateful he was for the gift of a blanket and, even more, for some pots and pans which a local manufacturer presented to the Leipzig party. Gradually, by making themselves useful, the refugees wore down the villagers' hostility and were able to start looking for work.

There were several Pittler machine-tools in the neighbourhood and the party began to earn a few marks by repairing them. Fehse was unable to recover the drawings which the Americans had taken from Leipzig and so new drawings had to be made from the machines which were being repaired. By degrees the skill of the Pittler men became known and they were able to come to an arrangement with an engineering firm by which they could jointly do the work in the one factory. Even this needed capital and the former Pittler representative in Frankfurt went the rounds of his old clients and managed to raise a loan of DM 8,000 – about £200 ($500) at the then rate of exchange. The most that the engineers themselves could earn was the equivalent of tenpence or some twenty-five cents a day.

However, this was a beginning. Gradually firms using Pittler tools heard of the little group and soon a Pittler engineer was working in five other small factories in different parts of Germany. Instead of being resented the refugees were in demand and out of the demand grew the idea of re-founding the whole firm of Pittler in the West. There were considerable difficulties. Apart from lack of funds the fate of the Leipzig works was unknown and the question of ownership uncertain. After a year or so, however, Fehse learned that the Leipzig factory had been wrecked by dismantling, that future plans were nebulous and that, in any case, what was left of the works and its subsidiaries had been confiscated. The Russians were now the owners.

This and the currency reform simplified matters. Fehse had already seen his old chairman and vice-chairman, Abs and Pilder, and both had been full of encouragement although at the time Abs himself was out of work. After the currency reform the province of Hesse promised a loan of DM 500,000 and, with the help of the banks and a direct grant from the Reconstruction Finance Corporation, the new Pittler Company was formed. Langen was chosen as the site for the new factory and Abs once more selected as chairman of the Supervisory Board. Alone among those who had left Leipzig, the widow of the largest shareholder in the old company had insufficient confidence in the new, and sold her interest. However, success was immediate. Even before the new factory was finished in 1953, Pittler machine tools were being shown in the trade fairs of Europe and orders were pouring in. An old connection with the National Acme Company of Cleveland, Ohio, was revived under which Pittler were licensed to make their products and by 1962, with 40,000 square metres of factory space, 17,000 employees, most of whom had come from Eastern Germany or Eastern Europe, and a turnover of DM 60,000,000 a year the new Pittler company was nearly as productive as the old.

Although Dr Fehse has retired he still greets visitors and shows them round the works he founded and still goes to the village of Michelbach in Taunus from which he used to bicycle into Langen to repair the old machines. Most of the new houses in Langen have been built by the firm which, like Burda's printing works in Offenburg or Grundig's factory in Furth and a hundred others, dominate this small town. Something of the excitement of those days of reconstruction still survive among Pittler workers. 'We are proud of the old man as he is of us,' said a machinist nodding at Fehse's back. Abs, honorary life Chairman of the Company, said simply: 'Fehse is one of the best Germans I know.'

CHAPTER XI

Spreading Wealth Downwards

For all its romance 'the miracle' was constantly under attack. Erhard was criticised by the British for not directing enough capital into basic industries and public services, by the Americans for lack of 'social conscience' in not doing more for pensioners and refugees, by Germans for allowing extremes of wealth and poverty to exist side by side and neglecting the cure of the German soul in favour of material prosperity.

The German criticisms were the most telling. The disappearance of the Jews and subordination of churches and universities to the Nazis had so impoverished intellectual life that widespread soul-searching was scarcely to be expected; but a minority of journalists, broadcasters, writers and academics protested ceaselessly against the general amnesia which 'the miracle' had induced. It might just be tolerable that men who had paid the penalty for promoting Hitler should again play a part in the national life, but at least they must not be allowed to set the tone.

The financial skill of a Blessing or a Flick, both of whom had bought a degree of immunity by contributing to Himmler's special fund, was acceptable only because they led discreet private lives. In spite of his notorious commentary on the Nuremberg Laws against the Jews, Hans Globke, Adenauer's State Secretary, won good opinions even among the Opposition; he seemed to wish to expiate the past by dedicated service to the Chancellor and the new Republic. But the knowledge, confirmed so dramatically by the Auschwitz trials held at Frankfurt in the early 1960s, that seemingly honourable officials, doctors, business men, professors or just ordinary neighbours 'like you and me,' had spent years shovelling corpses into mass graves or committing other crimes against humanity, haunted many of those who reported the West German scene.

It was a young Munich journalist who compiled and published

the dossiers of more than fifty professors holding chairs in the resuscitated universities whose past utterances might have been expected to disqualify them from ever teaching again. Marion Dönhoff, a countess who had spent the war looking after the family estates in East Germany but who had since become chief writer and co-editor of the Hamburg weekly *Die Zeit*, was tireless in her exposure of Nazis in high places. It was largely because of her that Herr Oberländer, leader of a tyrannical Association of East Germans under Hitler who had become Adenauer's Minister for Refugees, was forced to resign. *Die Zeit* revealed the fact that West German security police were illegally using special N.A.T.O. equipment to tap the telephones of leading German politicians, and waged an unsuccessful war against Professor Hugo Moser, Chancellor of Bonn's new university. The aura surrounding a German professor was such that, although Moser had attempted to provide Nazi ideology with a respectable historical basis, he retained his job.

It was not necessary to expose the neo-Nazi, Gerhard Frey, because he published his own weekly which achieved the third largest circulation for any such magazine. Buoyed up by 'the miracle', Frey revived all the old Nazi slogans about 'blackmail by international Jewry' and 'the sadistic Czechs with their love of human blood' and called for 'German' politics again. He was bitterly attacked by every liberal paper and so roughly handled on radio and television that he soon lost his following. But the echoes which Frey generated in high places were disturbing. Whereas President Heuss had tried to change the National Anthem out of shame for 'the things we knew about,' his successor, President Lübke, shocked the more articulate critics by calling for more patriotic songs and denying that what had happened under Hitler had been 'with the mandate of the German people.' When, in an effort to stimulate recruiting for the new German army he went farther and wondered 'whether the present generation of Germans is a match for its fathers,' he became the subject of lampoons.

Yet Lübke was only reflecting the self-satisfaction which 'the miracle' had produced. It might have been expected that the word 'crematorium' would have sent a shiver down every German spine; but Dachau had already become a new country town with the crematorium as its chief tourist attraction and Auschwitz was to supply an even more macabre example of insensitivity. During a visit to the site of the concentration camp to verify evidence for the Frankfurt trials, Amos Elon, a Jewish writer who had returned to Germany from Israel, noticed that the crematory ovens had been manufactured by a firm called J. A. Topf and Sons. The fact that the ovens had been unable to cope with the mass of corpses had apparently worried the firm of Topf and, in 1942, they had applied for a patent on a new mammoth apparatus into which the corpses could be carried 'uninterruptedly' by means of electrically operated conveyor belts. It seemed that the application was refused. Undeterred, Topf and Sons continued work on their invention and ten years later, in 1952, renewed their application. It was granted, apparently without comment, by the new Federal Authorities in January, 1953.

It was against this crass complacency that the few talented West German authors, dramatists and poets inveighed. Inevitably most books and plays produced since the war were written by foreigners. The only German-speaking playwrights who made a hit in the 123 subsidised theatres were Swiss, or former German Jews who had assumed foreign citizenship. Marcel Reich-Ranicki, the most biting and inspiring critic, was a Polish Jew. But more than one of the small theatres in Munich and the *Stachelschweine* in West Berlin provided a satirical commentary which delighted a small but influential audience. 'We are all democrats now, for to be a democrat is to be up-to-date,' sang four former prominent Nazis in one of the reviews. 'Our past was not held against us, on the contrary . . . in our case the past was worth it.'[1]

The hero of a film made by Alexander Kluge, novelist and member of the College of Design at Ulm, was a West German policeman who had faithfully done his duty under the three régimes which had ruled Germany during his life. He had arrested Nazi demonstrators for the Weimar Republic, Jews for the Nazis and now, at the end of his career and in the closing scenes of the film, was threatening to 'bash in the head' of everyone who was not a democrat.

Kluge, Gunter Grass, Heinrich Böll and the poet Hans Magnus Erzenberger were among those who were invited by Hans Werner Richter to the meetings of the 'Group '47' whose object was to keep alive the social conscience of German literature. Although Richter's writing was of minor importance the Group, described

1 Amos Elon, Op. Cit., pp. 26–8.

by Erzensberger as a 'travelling coffee house of a literature without a capital,'[2] had considerable influence. Grass and Böll, in their best-selling novels, constantly reminded their now prosperous readers that it was the beast in themselves rather than the demon in Hitler which had been responsible for the degradation of their country. The whole Group pilloried the schizophrenia which allowed German intellectuals to lecture on Goethe and Kant but at the same time separate 'culture' from their daily lives.

Neither Adenauer nor Erhard really understood what their countrymen were saying. Although Adenauer had spoken of 'the devil that lurks beneath the skin of every German' he saw himself as the embodiment of democratic virtue and resented moral criticism. *Der Spiegel*, which attacked the general amnesia as furiously as *Die Zeit*, he called 'an abyss of treason.' Even Erhard, who by temperament was a more genuine democrat, poured scorn on journalists and authors who reminded Germans of their past, abusing them as 'runty dogs' or 'idiots.' His weakness lay in thinking only in terms of 'economic man' and believing that all other virtues sprang automatically from physical well-being.

Yet Erhard had a conscience. He had not put the prefix 'social' to his market economy as an empty political gesture. He accepted Röpke's dictum that the fiscal policies of most Western countries had shorn businessmen of their profits and left them with their losses, and he wanted profits to be high; but he did not accept that economic imbalance or social injustice should follow. Although in his speeches he often seemed to suggest that all government action was an evil, his Ministry contained a maze of departments and committees, including an Economic Policy Bureau, which, under his two state secretaries, Ludger Westrick and Alfried Müller-Almack, regulated or supervised every aspect of economic life. When Erhard intervened he did so drastically.

Erhard was well aware that basic industries were the least profitable and had suffered such damage that the capital needed to rehabilitate them would be beyond the resources of the owners. But instead of nationalising coal and steel, as the British Labour government was urging, he devised a whole series of schemes through which surplus profits and individual savings could be used to stimulate private investment. In many ways his methods worked better than those of his critics.

2 Amos Elon, Op. Cit., pp 240.

First he imposed a levy of 3.5% of profits on all distributive and manufacturing industries to be invested for three years into an Industrial Bank which would then distribute it where it was most needed. This produced a sum of more than DM 3 billion.

Marshall Aid was used for the same purpose. Although Germany received proportionately less aid than other countries, it came in the nick of time and allowed German importers to buy just the mixture of raw materials and consumer goods which could get industry going. But the aid was strictly controlled. German users of dollar goods had to pay the equivalent in marks (1 deutschmark then=30 U.S. cents) into a special Counterpart Fund, which, at its peak, reached DM 20 billion. This fund, which played a crucial part in German recovery, was administered by the government-owned Reconstruction Loan Corporation, run by Abs. It built houses, ships, repaired bridges and docks, rehabilitated public services like gas, water and electricity, and also met some part of the compensation claims for which the government made itself responsible. Since the fund was wisely administered and many of its loans paid off, it still exists and is used to-day to help underdeveloped countries or promote any cause or concern which the Federal government feels needs encouragement.[3]

Perhaps the most ingenious of Erhard's schemes were the interest-free loans which firms and individuals were encouraged to make for housing, ship-building, or for the 'equalisation of war burdens' which could be wholly written off against tax. If the loans were recalled, then tax had to be paid, but as taxes in Western Germany were reduced almost annually, the longer the loan was left in the hands of the borrower the less was paid to the Exchequer. DM 5 billion were allocated to housing alone from this source in the first five years of the Republic's existence, and the number of dwellings built annually passed the 550,000 mark. By then private finance and private housing were predominant and in another ten years the housing problem had virtually disappeared.

The coal mines were a special problem. The machinery was out of date, most of the miners' houses had been destroyed and the miners themselves were too old. Rehabilitation took time. It was lucky that it did. While in Britain the newly nationalised coal industry, working to statistics which showed that the country would never

3 In 1971 the Federal Republic spent as much as the United States on aid to underdeveloped countries.

again be able to produce all the coal it needed, was investing £1,500 m. ($3,750 m.) in modernisation, which included the sinking of thirteen brand new shafts most of which were to be closed over the next two decades, in Western Germany the pits just about kept pace with the demand. Meanwhile the vastly increased use of oil, gas and electricity was making nonsense of the plans originally drawn up. When in 1952 the Federal Republic joined the High Authority for Coal and Steel, production was immediately stepped up with the result that coal was piling up at the pit-heads and 30,000 German miners had to be laid off for one day a week. Erhard's refusal to be stampeded into nationalisation had saved the Republic a lot of money.

It was much the same with the railways. Essential repairs to the system had been completed largely by the Occupation forces, but most of the war damage was still to be made good when the Federal Republic came into being. Social Democrats, economists and officials of the occupying powers inveighed against the lack of rolling stock and the slowness and unpunctuality of a service starved of modern equipment while vast sums of private and public capital went into roads, lorries, cars and motor coaches. But again, the barometer of the social market economy stood the Federal Republic in good stead. Germany had never had such a glut of railways as Britain and comparatively few railway lines have been closed; but because rehabilitation of the West German railway system proceeded gradually it was able to take account of road and air travel and avoid some, at least, of the mistakes made by countries in which too great a faith in planning committed governments or public authorities to inelastic schemes.

Steel is a slightly different story. When in occupation the Allies had argued furiously whether Western Germany needed to produce 5, 7, or 11 million tons of steel to satisfy an economy devoted to peaceful purposes. Had their limits been imposed strictly the Federal Republic would have been crippled. The shortage of ships, turbines, cranes, locomotives and machinery and machine tools of all kinds, the vast expansion of the automobile industry which the Federal Republic was peculiarly fitted to supply, created a demand for steel which no planner had foreseen.

However, vast though the sums needed were, three-quarters were found privately, mainly by the steel owners themselves once the initial investment from the reconstruction Finance Corporation had been made. By 1970 production of steel had reached 44,000,000 tons a year.

Nevertheless, there were moments when disaster threatened and it looked as if all Erhard's policies would have to be reversed. The first was the crisis of unemployment. By the spring of 1950, more than two million Germans were registered as unemployed and the numbers kept rising. Not only the Social Democratic opposition but most British and American economists thought the situation was becoming explosive and urged the Federal government to embark on a planned internal expansion so that low wage-earners could benefit and the unemployed be absorbed. Erhard stoutly resisted them.

For the Germans the maintenance of the value of the currency was paramount. The Federal Republic had already survived a twenty per cent devaluation following the British and were determined to avoid another. Erhard argued that the reason for unemployment was the never ending influx of refugees, that total employment was rising and that the need for goods and services in Western Europe was still so great that even this human tide would soon be absorbed, provided prices were kept down and exports up. He therefore supported the banks and refused to embark on grandiose schemes of public works. He was soon shown to have been right. Unemployment remained high for another five years, but those out of work were not the same people. By the summer of 1954, three million more Germans were at work than in 1948; but another two million refugees had arrived. By the end of 1961, when the Berlin wall was built and the flood of refugees was reduced to a trickle, the number in employment had risen to 21,000,000 and those out of work had sunk to 95,000. The Allied advisers were still living in the shadow of the 1930s; Erhard and the bankers were dealing with an entirely new situation.

The Korean war produced a different sort of crisis. As the result of initial American reverses most Western Germans believed that they would soon be crushed between the two world powers in a third world war – probably, in the end, to be over-run by the Russians. Savings dried up, people spent furiously so as to lay in stocks against rationing or starvation; entrepreneurs expanded their industries feverishly to make the most of a situation which might at any moment dissolve in a further defeat of the Western World. Raw material prices rocketed.

The Germans, who had spare manufacturing capacity, bought earlier and cheaper than most, but imports rose so fast that they had soon exhausted their quota in the newly formed European Payments Union and ate up the extra $120,000,000 which they had been specially granted. This time the Occupation Authorities demanded direct control over raw materials, rationing and price control of consumer goods and restriction of credit. Erhard fought them again.

'The air in my office is thick with disaster from morning to night – but I am still waiting for the disaster to happen . . .' he said in one of his speeches. When China came into the war at the end of 1950, the scare was so great that Erhard was obliged to impose some import restrictions and the banks further to curtail their credit; but by the summer of 1951, Erhard was able not only to remove the restrictions but to repay the European Payments Union their loan. By then, in spite of a rise in wages, the cost of living was going down and the balance of payments up. Erhard had been proved right once more.

At one time the refugees were the greatest threat of all. By 1918, ten million had already entered the Federal Republic and they were still coming in at the rate of thousands a month. Unemployment was inevitably higher among them than the rest of the population and with the formation of several radical refugee political parties in the early fifties, it looked as though they might be going to become a revolutionary force. A tremendous effort had to be made to assimilate them.[4]

Sensibly, but none the less generously, all refugees who could claim to be of German descent were immediately granted full citizenship, whatever their previous nationality (Germans in the Ukraine had been Russians, in Poland Poles, and the Sudetens in Czechoslovakia had been Czechs). This meant that, as far as social security and therefore immediate survival was concerned, they could claim the benefits to which their previous status entitled them. State and civil service pensions were at once honoured and there followed a whole series of measures to resettle those who found themselves in rural districts (in particular Schleswig Holstein) where there were

---

4 To-day the Federal Government puts the total of refugees at 13 million, but all figures are suspect, partly because children born of refugee parents in the West are often included and partly because the original census was inadequate.

no prospects of work, and to provide immediate assistance with housing, clothes and furniture. Four million refugees were moved under these resettlement schemes in the first three years after the war, and by the mid-fifties the planned migration was completed at a cost of DM 10 billion.

Special banks were created to provide credits for refugees to set up businesses, to finance industry in 'distressed areas', to grant house mortgages and personal loans. By 1952, a rural resettlement programme had enabled forty thousand farmers from Eastern Germany to buy or lease farms and the scheme was then enlarged. As so many West German farms were being run by widows, many of them elderly, production increased through the change.

All this cost money. Social service charges rose from DM 5.2 million in 1951 to DM 8.5 billion in 1954 and provincial and municipal charges increased proportionately. As Schaffer explained in an 'open letter' to the taxpayer in 1952, of every DM 100 spent by the Federal Government, DM 39 went on social services and the amount kept rising. The burden was only supportable because the national income rose faster still.

When in 1950 the Western Allies had objected to Schäffer's tax concessions because they felt that not enough was being done for the poor, they were assured that a scheme to 'equalise the burdens' caused by defeat would be introduced as quickly as possible. However, it was a huge problem.

Total losses sustained by the German people from the war and currency reform were roughly estimated at eighteen billion deutschmarks, more than twice the national income at the time. But these losses were haphazardly distributed. Those who still owned property, even if it was in ruins, could put it to profitable use, whereas one in four of the population was a refugee who had lost everything and millions of others were also destitute. 'Is it not enough that we have lost our entire families, our homeland, our livelihood and everything we possessed and that currency reform devoured our last reserves? Must we now die of starvation?' ran one of the hundreds of letters Adenauer was receiving. 'You cannot kill a cow, eat it and then go on milking it,'[5] answered a businessman in despair at the prospect of industry, which was desperately short of capital, being further denuded to help refugees. It took a

5 Paul Weymar, Op. Cit., pp. 403-7

commission of experts four years to devise a workable scheme and it was not until August, 1952, that it was passed into law.

The principle of the Act for Equalising War Burdens was that pensioners (of whom there were seven million including war widows and disabled) and those who had never owned property but had lost their livelihood, should be compensated through an emergency form of National Assistance augmented by special taxes; losses in property were to be met by a levy on capital of all kinds, including chattels. Since the community had lost approximately half its assets, every individual and every company or association which was a legal entity, with the exception of public corporations, the central banks and religious or charitable trusts, had to pay into the fund half of what they possessed in property and income in the year 1948-9, the payments to be spread over thirty years.

The base year was important because it was then that every citizen had to register his or her possessions and income so as to qualify for the new currency. There was no escape therefore, unless one was prepared to admit having exaggerated one's currency claim, itself a criminal offence. Since the ninety billion deutschmarks which the fund might eventually receive could only meet a quarter of the claims likely to be made, a limit was set to the amount any one person could be paid and compensation was assessed progressively, in favour of the poorest. People who had lost from 500 to 1,500 *reich*marks received a minimum of 800 *deutsch*marks – in other words very much more than they had lost. (One deutschmark was worth about 16 reichmarks). On the other hand a man who had lost 1,000,000 reichmarks received only 50,000 deutschmarks, considerably less than half.

The method of making a claim was simple. Since any detailed evaluation was impossible, people often had to be trusted. A farmer from East Prussia would have to state the number of hectares he had owned, the beasts his land had carried and the crops harvested, the size and condition of his home and his debts – facts which could sometimes be checked through other refugees from the same village. The same applied to people with shops, businesses or factories; they would give the size of their holdings, the number of employees, annual turnover and profit. A rough estimate of capital value would then be made for which a claim could be lodged.

The size of the levy and the rough and ready method of assessing claims produced a torrent of criticism from opposite points of view.

Social Democrats and many refugees felt that to base compensation on property was wrong and that the equalisation fund should have been used for a peaceful revolution through which everyone could start again at the same level; others wanted quotas so that all property owners received the same proportion of what they had lost.

In practice, however, the Act worked well. The categories of those who could benefit were constantly enlarged by amendments until not only those who had fled from Hitler in the early 'thirties' but all who had suffered war damage or loss through the currency reform were included. Although this meant that many former Nazis became beneficiaries – in March, 1969, the trade union magazine *Welt der Arbeit* (*World of Work*) stated that Field Marshal Milch, Göring's deputy, had received DM 280,000 and a former judge of the infamous People's Court, Dr Rehse, DM 270,000 – this was certainly fairer than perpetuating discrimination against people who had served their prison sentences or paid the penalties of de-Nazification.

Nor was the levy quite so drastic as had at first appeared. The spread of the payments and the fact that in the base year the value of property was at its lowest meant that, with the sudden boom in incomes and values due to the recovery, most people could pay their instalments without difficulty. Those who could not almost always found that, for one reason or another, they were eligible to draw from the fund as much, or more, than they were due to put in.

Long before the equalisation fund was in full operation the re-fugees had ceased to be a threat and become an asset. Abs is fond of saying that 'the miracle' could not have happened without them. This is true, although not quite in the sense in which his remark is often quoted. At first the refugees would do almost anything for something to eat or some form of shelter, and as their ranks were constantly swelled by thousands fleeing from the Russian zone, a supply of cheap labour which, incidentally, would undermine the bargaining power of the trade unions, seemed inexhaustible. But it did not work out like that. There were occasional instances of local strikers being dismissed and refugees taking their place, but at all times the vast majority of unemployed were new refugees rather than workers who had lost their jobs. When Germans quote Abs to-day, therefore, they do not refer to a pool of cheap labour but to a continually recharged pool of skilled labour which took jobs at union rates and allowed expansion to continue at a speed which would otherwise have been out of the question. In other words the refugees helped the Federal Republic in the same way that a million French subjects from Algeria helped France, by supplying an enterprising and hard-working addition to the population at the moment it was most needed.

Many Germans came to regard Erhard as a magician, but not even he could prevent inequalities arising from 'the miracle'. Inevitably there were black spots, industries which lagged, people on whose heads manna fell lightly or not at all. Equally inevitably there was a huge disparity between the new rich and the poor. Luxury and squalor lived side by side in the streets of any sizeable town. By 1954, there was nothing you could not buy in Dusseldorf's Königs-allee, and there were night clubs, some of them still in the cellars of ruined buildings, selling more champagne than anywhere else in Europe; a few hundred yards away in the Kölnischestrasse refugees and war widows were having a hard struggle to keep alive.

There were also eccentrics and vulgarians among the new millionaires. Parties which cost DM 100,000 or more have been frequently reported in the press. Gunter Sachs, one of the heirs to the firm of Fichtel and Sachs, is said to have designed a water closet in his house in Paris which gave the occupant the impression of being in a magnificent courtyard open to the sky. Outwardly modest villas may contain a swimming pool in the living-room, an organ in the bathroom or a private film studio. One banker's sense of thrift was so great that he was said to have given his wedding party in an aeroplane at the airline's expense. In 1971, a long article appeared in *Der Spiegel*, listing the millionaires who register their companies in Lichenstein so as to avoid tax altogether. People began to speak of 'poor' millionaires whose incomes only amounted to a few hundred thousand deutschmarks, and 'bejewelled' million-aires, like Helmut Horten, the department store king, whose assets were estimated in 1971 at more than DM 2,000,000,000. Since even the richest citizen still keeps more than 40% of his income, the gap between them grows steadily wider.

Erhard was not in the least dismayed by such disparity. The Social Market Economy did not aim at egalitarianism but at the creation of wealth. Erhard answered those who pleaded for 'fair shares' by pointing out that every household gadget had been a luxury at some time and that if you tried to regulate production so as to be 'fair', you would soon reduce everyone to a level of subsistence.

When a woman complained in an article in *Welt der Arbeit* that old-age pensioners could not afford the refrigerators which were pouring on to the market, Erhard boldly replied that, of course, they could not be the first to have such things but that if the State tried to regulate production so that those who had least were satisfied first, then the whole economy would stagnate and high unemployment would become chronic. 'We must have the courage to cast out social resentment and petty jealousy. Some people benefit more than they deserve, others go short through no fault of their own. These things cannot be avoided and if we are not prepared to put up with them we shall find ourselves in a permanent state of artificial impoverishment.'[6]

The Germans responded to this sort of talk. Under Hitler they had had twelve years of regulation and control leading to disaster; under the Occupying Powers they had had three years of even tighter control associated with starvation and misery. Every week tens of thousands of their compatriots were fleeing the Russian zone where these controls were being maintained and strengthened, allegedly in the interests of egalitarianism. The concept of apportioning fairly what government considered the essentials of life and hoping and planning for nothing else, was anathema even to the poor. They had done better fending for themselves on the black market than under rationing; they believed that if others got rich they might do so too. Envy was not an over-riding emotion.

They had their reward. As Erhard had prophesied, wealth spread downwards rapidly. Because money was kept in short supply, prices remained stable and real wages slowly but steadily rose. Not only the refrigerators, but the washing machines, vacuum cleaners, mixmasters appeared in most wage-earners' homes. By the beginning of the nineteen-sixties middle income Germans, the skilled and clerical workers, were buying a second house and taking two holidays, one of them abroad. So as to spread the expansion even wider and make it worthwhile for manufacturers to convert what had begun as luxuries into mass produced household necessities, Erhard had to overcome the German disinclination to incur debt and campaign openly for consumer credit and hire purchase. Gradually he succeeded and by the end of the decade manual workers too were

6 Erhard, Op. Cit., p. 142.

demanding a forty-hour week, buying television sets and motor cars, and travelling abroad in even greater numbers than their bourgeois compatriots.

It is impossible to prove conclusively that Erhard's system raised the West German standard of living faster than would have been possible under any other because Western Germany possessed resources in an established coal and steel industry which gave it special advantages. It is, however, true that, in the decade from 1950 to 1960, real personal incomes in Western Germany rose faster and farther than anywhere else in the world, including Japan, and that compared to any socialist country its progress was phenomenal. The contrast between life in the Federal Republic and in the neighbouring states of Eastern Europe, including Eastern Germany, has caused a disillusion and discontent which is still a threat to communist domination.

As a young lorry driver said to two foreigners whom he insisted on entertaining to a third litre of beer in Munich's famous Hofbräuhaus: 'I have a good life. I get good wages, live in a good house, buy my wife good clothes, send my children to good schools and take them abroad for their holidays. When I remember what it was like after the war, it seems too good to be true.' To him, Western Germany's recovery is still a miracle.

CHAPTER XII

Change Without Destruction

The romance of 'the miracle' was not confined to bankers and entrepreneurs; it was shared by millions of Germans in every walk of life who suddenly took a pride in themselves once more and in their capacity for work. Once money again had value and the effort was worthwhile, they made nonsense of every calculation and confounded every prophecy. Looking back over the first decade after the currency reform, statisticians came to the rather surprising conclusion that German productivity had not been particularly high; but the truth was that published figures had not measured more than a fraction – perhaps not even half – of the work done. Most able-bodied Germans did two jobs and no doubt at the end of a sixteen- or eighteen-hour day were less 'productive' in statistical terms than they had been at the beginning, but they were doing work that otherwise would have had to wait. Millions of other men and women, the aged, the wounded and the unfit, spent their spare time repairing their own or other people's homes, clearing rubble or just mending and decorating. The so-called 'unemployed' were seldom idle. Thousands of refugee families, billeted in villages or small towns, paid their rent in kind by rebuilding farm bridges and culverts, teaching or tending children while their parents worked, or acting as unpaid gardeners, secretaries or accountants. Such work was never recorded but was as much part of the foundation of 'the miracle' as work for which people were paid. It alone explains how the rubble and ruin of 1945, which experts calculated would take thirty to fifty years to clear, was removed in one decade and how in the next, jobs and homes were provided for ten million refugees and two million visiting foreign workers. It also explains why many Germans demur at the use of the word 'miracle' at all. 'A miracle implies luck,' they say, 'but we worked our way out.'

But although Germans to-day may see nothing miraculous in the conscious effort of a whole people, they would not deny that they were often inspired and helped by a group of men who did not share the ideals of the Social Market Economy, yet loyally collaborated in deference to the wishes of the electorate. If a medal were to be struck to commemorate the beginnings of the Federal Republic, on one side might appear with equal justice the head of Adenauer or Erhard, on the other undoubtedly should be stamped the rugged features of Hans Böckler, the first chairman of the Federation of German Trade Unions.

Böckler had begun life as a metal-worker but under the Weimar Republic had moved through his union into politics, first as a municipal councillor of Cologne, of which city Adenauer was then Lord Mayor, and later as a deputy in the Reichstag. Inevitably he suffered persecution under the Nazis, but although arrested more than once, somehow managed to avoid being sent to a concentration camp. As a known leader of the underground Trade Union movement he escaped with difficulty after the July plot of 1944, but survived by hiding in the mountains.

Like many of his contemporaries, Böckler had been disillusioned by the failure of the Social Democrats to make a firm stand against Hitler, and was determined not to repeat the mistakes of the past. In the Weimar era the Trade Union movement had been divided. There were not only three different types of union – the 'free' socialist unions to which anyone could belong, the Christian unions, and the Liberal or 'yellow' unions – but each, in his opinion, had been too closely tied to a particular party. This made it difficult to frame a policy even on strictly trade union matters.

In 1945, therefore, Böckler had three aims. He wanted to unite all German workers in one big union; he wanted that union to be completely independent of any political party; and he demanded for that union an equal share with employers in the economic life of the country. In the few short years that were left to him he came remarkably close to his goal.

During the Occupation the Allies, and particularly the British, helped him. All the Western Allies were agreed that trade-unionism was fundamental to democracy and encouraged the Germans to revive it immediately. Böckler and colleagues like August Schmidt of the coal miners took advantage of this situation to establish the complete independence of trade unions before the political parties had been properly formed.

However, for his cherished idea of a single giant union, Böckler ran into opposition from his most sympathetic well-wishers, the small group of British officials who had taken over the Nazi Labour Front and were trying to re-establish trade-unionism on a democratic basis. They warned Böckler that a single union would be unwieldy, would almost certainly give rise to splinter movements and probably become too powerful politically, causing resentment within the parties. The British, therefore, summoned to their aid, Mr William Lawther, President of the British Mineworkers' Union and Mr Jack Tanner, President of the Amalgamated Engineering Union. During a visit to the British zone in 1945 these two men managed to persuade Böckler to opt, not for one giant union, but for a single union for each industry – something one cannot help suspecting that they would dearly have liked to institute in their own country.

Böckler then came to the British authorities with a plan for thirteen unions, bound together in a federation whose central organisation would have real power. His plans were accepted, but the wisdom of his advisers was immediately demonstrated when three groups, the railwaymen, teachers and postal workers, refused to join the industrial unions for the public services, transport and communications and insisted on each having one of their own.

Böckler then returned with a revised plan for sixteen unions – his original thirteen, plus the three breakaway groups formed into separate unions – and again his plans were accepted. In October 1949, just after the birth of the Federal Republic, a trade union congress was held in Munich at which the Federation of German Trade Unions (D.G.B.[1]) was formed and Böckler elected its first chairman.

As a result of Böckler's success the Federal Republic embarked

1 The composition of the *Deutschergewerkschaftsbund* has not changed, but later three more splinter groups formed their own unions outside the Federation. The civil service union (the' *Deutsche Beamtenbund*), with a membership of some 700,000 and a union consisting mainly of clerks in businesses and banks with a membership of about 500,000 (the *Deutsche Angestelltengewerkschaft*), are what would be known in England as white-collar unions. There are also three much smaller police unions.

The D.G.B. also caters for white-collar workers within its industrial unions and claims to have slightly more civil service members in its public services union than the independent *Deutsche Beamtenbund*; it has nearly twice as many bank clerks as the *Deutsche Angestelltengewerkschaft*. Nevertheless, the independent unions are quite powerful and assert the right of people with a certain status to have an organisation of their own rather than be lumped together with all non-manual workers. Both the civil service and the police unions have renounced the right to strike.

upon the reconstruction of its ruined country with a far more homogeneous framework for industrial relations than that possessed by any of the Western Occupying Powers. It had no avowedly political unions like the communist-affiliated C.G.T. in France or the Trade Union Congress in England. It had no religious unions, as in France, Belgium and Holland. Instead of a multiplicity of craft unions, each jealous, not only for its existence but of the wage differential it must keep for its members, industrial unions could negotiate for all grades of workers within their industry. And instead of rival federations like the A.F. of L. and C.I.O., as they then were in the United States, all sixteen industrial unions were members of the D.G.B. Every attempt to create a rival federation based on political or religious allegiance failed.

Quite as important as the creation of industrial unions, was the strength given to the D.G.B. itself. The D.G.B. was not, like the British T.U.C., a loose association whose officers have no power other than that of persuasion.[2] The eleven permanent members of the Federal Council sitting in their huge ultra-modern headquarters in Dusseldorf with the sixteen representatives of the affiliated trade unions at their side, virtually rule Germany's trade union movement. Theoretically, each individual union is autonomous and only has to inform the Council of its actions. In practice no union has for long defied the D.G.B. and only in the rarest instances does a union take action of which the Council disapproves.

The D.G.B.'s power is part financial, part constitutional. In 1949, Böckler managed to insist that 15% of all dues received by unions must be paid to the General Council; as dues are graduated according to income and the top grades pay as much as £5 ($12.50) per month this gave the D.G.B. very considerable reserves.[3] In addition it was laid down that every individual trade-unionist should pay 15 pfennigs (roughly 3d or 8 cents at the then rate of exchange) quarterly to a 'solidarity' fund, which, in reality, was a reserve strike fund. Since trade union membership has averaged more than 6,000,000 since 1950 this means that the solidarity fund of the Council alone has been in receipt of an income of more than £700,000 ($1.25 m.) a year for the past twenty-one years. It is not

2 The powers granted by the individual unions to the T.U.C. in the Bridlington Agreement reached after Mr Harold Wilson's abandonment of his proposed trade union legislation in 1969, were not used with effect until Mr Heath's government came to power in 1970. Even so, the T.U.C. is a far weaker body than the D.G.B.
3 By 1952 the percentage was reduced to 12 per cent.

surprising, therefore, that the D.G.B. has built up huge reserves which it now employs in profitable commercial enterprises.

This financial strength reinforces the D.G.B.'s constitutional powers. It is not illegal to form unions which are not affiliated to the D.G.B. – the white-collar and police unions are examples – but as craft unions which have voluntarily renounced the right to strike they do not need extensive reserves. Industrial unions, for whom the strike is the ultimate weapon, cannot do without the support of the D.G.B., but they get it on the D.G.B.'s terms.

The union must be a member of the federation,[4] and membership involves obedience to the 'instructions' which the D.G.B. issues on the conduct of industrial disputes. If a union disobeys, it gets no financial aid and risks expulsion. And the instructions lay down first that no local union may call a strike without the authority of its own National Executive, and that executive must not authorise a strike until every attempt at negotiation has been made. Even when an executive does authorise a strike, there must still be a ballot of all members of the union and a majority of 75% in favour, before the strike can take place. Even after the vote, unions are enjoined by the D.G.B. to 'take into account' the state of business and the 'repercussions of a strike upon other sectors of the economy' before actually bringing their men out.

Once a 75% majority has voted for a strike, the strike has always taken place, but it is the D.G.B. rather than a single industrial union – even as powerful a union as the metal-workers' – which ultimately controls it. The D.G.B. will only support official strikes and, if a strike has not been properly authorised, it will instruct the union to see that there is a prompt return to work. If the strike is official it is the D.G.B. which supervises the way it is called, run, and terminated, and termination requires the same 75% majority in favour as does the beginning.[5]

Böckler's purpose in creating this unprecedented instrument of industrial power was to win for the unions an equal share with the employers in the direction of Germany's economic life. This was a revolutionary concept. He did not discard the orthodox political

---

4 All the industrial unions are, in fact federations of separate unions belonging to each German province. The D.G.B. is the Federation of all the industrial federations. I have used the term 'industrial union' to cover the industrial federations.

5 Strike pay, which is obligatory during an official strike, is high – from £16 to £20 ($40 – 50) a week for the lowest paid workers and as much as £40 ($100) a week for the highest. Even the richest union needs help, therefore, if it is planning a long strike.

philosophy of trade-unionism; along with his colleagues in the rest of Western Europe he believed that a concentration of economic power in the hands of private individuals was one of the main causes of war, and that the support of 'financiers' and 'industrialists' had made Hitler's rise to power possible. His programme, therefore, included an extension of public ownership, which had existed in Germany for decades, and what he called the 'socialisation' of industries commanding the 'economic heights' such as coal, steel, banks and insurance. However, Böckler and his colleagues were more flexible and imaginative than their contemporaries. Realising, after the elections of 1949, that such a programme would have no chance of being passed by parliament, they decided to try and transform society from within rather than adopt a policy of obstruction.

Co-determination, or *Mitbestimmung*, to give it its German name, was first put forward as a political demand during the revolution of 1848. Forgotten under Bismarck, it was revived as a serious proposition by a German Jew, Herr Napthali[6] at a trade union congress in Leipzig in 1929. Its principle is straightforward. Instead of accepting conflict between labour and capital as inevitable and therefore intensifying it in order to force a new synthesis, as Marx recommended, Napthali accepted their co-existence and sought to make them equal partners at every level and in every enterprise. He therefore proposed equal joint councils or committees from the factory floor to the boardroom, from the hospital floor or the courtroom to the Medical or Bar Council, with responsibility fully shared at each stage. Those who had only their skill to sell should be given an equal voice, through their representatives, with those who commanded money or traditionally exercised power.

In the 1930s the idea was soon overtaken by Hitler's Labour Front and the slogan 'Strength through Joy,' but it had been cocooned rather than killed. After the war it was first revived by the British, who saw in it a means of preventing huge industrial combines from ever again supporting a dictator, as well as a first step towards socialism. British Military Government imposed co-determination upon the heavy industries in the Ruhr and many British politicians hoped that it would be extended to all industry when the province of Rhine-Westphalia was formed.

It might have been expected, therefore, that when the Germans began to manage their own affairs, the idea would have dis-

6 Herr Napthali, who later became a Minister in Israel, died there in 1969.

appeared along with all the other forms of foreign control. Just the reverse happened. Böckler had already shown his independence when, to the fury of Schumacher and the S.P.D., he had backed Adenauer in his acceptance of the Petersberg Agreement which committed the Federal Republic to send a representative to the International Authority for the Ruhr; he had also steadily resisted his more militant members who urged him to make wage demands which might jeopardise recovery. In both cases he put full employment and security against communism before any other consideration. Now he was to exact his price.

Böckler knew that a law would have to be prepared to take the place of the regulations through which the Allies had controlled German industry, and in 1950, a few weeks after the D.G.B.'s first congress, he persuaded it to formulate proposals for a Co-determination Act. Böckler and his colleagues argued that democracy could only be preserved if its principles were applied to a citizen's whole life. Why, he asked, should economic decisions, which are every bit as important as political decisions, be taken autocratically by a hierarchy, part hereditary, part self-perpetuating which, if it owed responsibility at all, owed it only to a small fraction of the population – the shareholders? To those who replied that workers were incapable of taking such decisions, Böckler answered that in the nineteenth century the same had been said about politics – and in any case workers could be trained.

The argument raged in the press and in thousands of meetings up and down the country. The employers were hostile and although Adenauer had declared himself favourable in principle, he faced formidable opposition within his own party and from his coalition partners, the Free Democrats and the German Party. The majority of the S.P.D. was well disposed but lukewarm. The issue was still in doubt when it finally reached Parliament.

Böckler then decided to act. First he held a referendum about the proposed Bill among coal miners who had already had experience of co-determination under the British. The result was a vote of 95% in favour of the Bill. Armed with this backing and alarmed at the hesitation in Parliament, he approved the three weeks' notice of a strike in the coal and steel industry which was announced by the leaders of the miners' and metal-workers' unions to begin on 1st February, 1951. Böckler then asked for a personal interview with his old colleague, the Federal Chancellor.

Although Adenauer and Böckler had often opposed each other, they shared a mutual respect. Adenauer knew that Böckler was both a patriot and a democrat and Böckler that Adenauer was by no means the hard-faced right-winger he was so often depicted, and as often looked. Böckler came straight to the point. He did not mention wages but said bluntly that, unless the Government introduced the long-promised 'economic reforms' immediately, he could not answer for the unions. As Adenauer knew, they had plenty of money for a prolonged strike.

Adenauer agreed that the Federal Republic needed 'an economic system suited to our times' but, equally bluntly, said that a strike aimed at forcing Parliament's hand was not the way to get it. Böckler, illogically in view of his passionate advocacy of the democratic principle, defended political strikes but when challenged again by Adenauer, said that what he had come to propose was a joint conference of employers and trade unionists under Adenauer's chairmanship to agree the terms of the Bill that would be presented to Parliament. If employers and workers agreed, Böckler argued, then it would be virtually impossible for Parliament to go on procrastinating.

Adenauer agreed to Böckler's proposal and called the conference the following week. But before parting from the trade-union leader he pointed out that, if he won his co-determination, there could be no question of further 'socialisation.' If municipalities or the State were to own and control industry, they could not share that control with trade unions any more than with any other private association. Böckler must accept one thing or the other, and Adenauer made it plain that he believed co-determination was likely to be a far more productive form of economic democracy than 'socialisation.' Böckler gave no undertaking but was so persuasive at the conference that full agreement was reached by 19th January and the proposals were approved by the Cabinet that same day.

The Bill for the co-partnership in the coal and steel industries was in essence very simple. Already limited companies of any size were run by two boards, a supervisory board and a management board. In future this practice was to be extended to all firms with more than 1,000 employees. The supervisory board was to consist of eleven members, five of whom were to represent the shareholders and five the workers. The eleventh man, who need not but in practice, has often turned out to be chairman, must be nominated jointly with not less than three votes on either side.

Of the representatives of the workers on the supervisory board, two, one manual and one clerical, must be members of the firm concerned, chosen by the factory committees after consultation with the union; two could be full-time union officials not employees of the firm, and the fifth must be an outsider, neither a trade-unionist, nor someone who worked in the firm or had any financial interest in it.[7]

The management board, which was to run the company from day to day, must include three people all of equal standing, the business manager, the production manager and the personnel or labour manager. But the personnel manager was given a special safeguard; whereas the business or production manager could be changed at the discretion of the supervisory board, the personnel manager could be appointed or dismissed only with the consent of a majority of the workers' directors.

The Bill was greeted with a storm of criticism inside and outside Parliament. The Free Democrats and the conservative 'German Party', Adenauer's partners in the coalition, denounced it first because it gave the unions and the D.G.B. a power to influence every board in the coal and steel industries in a manner which, had it belonged to an employers' federation, would have been denounced as dangerously monopolistic; secondly, because the Bill was being debated under duress. To threaten a nation-wide strike in order to force government to adopt a policy desired by the unions was, said Herr Dehler, the leader of the Free Democrats, a violation of every democratic principle and as vicious a form of intimidation as those which Hitler practised in the years just before he assumed power. The D.G.B., in conservative eyes, was being recognised as a state within a state and given powers in no way justified by the number of citizens it represented.[8]

The communists, on the other hand, backed by the Russians and East Germans, stigmatised the whole idea as a betrayal of socialism and a 'sell-out' to capitalism. The unions had become the 'lackeys' of big business and were branded with every epithet familiar to the

7 Broadly the same rule applied to the fifth shareholders' representative. He must neither be an employee of the firm nor a member of an employees' association.
8 Theoretically this was true, but the unions could reply that their members constituted the largest single group in Parliament – more than one-third of its elected representatives – and therefore had a right to make their voices heard.

Communist repertoire. The other occupying powers were sceptical. The members of an American trade mission visiting the Republic thought the Bill would stifle investment; the French feared it would kill the Schuman Plan for the amalgamation of Western Europe's coal and steel industry, since no other country would be prepared to follow Germany's example; the British doubted whether it would work and thought that the workers' representatives on the supervisory boards would become the pawns of management and lose contact with the unions. Nevertheless, when M. François Ponçet, the French High Commissioner, tried to insist that the act be submitted to the High Commission before it became law, Sir Ivone Kirkpatrick, his British colleague, opposed him, saying that he did not think it was a matter in which the Allies should interfere.

The debate carried over through February and March into April. Adenauer outspokenly denounced the strike threat which had preceded it but equally firmly maintained that the Bill represented 'a great step forward' in human and industrial relations. For once he was supported by Schumacher and the S.P.D., and together the two major parties carried the measure clause by clause. On 21st May, 1951, the Bill became law.

Hans Böckler did not live to watch the seal being set upon his work. He suffered a heart attack just before the Bill was introduced into Parliament and died during the debate on the second reading. But the extent of his influence and the measure of his triumph was seen at his funeral. All over the Federal Republic flags were flown at half mast. Although Böckler had never held office and was by no precedent entitled to a state funeral, the President of the Republic, Theodor Heuss, the Chancellor, Konrad Adenauer, the Leader of the Opposition, Dr Schumacher, industrialists and bankers like Abs, joined the thousands who marched behind his coffin. It was as if a renascent Germany sensed that the life of this great man marked a step forward in civilisation which had been achieved, not by revolution but by agreement. The next twenty years were to show just how important an achievement it was.

The Act of 1951 was a first phase; the second came with the *Betriebsverfassungsgezetz* (Works Constitution Act No. 5) the more general law extending a rather different form of co-determination to the whole of industry, which was passed in 1952.

The trade unions had wished to apply the 'parity' system of workers' representation established in coal and steel to the rest of industry, but opposition to their proposals had increased since Böckler's death. The Christian Democrats were indignant that co-determination had been passed under the threat of a strike and the employers were genuinely fearful that too much power was being given to the unions. It was also widely felt that, for small firms, of which there were many thousands, a rather more intimate form of collaboration was required.

The Government, therefore, decided that for all limited and joint stock companies with 500 or more employees, a third of the supervisory board should consist of the elected representatives of labour, with a progressively decreasing proportion for smaller companies. On the other hand, all companies employing five or more people must have a works council endowed with statutory rights, and those employing more than a hundred, an economic committee as well.

Works councils, which were to consist solely of workers' representatives (members of management could attend if invited) had considerable powers. Its members, who need not be but almost invariably had been trade unionists, could not be dismissed while holding office, had to be allowed time to attend meetings and, in large companies, might be excused productive work altogether. Whether the council consisted of one man or thirty-five, it had joint and equal responsibility with management for all decisions affecting hours of work and overtime, holidays, job evaluation, piece rates and wages structure, training, accident prevention and welfare, the allocation of homes provided by the employer and the conduct of workers on the shop floor. In case of disagreement the works council could go to arbitration, or in the last resort, to the Labour Court.

These two Acts, which laid the foundations for Böckler's Grand Design, were supplemented by a third which set the tone for West German industrial relations. Böckler's object in giving the trade unions a share in the direction and management of industry had not been to replace negotiations on wages and conditions by some system of agreement reached at the top, but to arm the representatives of labour with enough knowledge and constitutional power to conduct those negotiations on a more equitable basis. However both he and his successor, Christian Fette, recognised that the sharing of power meant also acceptance of increased responsibility. The mutual obligations of employers and unions were spelled out in the Wages Agreement Act, which had been passed originally in 1949, while the Allies were still the effective power, but was now amended to take account of the new situation.

The object of this Act, explicitly stated, was to keep 'industrial peace' through collective agreements on wages and conditions freely arrived at. All collective agreements, therefore, were made legally binding on both sides and, on application by either party through a joint committee within the industry, could be applied compulsorily by the Federal Ministry of Labour to the whole cognate industrial field. More than 2,000 agreements have been so applied since the Act was passed and, as a trade union has to be a party to each, whatever the strength of its membership, this has enormously increased trade union influence.

Even with these three Acts, trade union legislation was not exhausted. During the first two parliaments of the Republic, specific Acts granted workers the right to appeal against dismissal, the right to paid holidays, sickness pay over and above that provided by social insurance (because of the high sickness incidence after the occupation), and special protection for mothers and disabled. In case some workers might not be covered by an extension of collective agreements, the Federal Government passed a law enabling it to impose minimum conditions of employment by decree; but the influence of the unions has been such that this law has never been used.

These laws were neither passed nor applied without conflict. Aggressive employers opposed them throughout and militant trade unionists regarded anything less than parity of representation throughout industry as a betrayal of Adenauer's undertaking with Böckler. It needed all the skill of the government, the bankers and Böckler's successors to keep the spirit of that understanding alive.

At first Fette himself had been opposed to the Works Constitution Act and had not only organised a massive demonstration against it but brought out his own printing union in a two-day strike in May, 1952 in protest. His union was at once sued by the newspaper proprietors for using the strike weapon to influence legislation, contrary to the Basic Law of the land, and Fette gave way. He agreed to the Act a few days before judgement was given against his union.

However, Fette was doubly unlucky. The argument over the Works Constitution Act coincided with the great debate over the Federal Republic's participation in European defence and in this too, Fette was at odds with many of his followers. The Social Democrats, on so many of whose parliamentary committees trade unionists sat, were opposed to any form of defence contribution until every advance made by the Soviet government had been exhaustively discussed. Fette believed that free trade unionism itself depended upon rapid integration with the West and came out in support of Adenauer. In the second post-war trade union congress of October, 1952, he was voted out of office in favour of Walter Freitag.

Freitag's accession provoked a new series of crises. He was one of the old guard of trade unionists who had entered the movement in 1908 at the age of nineteen and, under Hitler, had spent many years in concentration camps. But Freitag, like Böckler, was more concerned with preserving the newly-won status and independence of the trade unions than in exercising naked industrial power. To the disappointment of his militant followers he refused to try to influence the elections of 1953, beyond saying that he 'hoped for a better parliament,' and when the result confirmed the Christian Democrats in power, he ungrudgingly accepted it. He was at once attacked from both right and left.

Flushed with victory, the Christian Democrat trade unionists in Parliament founded a Christian Trade Union Movement and demanded that its members should be appointed to every trade union committee in the country. Fortunately so many churchmen spoke out against it that the movement, which would have caused a fatal schism, never got off the ground. Adenauer, by attending the fifth Trade Union Congress in Hamburg the following year, signified his approval of its failure.

Simultaneously Freitag had to withstand a revolt in his own ranks. Dr Victor Agartz, the able chairman of the Trade Union Research Institute, suddenly attacked the whole conception of industrial peace on which Böckler's Grand Design was based. In a speech at the Trade Union Congress which was wildly applauded, he revived all Schumacher's old slogans against 'monopoly capitalists' and cartels and, in defiance of the Basic Law, demanded that strikes be used for political purposes. Seeing their chance, the coal and steel employers at once replied by denouncing co-determination which, they alleged, had been introduced under brutal duress when the State was too weak to assert itself.

However, Freitag had a new and powerful ally in the man who had succeeded him as Chairman of the Metal-Workers' Union, Otto Brenner. This bespectacled, round-headed man who looked like a diffident bank clerk, was born in the slums of Hanover in 1907. His father, having been a prisoner of war, was out of work through much of the twenties, and his mother took in washing. Otto left school at fourteen, became a qualified electrician, joined the Social Democrats and a trade union and was already so ardent a Republican and Socialist that, when the S.P.D. voted for naval rearmament in 1929, he left it and founded a new Independent Workers' Party.

Under the Nazis, Brenner was arrested time and again and was finally imprisoned for two years for carrying on illegal trade union work. These experiences both hardened and refined him. In 1945, he emerged, not only as a dedicated trade unionist, but as a passionate democrat bitterly opposed to both communism and fascism. Within seven years, and when he was still only forty-five years old, he had become a Social Democratic Member of his State Parliament, the leader of I. G. Metall, the largest trade union in Germany (now the largest in the world) and President of the ten-million-strong International Metalworkers' Federation.

Brenner was not an admirer of Agartz, but as a whole-hearted believer in *Mitbestimmung* he was determined that the unions should not lose a particle of the rights they had won. Since Hermann Reusch had been one of the employers' chief spokesmen, Brenner immediately brought out on strike 30,000 workers in Reusch's metallurgical factories. The employers replied by demanding the outright repeal of co-determination. In January, 1955, Brenner retaliated by telling 800,000 metal workers to down tools for twenty-four hours in protest. They answered him to a man. It seemed as if the whole framework for industrial relations which Adenauer and Böckler had constructed with such care was about to collapse.

But neither the government, Freitag nor Brenner really wished this to happen. Adenauer went on the air to assure the unions that co-determination was in no way threatened, Freitag and Ludwig Rosenberg, the D.G.B.'s international representative who had spent the war in London and was deeply imbued with the spirit of men like Bevin and Lawther, declared the twenty-four hour strike illegal, reasserted their control over the metal workers' union and, by a combination of lobbying and luck, managed to get Agartz replaced as Chairman of the Research Institute.

In the following year Freitag, Rosenberg and Brenner came together to consolidate their gains. To the fury of the employers, Adenauer extended the principle of co-determination to holding companies, blocking at a stroke a convenient loophole. Freitag rewrote the rules governing strikes so that in future the D.G.B. Executive could itself call a strike without the normal ballot, if the existence of trade unions or the democratic basis of the Federal Republic were threatened.

In the autumn, Brenner, this time backed by the D.G.B., put in demands for higher wages, shorter hours and full pay during the first weeks of illness on the same terms as those enjoyed by salaried staff. When the employers refused he declared an official strike in Schleswig-Holstein and maintained it for one hundred and fourteen days, from 24th October, 1956, to 15th February, 1957. The strike was admirably organised. As obliged by law, the strikers received more than half of their normal pay from the union. In addition the union and the D.G.B. published a free daily paper for strikers' families and laid on an elaborate cultural programme of concerts, films and lectures so that the strikers should not get bored or feel that they were wasting their time. The cost to the union and the D.G.B. was more than £3 m. ($7.5 m.), but it was well worth it.

Although in the end the strike was declared illegal on a technicality and had to be called off, the employers refrained from collecting the considerable damages they had been awarded in the courts and granted the metal workers shorter hours which were soon to lead to the forty-hour week; they also conceded full pay for the first two weeks of any sickness.[9]

Meanwhile Freitag and the D.G.B. had resumed the campaign for the completion of Böckler's Grand Design. In order to negotiate from strength the D.G.B. had first to ensure that the German worker had the highest wages and the greatest security of employment the country could afford. This Freitag and his successors can

---

9 Having established the principle, the union pursued their aim so doggedly that in 1972, fourteen years later, they wrung from the employers the right they had originally demanded – full pay throughout industry for the first six weeks of any worker's illness, just as for salaried staff.

fairly claim to have achieved. Average gross hourly earnings have doubled in each of the decades since 1950, and have risen even faster in the seventies; as prices have increased by only about half as much the German worker is basically better off than most of his contemporaries. Even in 1971, when wage increases outran the annual increase in productivity, the re-valuation of the deutsch-mark kept the price of imports, and so the cost of living, down.[10]

He is also better off when fringe benefits are taken into account. The standard of living of the German worker does not depend only on his earnings, but on the degree of paternalism shown by his employer; and this, in turn, may arise from tradition, post-war ex-perience, or the need to keep labour where there is a national shortage. Only twenty years ago many employers were themselves penniless and had accepted the most menial jobs to keep alive; the memory often creates an affinity with those who now work for them; and since, to most Germans, work is not just an unpleasant necessity but of great importance for its own sake, employers and workers tend to agree that the place where they work should be made as attractive as possible.

By law employers are responsible for a major share of social insurance but successful firms add lavish amenities of their own. With tax-free money they have built workers' houses, Olympic swimming pools, sports grounds (attended by professional coaches) excellent clubs where employees can get subsidised meals, chil-dren's kindergartens and gymnasiums equipped with sauna baths and a masseur. Almost any large company will have its orchestra and music rooms and often an Old People's Home for which the company pays half the bill. It is impossible to strike an average, but it is not at all uncommon for a firm to spend £15 ($37.50) a head per week on such social services beyond what is provided by the State, and many spend much more.

A majority of German workers reciprocate by making the com-pany not only the place where they earn their living, but a part of

10 In December, 1971, the average wage for all German workers, manual, skilled and white-collar, was £2,400 ($6,000) a year. The average among the least well-paid, dustmen, waiters, porters, etc., was between £1,100 and £1,200 ($2,750-3,000). Unskilled workers in banks, insurance, transport, manufacture and construction, averaged between £1,200 and £1,550 ($3,000-3,875); in the Public Services, £1,660. Skilled and white-collar workers (those who earn wages rather than salaries) averaged between £1,600 and £3,000 ($4,000-7,500). Aver-ages conceal wide differences but, in this case, give a broadly comparable picture. German wages are only marginally ahead of those in neighbouring countries; but the Germans work little overtime and with the shorter week and fringe benefits they have an advantage.

their social and cultural life. They drink at the club, play in the orchestra and take part in sport or hiking expeditions. Long-service medals are gratefully received and proudly worn. Company rules are obeyed. Smoking on the job is considered dishonourable and if a man is absent without reason he expects, and gets, the sack.

Of course there are militants and probably militancy is growing, but many British workers testify to the good spirit in German industry. 'Here one can *really* work and get rewarded for it,' said an electrician from Derbyshire employed in Burda's printing works in Offenburg. 'Unless there is a great change of heart at home I shall not go back.' His feelings were echoed many times by compatriots in other factories.[11]

Nevertheless, consciously or unconsciously, paternalists cling to power and it is this power which the D.G.B. is determined that the German worker shall share. In almost every issue of *Welt der Arbeit*, the trade union magazine, in the papers of the Trade Union Research Institute and in the D.G.B.'s *Basic Programme*, published in 1963 and amended several times since, Böckler's dominant idea of sharing equally the planning and control of the whole economy (in his view this included schools, universities, newspapers, magazines and publishing houses), is reiterated. Phrases like: 'The vast majority of people are still excluded from control of the instruments of production,' and 'the function of every national economy is by its very nature social, it must not be allowed to be determined solely by the profit motive,' occur over and over again.

Yet instead of leading to a demand for the usual crude form of Marxist socialism, the D.G.B. thinks in terms of a 'dynamic' economy in which, certainly, public ownership is extended and developed 'into a national system,' but in which private enterprise has its place and private ownership can be extended to the humblest worker. 'The object of trade unionism is the emancipation and self-improvement of every individual worker in a constantly changing economic, social and political structure . . .' says the Research Institute in a survey on social and economic development, and it goes on to state that the better distribution of wealth must be achieved partly through a 'reduction of taxation privileges' granted to the entrepreneur in the early days of the recovery, but also by encouraging the savings and 'possession of property' by the workers.

Successive German governments have made shares of small

11 In conversation with the author.

denominations available to those with small incomes in concerns in which the State has a major interest like Volkswagen; Preussac, the Prussian mining and quarrying combine; or Veba, the 'united electricity and mining stock company,' whose subsidiaries produce electricity, coal, chemicals and crude oil. Each scheme varies, but broadly anyone with an income of less than £1,500 ($3,750) a year can not only buy shares at a special discount, but can often get a government subsidy of one-third of the value of the shares as well. There is a limit of £50 ($125) to such holdings and the owners must retain them for at least five years, but the shares are virtually free of all tax. Each of these schemes was heavily over-subscribed when published and the government had to make extra shares available. There are also investment trusts for people with small incomes in which the companies are obliged to buy back the share certificates at par at the owner's request. Willy Brandt's government strengthened these schemes by increasing the limits of tax exemption for wage-earners and also the number of shares which they could hold.

However, the trade unions, while accepting the idea of a property-owning democracy, do not place too much importance upon it. There are between five and six million small shareholders in Western Germany to-day, but the amounts they hold are an insignificant proportion and their voting rights (usually exercised by the bank which holds their certificates), so negligible that they can in no way counteract the tendency of money to accumulate in a few hands. The unions, therefore, hold to co-determination as their main goal.

To achieve it, they train their members. The D.G.B. and the individual unions run twenty training schools for trade union organisers and officials through which several hundred rank-and-file members pass annually on full pay which, if it is not met by the firms for which they work, is made up by the union or federation. The syllabus is broad enough to warrant a degree in Social Science. The elements of politics, philosophy and economics are taught as background to courses in legislation, social insurance, group psychology, public speaking, the organisation of meetings and discussions. It is not an Arts Council or Ministry of Culture which organises the Ruhr Festival, but the D.G.B. It lasts several weeks and the hundred thousand or more who attend have a sort of summer school cum Edinburgh Festival combined with concerts, plays, ballet and painting exhibitions alternating with lectures.

In research the D.G.B. is as well served as industry. The Trade Union Institute of Economic Studies employs about a hundred economists, statisticians and social scientists led by professors who carry out surveys and inquiries and provide data, not only for the D.G.B. but for workers' representatives on supervisory boards and even on works councils. The monthly magazine which the Institute produces, surveying German society and the position of the unions within it, has a standing as high as *The Economist* in Britain or any similar magazine in Europe. Brenner and some other individual union leaders also have their own 'think tanks' composed of specialists in trade union law, automation, management and method study, statistics, marketing, public relations and politics, which enables them to negotiate on a level with employers and also play their full part on the many supervisory boards on which they sit.

But training means more than sociology and research. The trade unions are not just plaintiffs at the Bar of West German society, they are large-scale entrepreneurs and public administrators. Out of the reserves they have accumulated through good industrial relations they have created the fourth largest bank in the country (which may soon become the largest of all), a formidable insurance group, the biggest building society and construction firm in Europe, a publishing house which issues some four hundred new titles a year, a fast-expanding travel agency, an automobile club and a chain of more than 5,000 high quality food and furniture shops including fifty-two supermarkets, nine department stores and thirty factories.

This entrepreneurial role of the trade unions is not new. Ever since the time of Bismarck the idea that unions should use their 'monopolistic' control of labour or their 'privileged' position (and both epithets carry more than a kernel of truth), to found their own enterprises has been bitterly attacked by employers with whom they must compete. The official who licensed the first 'People's Life Insurance Association' before the First World War was challenged to a duel by the President of the existing Life Insurance Federation, Wilhelm Kapp.[12] More than half a century later industrialists and financiers were still protesting as vigorously, if less violently, at the thought of trade unions overstepping the 'natural limits' of their calling and forming their own bank.

12 In 1920 Kapp led a famous but abortive putsch to prevent an alleged alliance of communists and trade-unionists becoming the rulers of Germany.

In the nineteen-sixties, however, they were answered by a different sort of challenge from a very different man. The founder, architect and protector of this great group of trade union enterprises is someone who, but for his origins and experience under Hitler, might just as well have filled the role of Hermann Abs. Dr Walter Hesselbach, Chairman of the Trade Union Bank, Chairman or Director of a list of companies and federations which spans the gamut of West Germany's financial and economic life, was born of parents who were in domestic service; Hesselbach joined the Jewish banking firm of Dreyfus before the war and, no doubt, partly for that reason but also perhaps because, when attacked by members of the Hitler Jugend, he retained enough of his schoolboy boxing and Judo skill to send them packing, he was soon on the Nazis' black list. However, in 1939 he was taken up by Georg von Opel and worked as his personal assistant in the Opel Works (which were already a subsidiary of General Motors) until he was called up and, in 1943, sent to the Eastern Front. Taken prisoner by the French in 1945, he returned to Frankfurt in 1947 and, within a week, had joined the Social Democrats, a trade union and the Central Bank of Hesse. From then onwards he had one purpose, to use his skill as a banker to enable trade unions to compete with employers in every kind of enterprise.

First, in the teeth of the opposition of men like Abs, who was afraid not only of competition but also for the good name of banking, he consolidated the small regional trade union banks which had sprung up since the war into a single central bank. He won the favour of the unions by paying them a flat 10% return on the money they invested and by keeping sufficiently liquid to meet any demands for benefit or strike pay they might make; he gained the confidence of the general public by otherwise running the bank on strictly commercial lines. Gradually even those firms which had been most critical of his enterprise became his clients until in 1972 the deposits in his bank amounted to £1 billion. With the bank as his base, Hesselbach then set about encouraging, financing and directing the whole complex of enterprises through which the unions are taking an ever-increasing share in the social market economy.

The principle on which these concerns is run is broadly co-operative in that management is more interested in keeping prices down and performing a social service than in maximising profits. For example, the tenants of *Neue Heimat*, the building society which has housed more than a million people since 1945, cannot be given notice so that, in effect, they are in the position of owner-occupiers. Yet the society is a commercial undertaking and so successful that it can offer, at competitive prices, a whole range of services to local authorities such as the building of hospitals, swimming pools, kindergartens, homes for pensioners, town halls and shopping centres for which it provides not only technical advice but finance as well if needed.

Hesselbach, therefore, has been able to answer his capitalist critics by claiming that the enterprises run by the trade unions set the best example of fair practice and provide the cleanest competition in Germany. So far no one has challenged him to a duel and Abs, at least, now speaks with pride of the trade union bank's achievements.

A more serious charge is that this great industrial empire has created a hierarchy which is remote from the ordinary trade union member and blurs trade union objectives. But even this is only superficially true. Certainly Hesselbach, and many trade union leaders, live in attractive villas, enjoy an income of from £20,000 to £30,000 ($50 – 67.5 m.) a year, are taken to the office in a chauffeur-driven car, go to good tailors and restaurants and spend most of their working lives in high level meetings. But there are many differences between them and their fellow directors. The 'manager' who works sixteen hours a day is endlessly making money for himself or his employer; a trade union director spends many evenings and weekends at trade union functions meeting the rank and file. They seldom own properties abroad and are far more likely to take their holidays at a convention than on a beach. If German workers really felt that co-determination had corrupted their leaders, as is so often alleged, they would elect others to pursue a different policy; but so far only a small fringe of revolutionaries and anarchists has shown any such desire. With a slow but steady increase in membership, German trade unionism is growing stronger every year.[13]

One further attraction which German trade unions can offer their members is due more to Bismarck than Böckler; jointly with management they run what is virtually an industrial civil service. In 1972 more than £20 ($50) billion were spent in the Federal Republic on social services, excluding education, and by 1975 this

13 In the spring of 1972, membership of the sixteen industrial unions affiliated to the D.G.B. was just short of 7,000,000 – of the un-affiliated unions a little more than 1,000,000.

figure will have reached £27 ($67.5) billion. Owing to a tradition established in the nineteenth century, these services, health insurance, old-age pensions, industrial injury and unemployment insurance, occupational training and rehabilitation are financed and run by public corporations composed of equal numbers of employers' and workers' and consumers' representatives.

The Government appoints the chairman and leading officials, and basic policies are determined by statute, but it is the Board of the Corporation which manages the day-to-day business of the Federal Institute of Labour and the various health and other social security funds. This means that public funds representing more than a quarter of Germany's total gross national product are to a large extent administered by men and women from both sides of industry. For young trade unionists this opens up a wide field of opportunity.

A climax to the D.G.B.'s campaign, of which this diverse training and experience form a vital part, came when Willy Brandt was elected Chancellor. Although not affiliated, the unions and the D.G.B. had given increasing support to the Social Democrats since Brandt became their leader and when he formed a government and Walter Arendt, President of the miners' union to which Vetter also belonged, became Minister of Labour,[14] the D.G.B. could reasonably hope that its wishes would be met and 'parity' be accorded throughout industry.

Partly because this seemed likely, the union leaders first had to meet a challenge from the left. To marxists and anarchists every stage in the growth of 'co-determination' has been anathema because it strengthened both liberal democracy and capitalism. The students who had revolted in 1968 and been balked of their prey – Axel Springer is still very much alive – now turned their attention to the unions, some of which they had since joined. They were welcomed by the newly legalised Communist Party which was not only anxious to make its mark, but at its first congress, had already adopted the classical tactics of penetrating the trade unions as the first step on the road to power. In 1969, urged on by some hundreds of small communist cells, several groups of workers in coal, steel and shipbuilding suddenly laid down their tools

14 In 1972, ten members of Brandt's Cabinet, including himself, and almost half the members of Parliament belonged to trade unions.

without consulting their unions or works councils, and claimed higher wages.

Both employers and trade union leaders were taken completely by surprise. A Personnel Director in one of the firms affected was in Tokyo at the time and had just delivered a lecture showing how admirably the system of co-determination worked in Germany when he was summoned home by telephone to deal with a situation which had not occurred since the Occupation ended. Trade union leaders were badly shaken and employers so startled that they conceded the militants' demands immediately. None of the strikes lasted more than a few days and the D.G.B. and the unions were able to reassert control and supervise the return to work.

Meanwhile the campaign for the extension of 'parity' had been launched. Vetter saw it as the coping-stone to Böckler's great edifice and threw the whole weight of the D.G.B. behind it. He was unwilling, however, to threaten a strike and embarrass the first post-war government he could call his own. Had Brandt had a clear majority there is little doubt that he would have agreed; trade unionists, after all, formed more than a third of his parliamentary party. But his government rested on a coalition with those champions of *laissez-faire*, the Free Democrats, and had the latter made further concessions to what many of their supporters considered an extreme form of socialism, they would soon have ceased to exist as a party. Brandt bought time by waiting for the report of the Biedenkopf Commission but, when it gave a neutral verdict, came down on the side of strengthening Works Councils.

However, this 'strengthening' meant further considerable gains for the unions. Under the Act of 1962, management needed only to 'consult' Works Councils about dismissals, the introduction of new machinery or major changes in the structure of a firm. To-day no employee can be dismissed without the agreement of the Works Council and if that agreement is withheld the worker must keep his job until the case is decided in the Labour Court.[15] Major changes in the policy of any firm which might result in a contraction or expansion of business must be subject to the agreement of the Works Council and a formal plan to resolve the social consequences be submitted to it.

15 Although the Courts normally settle cases without any formal judgement, this may take up to 2 or 3 years. In 1971 thirty-two courts in North Rhine-Westphalia dealt with 31,000 cases.

Trade Union representatives have an absolute right of entry into any undertaking and need only inform the employer of an intended visit; and although fairly strict limits to political activity within business hours have been set, the right of Works Councils to discuss general political questions which affect their interests is safeguarded.

But the issue of parity is still very much alive. In saying that there was little to choose between 'parity' as it exists in the coal and steel industry and the system which centres upon the Works Council, Biedenkopf was not denigrating co-determination. On the contrary, he was saying that both forms had served Germany well. No doubt there will always be a conservative Old Guard which regards the whole idea as a first step towards Communism and an *avant garde* which sees any sharing of responsibility as a 'sell-out' to monopoly capitalism, but there is no question of going back to the position the trade unions have won. If Brandt wins a clear majority for the Social Democrats in the 1970s then the D.G.B. will have its way and 'parity' will come to all German industry; if Rainer Barzel, the present leader of the Christian Democrats, forms a government, to-day's dichotomy will probably continue. In either case co-determination is there to stay.

The question for the future is how much farther it will be extended and whether it will spread beyond the frontiers of the Federal Republic. Brandt has already said that, as soon as Britain and the other aspirants have signed the Treaty of Rome, he will press his partners to adopt co-determination as the basis of industrial relations for the Community as a whole and he has been supported by the European Confederation of Free Trade Unions. Barzel could scarcely do less without antagonising both the German unions and a powerful group of employers who approve the Works Constitution Act.

So far, admittedly, the other countries of Europe have not shown much enthusiasm. France has Works Councils and special Labour Courts in which, among other things, workers can appeal against dismissal, but neither the *Patronat* nor the communist-dominated C.G.T. wish to share power in quite the way the German system envisages. Britain also is experiencing great difficulty in harmonising militant trade-unionism to a modern technological society. The United States is no analogy since there the unions accept the capitalist system unreservedly and see themselves simply as the other parties to a deal.

Nevertheless, if representative government is to continue and democracy be enabled to fight off the communist challenge, a way has to be found of inducing trade union leaders to accept a far greater measure of responsibility in a mixed economy. Stark confrontation can only lead to authoritarianism in the end; equally, democracy will die if it remains static. It is entirely reasonable to wish to apply democratic principles to economic as well as to political life and employers and property-owners will resist this at their peril. Since nothing as far-reaching as co-determination has yet been practised and few industrial countries have made such rapid or harmonious progress as Western Germany, it is possible to hope that it will prove the solution.

CHAPTER XIII

The Great Divide

The dazzling success of the Federal Republic is even more remarkable for having been achieved under a continual threat of extinction. The Russians not only refused to accept the existence of a separate West German state, but waged a campaign of intimidation and subversion against it every bit as ruthless as any that Hitler unleashed against Czechoslovakia or Hungary in the days of his notorious Fifth Column and for a far longer period. For twelve years after the war the Soviet Government remained confident that it could drive the Western Powers from Berlin and eventually from the whole of Germany by a combination of force and diplomatic pressure; when that attempt finally ran into the ground with Khrushchev's retreat from belligerence in both Berlin and Cuba, the Russians fell back upon a war of nerves, made easy by the division of Germany, of an intensity and sometimes of a savagery that has seldom been equalled.

The object of this underground warfare, which was carried on by thousands of Russian and East German spies, agents and even assassins, was to undermine morale so completely that West Germans would come to prefer a reunited country under communist 'protection' rather than live in a perpetual state of fear and suspense. If it is still too early to judge how far the campaign has succeeded, there can be no doubt that the bitterness and fear it engendered was largely responsible for the hostility to the treaties with the Soviet Union signed by Chancellor Willy Brandt in 1971, ratified the following year only through a massive abstention on the part of the official Opposition. Although the intention of the treaties was to improve relations between the Federal Republic and the communist world by recognising the existence of two separate German states, there is little sign of any relaxation in the clandestine struggle.

As in all the satellite countries of Eastern Europe, it is the Russians who direct the policies of the Peoples' Republic and it has been the Russians who, from the start, have directed the subversive campaign. As soon as Berlin was conquered the N.K.V.D. (as the Soviet Committee for State Security was then called) installed itself in St Antonia's Hospital and quickly recruited a staff of 800 people distributed throughout the zone. Soviet Military Intelligence, with a further 250 employees, had its headquarters in the suburb of Wunsdorf and branches in the main cities. These two organisations immediately began supporting their government's policy by a campaign of open intimidation.

While the communist-controlled radio and press hurled abuse at the Americans, accusing them now of instigating a third world war and now of preparing to quit Europe and leave the Germans in the lurch, Russian agents spread into West Berlin and the Western zones, hunting down 'enemies of the people' and terrorising the population. Those who had stood out against the merging of the Social Democratic and Communist Parties, who protested against Soviet ruthlessness, appealed for basic human rights or had fled to the West rather than work for the Soviet forces of occupation, were traced to their new homes, kidnapped, shot in broad daylight in the streets of West Berlin or lured to the Russian zone to disappear into concentration camps, often never to be heard of again.

In these early days it became quite common for West Berliners to see a car draw up to the pavement, men in plain clothes jump out, seize a man or woman who was passing by, bundle them into the back seat and drive off at high speed towards the Russian sector. Sometimes the victim screamed and struggled, but as the men were armed there was nothing a bystander could do. Occasionally an Allied patrol car would give chase but the barriers at the check points were always raised in preparation for the Russian car, showing that the kidnapping had been carefully planned. There is no record of any car being successfully intercepted. Protests by Allied commanders were invariably met by a complete denial that any such incident had taken place and often a counter protest was lodged against the 'base accusations' being made against the Soviet authorities.[1]

---

1 No records were kept by Germans in the Russian zone between 1945 and 1949, but, according to Allied and West German Intelligence, 900 cases of abduction have been recorded of which 600 took place before 1949, 300 between 1949 and 1961 and 16 since the building of the wall. Hundreds more abductions were planned but failed, often because those who were to have carried them out fled rather than do so and revealed all the details of the scheme

The failure of the Berlin Blockade forced the Russians to alter their methods. They still believed that they could drive the Americans from Europe – as late as the summer of 1960 a defector from the East German army brought with him detailed plans which had recently been issued for the conduct of troops after the conquest of the Federal Republic – but they realised that it was going to take longer than they had first imagined and that more deliberate and subtle means of persuasion would have to be employed. They had also learned to have more faith in the East German communists.

Stalin's opinion that communism was too good for Germans was faithfully reflected by the Soviet Authorities during the early months of the Occupation and although German communists were extensively used they were kept under the strictest control. But it soon became apparent that not even a thousand trained Russians were sufficient to protect their own forces from contamination and at the same time impose a new régime on the conquered people. German communists had to be given greater responsibility and, in any case, were more useful in tracking down Nazi criminals and penetrating the Western zones than members of the N.K.V.D. Fortunately for the Russians several had been trained in secret police schools in the Soviet Union. Wilhelm Zaisser, a German who had joined the communists when serving with the Occupation forces in the Ukraine in 1918, and Ernst Wollweber, ex-merchant seaman, had both been in the same espionage academy run by the Red Army. Erich Mielcke, an old reporter on the *Red Star* who had fled from Germany in 1931 after the murder of two policemen in Berlin and later fought in the Spanish Civil War, had also gone to Moscow in the late thirties. The three compatriots met and, on their own initiative, laid plans for a secret police and espionage service in Germany when the war was over. These were the men the Russians now proceeded to use.

Although all three later became successively Ministers of State Security of the People's Republic, Zaisser was the leader. He had attracted the attention of Beria who, having rescued him from the prison which he had entered during one of Stalin's purges, made him his chief adviser on Germany. In 1942, Zaisser was put in charge of

to the West German or Allied authorities. Occasionally a man or woman who was kidnapped subsequently escaped and returned to tell their story. Although the records read like a James Bond melodrama, all the cases are authenticated and most of the evidence has been given at first hand.

a training school at Krasnogorsk to which were sent German prisoners of war specially selected for future work in Germany. There, from Hitler's S.S., ex-officers, party officials and policemen, he had been able to select the team which now, under Russian supervision, he began to build into a German secret police force.

Zaisser made rapid progress. Revulsion among East Germans over kidnappings, resentment against communisation and excitement at the success of the Allied Air-lift had so increased resistance to the Russian Occupation that he was soon given powers of summary arrest and confiscation of property. Mielcke was put in charge of a special section to protect industry from sabotage and Wollweber headed another to do exactly the reverse in Western Germany. By the time the People's Republic was formed in 1949, Zaisser had earned the confidence of the Soviet Authorities to such an extent that he was allowed to fulfil the plan he and his colleagues had sketched in Moscow during the war and form a full-scale Ministry of State Security on the Russian model.

It is difficult for anyone brought up in a democracy to realise the scope of such a ministry. Security, in so far as it exists in countries like Britain or America, is a passive function. Special branches of the police keep dossiers on criminals and those who may be suspected of disturbing the peace but action against them, other than to quell a riot, can only be taken through the courts. The police themselves are subject to the law and to challenge in Parliament. In Britain, espionage and counter-espionage are in the hands of the Foreign Office and Ministry of Defence, and is normally conducted as a purely defensive operation.

The security services of the Federal Republic are essentially of this democratic character. Until the formation of the Federal Office for the Protection of the Constitution, of which Dr Otto John became the first President in December, 1951, there was virtually no West German security system at all. During the Occupation a private organisation financed by the Americans and run by former S.S. General Reinhard Gehlen, provided fairly extensive information about Eastern Europe and the Red Army and at one moment the C.I.A. toyed with the idea of using German refugees and ex-members of General Vlassov's anti-Soviet Russian division as an underground army of resistance behind the Iron Curtain; but it came to nothing. A German refugee organisation carried out a few isolated acts of sabotage, but their agents were soon caught and shot, or disappeared. Both John's office and Gehlen's organisation, which was finally incorporated into the Federal Chancellor's Office, were confined to a strictly defensive role. West Germans were prepared to admit the necessity for spying on foreign countries, including the other half of their own, but at the slightest hint of internal surveillance or a secret police, Parliament and Press were up in arms.

No such inhibitions hampered Zaisser or his lieutenants. The Ministry of State Security was responsible only to the Executive Committee of the Party and the Head of State. Its actions could not be challenged in the courts and if censure came from above it came after the event and not before. In planning and executing subversion, therefore, Zaisser virtually had a free hand. As the authors of a critical study of the Gehlen organisation wrote in 1972: 'The truth was that, in contrast to the West German secret service, the M.F.S. (Ministry of State Security) and its executive organ the State Security Service (S.S.D.) was able to arrest any opponent and read the letters of any citizen. It could engineer fake trials and manipulate indictments. It knew that it had the backing of an authoritarian State and Party machine and was immune from any public criticism. From telephone tapping to kidnapping the M.F.S. and S.S.D. could make use of the whole range of police practices, always with one end in view, expressed thus by the Minister of State Security: "We are a sharp sword with which our Party will inexorably strike down its enemy." '[2]

The most immediate enemy lived in East Germany. Zaisser and his deputy Mielcke soon had a network of cells and agencies spread across the People's Republic tracking down opponents of the régime in factories, state enterprises, the civil service and police. A special branch of their Ministry kept watch on all main post offices, opening letters and parcels, tapping telephones and following up the clues gained. As the executive arm, the S.S.D. could arrest without warrant and interrogate and imprison without trial; it soon had a tight grip on the daily lives of East German citizens. But internal security was not enough. The frequent exchange of visits with the West, the ebb and flow of refugees and the propaganda poured out over the radio, meant that East Germans were exposed to constant contamination. The more flourishing the democratic way of life in

2 *Network*, by Heinz Höhne and Herman Zolling. Translated by Richard Barry. Secker and Warburg, London, 1972, p. 194. Published in America as *The General Was a Spy*, Coward McCann, New York, 1972.

the West, the more essential it was to undermine and eventually overthrow it if communism was to take firm root. Therefore every department of Zaisser's Ministry, and its sister organisations in the Ministry of Defence and the Party, had a special Western Section whose duty it was to operate across the frontier.

Although that frontier was a barrier to the peoples living on either side of it, to Zaisser it offered unique opportunities. It was not just that the citizens of the two newly constituted German states spoke the same language – for more than a century they had been part of the same country and shared the same life. Thousands of families had been divided, parents living in one country, children in the other. Brothers were separated, sisters married to men serving respectively the Russians and the Americans. Civil servants who had spent a lifetime working together now found themselves in different administrations. Old comrades in arms occupied positions of responsibility in rival police or armed forces, old business associates ran rival concerns. Even the secret services themselves were manned by people who had done a similar job, often in the same department for Hitler. However hard the government of the People's Republic might try to segregate its subjects, an intimate and unofficial dialogue between the two Germanies was bound to take place at all levels.

As most of Zaisser's staff had been trained either in Russia or under that pastmaster of subversion, Heinrich Himmler, they knew just how to manipulate this dialogue and take advantage of the 'decadent' freedoms of speech and association on which democracies rest. West Germans by the thousands were blackmailed into the service of the communist powers for fear of reprisals against their relations still living in the People's Republic, or by a threat to expose some unsavoury incident in their past.

Zaisser could even make profitable use of the flood of refugees. Of course it was humiliating that so many East Germans fled from the communist state, but the tide did not flow entirely one way, nor did it include all the most highly qualified people. The majority of professional men, academics, doctors, lawyers, civil servants who could easily have found employment in the West, stayed where they were either from conviction or a sense of duty;[3] it was the young,

---

3 There was a mini-exodus of professors after the passing of the new model statute for the University of Jena in 1958 when several hundreds left East Germany; even so, the majority stayed on.

longing to be free of the tyrannies in which they had been brought up, property-owners, small business men, farmers or disillusioned Social Democrats who swarmed across the sector boundaries in Berlin. Of many of these Zaisser was well rid; they could only hamper the revolution or crowd the prisons if they stayed. On the other hand their going offered a unique opportunity to export picked men and women into West Germany who could work their way into key positions in the Federal Republic. The records of the West German courts and police files show how many hundreds succeeded.

The task of these agents was not simply to collect information, although that was always welcome; it was to undermine the confidence of West Germans in themselves and their system of government, and to impress upon them the inexorability of Russian power and the helplessness of the Allies in face of it. This they must do through a mixture of persuasion and intimidation, kidnapping and political murder where necessary, through sabotage and a carefully planned campaign of blackmail and slander assisted by deliberate lies and forgeries. The better the agents operated the more quickly, or so they were told, would follow either a Russian occupation of the Federal Republic or an internal revolution through which the Soviet Government would once again unite all Germans within the communist fold.

On 8th February, 1950, Zaisser was officially installed as Minister of State Security in new headquarters at 22 Normannenstrasse, Berlin-Lichtenberg. His deputy, Mielcke, was in charge of the S.S.D., really the secret police. Alongside the head of each department sat a senior Russian official and it was clearly understood that, although the Ministry could initiate and carry out its own operations, it was to co-operate with the Soviet authorities who might at any time intervene and take over. However, it was to the Ministry that the first success fell.

It was just at this time that the American C.I.A. was encouraging a refugee organisation called 'The Combat Group Against Inhumanity' to perform acts of sabotage in the Russian zone. Their efforts were amateur, but the group's agents managed to blow up a few railway lines and to burn some propaganda photographs in the headquarters of the S.E.D. Zaisser at once ordered the penetration of the group, and it was not long before the night-watchman at headquarters was one of his men. Not only were the group's agents soon identified and arrested but the night-watchman absconded with the records. These contained valuable further clues.

Some of the most intrepid opponents of communism belonged to the Investigating Committee of Free Jurists whose headquarters were in West Berlin. The West German committee belonged to the World Federation of Free Jurists which, ever since the war, had carried on a relentless fight for human rights in all countries behind the Iron Curtain. The cases which the Federation took up had provoked such unfavourable publicity for communist governments that Stalin gave orders for an example to be made of some of its more prominent members. Once again Zaisser managed to infiltrate one of his men, this time as secretary to the Committee itself and, on the information he provided, the Russians acted.

The first victim chosen was Dr Walter Linse, a prominent West German lawyer, economic adviser to the Federation of Free Jurists and acting President at the time of the Federation's annual conference in July, 1952. Although Dr Linse took the risk of living in West Berlin, he was on his guard and unlikely to accept any invitation which would enable his abduction to be carried out quietly. It was therefore decided by the N.K.V.D. to kidnap him in broad daylight, which meant handing the operation over to the 'liquidating branch' of the Russian secret police. This was S.M.E.R.S.H.,[4] an institution made famous by Ian Fleming in his James Bond books but, nevertheless, an all too genuine terrorist organisation. At the time S.M.E.R.S.H. had on its payroll a number of Germans who had been convicted of crimes of violence but had been released on condition that they carried out S.M.E.R.S.H.'s orders. Seven men were selected to kidnap Dr Linse.[5]

It was not a particularly difficult operation for determined criminals, and yet it nearly misfired. Dr Linse left his flat in the Berlin

4 SMERSH is a contraction of SMIERT SPIO NAM (Death to Spies). Its headquarters in 1950 were at No. 13 Svetenka Ulitza, Moscow.
5 The details of this case as presented by the West German police were corroborated by Pyotr Deriabin, a Russian defector who was Deputy Chief of the Austro-German section of SMERSH at the time of Dr Linse's kidnapping. In March, 1959, Deribain gave evidence before the House of Representatives Committee on Unamerican Activities which was inquiring into 'The Kremlin's Espionage and Terror Organisations'. In March, 1965, he gave evidence before the Senate 'Subcommittee to Investigate the Administration of the Internal Security Act and other Internal Security Laws'. A full account of Dr Linse's kidnapping, partly based on Deriabin's evidence, is given in *The Story of SMERSH* by Ronald Seth, Cassell, London, 1967, pp. 112 onwards.

suburb of Lichterfelde every morning at 7.30 and walked to the headquarters of the Committee of Free Jurists about ten minutes away. S.M.E.R.S.H. decided to capture him within a few hundred yards of his home. Having lured a West German taxi into the Russian sector and arrested its driver, the four kidnappers drove to a corner of the street near Dr Linse's flat just before 7.30 a.m. on 8th July, and waited for him.

The doctor was punctual and, as he approached, two of the men got out of the taxi. An eye-witness, who later reported to the police, said that it appeared that one of the men stopped the doctor, who was smoking a pipe, and asked him for a light while the other went behind and felled him with a savage blow on the head. The doctor's own account, brought back verbally by a fellow prisoner from Russia, makes no mention of a 'light' but says simply that the two kidnappers, whose faces the doctor particularly noticed as belonging to men he would not like to meet alone on a dark night, passed him on either side and immediately knocked him to the ground.

But however the blow was delivered, it failed to knock the doctor out and he put up a tremendous fight. It was not until the man driving the taxi leaned out and shot him in the leg that the kidnappers could get into the car. Even so they drove off in such a hurry that the doctor's legs were sticking out of the door which they could not shut. The shot had given the alarm and the driver of a commercial van, soon joined by a police patrol car, gave chase. Nails thrown into the road failed to stop the van, so the kidnappers leaned out and shot twice through the windscreen; but the van driver was unhurt and kept going.

Workers going to their offices now saw three cars travelling at a furious speed down the Giesendorferstrasse, one of them sounding a siren to get traffic out of the way. But the sector barrier was already raised as the kidnappers' car came in sight and the East German guards slammed it down as soon as it was through. Only prisoners were ever to see Dr Linse again.

Because of Dr Linse's importance this kidnapping caught the headlines of the world. The Americans, in whose sector he lived, made repeated protests. On the night before he left Berlin for good, Walter J. Donnelly, the United States High Commissioner for Germany, wrote a personal letter to Colonel Vasily Chukov, then Chairman of the Soviet control Commission for Germany, appealing to him, on behalf of Mrs Linse, to have Dr Linse sent home. In every instance the Russians denied all knowledge of Dr Linse and indignantly repudiated the suggestion that they might have had anything to do with the kidnapping. Then suddenly, in June, 1960, officials of the German Red Cross announced that they had received notification from the Soviet Red Cross of Dr Linse's death in a Soviet prison camp on 15th December, 1953. The Soviet statement was in reply to a routine German check on the whereabouts of missing persons.

No sooner had the Western press made the announcement given to them by the Red Cross than the Russians denied the authenticity of their own Red Cross statement. But subsequently defectors have not only confirmed Dr Linse's death, but have also revealed that no such kidnapping ever takes place without the full knowledge of the Central Committee of the Communist Party. In Dr Linse's case not only Stalin but six other members of the Politburo including Molotov and Malenkov knew all the details both of Dr Linse's kidnapping and of his subsequent imprisonment, interrogation and death.

Two of Dr Linse's kidnappers were caught, one after he had tried to commit suicide. During their trial it transpired that Dr Linse, under torture, had revealed the names of more than twenty people in East Germany who had given information to the Investigating Committee of Free Jurists. All were arrested and sent to concentration camps. Dr Linse's kidnappers, who had been paid the equivalent of £83 ($207.50) in West German marks, were both sentenced to penal servitude for life.[6]

While the Russians were dealing with the Free Jurists, Zaisser had one further success of his own; the documents from the combat group and statements from prisoners had revealed a great deal about the Gehlen Organisation. During the war, Reinhard Gehlen had been head of a department known as 'Foreign Armies East' which not only provided intelligence but organised resistance behind the Russian lines. Before being dismissed by Hitler in April, 1945, he had risen to the rank of Major-General. But Gehlen, a

6 The Free Jurists never recovered from this blow. They continued their work, but the East Germans continued their penetration. Some further attempts to kidnap leading members of the Committee failed because those selected for the job defected rather than do it, but by 1956 one of the members of the Committee itself, a certain Dr Werner, was reporting to the East German Ministry, and continued to do so for several years. Since then time has blunted the indignation of the Free World at communist police practices.

dedicated anti-communist, preserved and hid his records and then gave himself up to the Americans hoping that they would employ him against the Soviet Union. Instead they put him in prison. Only when the Russians themselves started asking for him did the Americans prick up their ears. By then Gehlen had been lost in the 'cages' and it took them several weeks to find him.

The upshot was that Gehlen was sent to America and a year later, when American faith in Russian friendship was becoming a little tarnished, signed an agreement under which he undertook to supply information on the Soviet Union and satellite countries for the C.I.A. Since all other German Intelligence organisations had been disbanded and Allied information about the Red Army and the Soviet Union was rudimentary, this private agency, financed by the Americans but working also for Bonn, soon became the most valuable service the Western Powers possessed.

In 1952, Gehlen was riding high. His organisation had accurately forecast Russian policy in Eastern Germany and the satellite countries and was almost the only source of information about the strength and morale of Russian troops in Europe. In the Federal Republic Gehlen's agents had uncovered many of Zaisser's operatives and denounced members of the illegal Communist Party. He had thoroughly earned the attention of Zaisser and Mielcke.[7]

Working closely with the Russians and with ex-officers who had served with Gehlen during the war, Zaisser's ministry built up a dossier which led them first to one of Gehlen's organisers in West Berlin, a former Major Wolfgang Höher. Since Höher was both loyal and suspicious, Zaisser decided to kidnap him, using as a decoy his 'contact', Hors Kirves, who had already been convicted as a West German agent and was therefore living under possible sentence of death. On 13th February, 1953, Kirves met Höher as arranged in a bar in West Berlin and gave him an impregnated cigarette. Höher collapsed and, under the eyes of passers-by and in an apparently drunken condition, was bundled into a car and taken to East Berlin. Under interrogation Höher gave so much away about the Gehlen organisation that his story was published in a brochure entitled *Agent 2996 Speaks*.

However, before Zaisser could follow up Höher's revelations,

---

7 In July, 1955, Gehlen's organisation was finally incorporated into the Federal service as an 'agency affiliated to the Chancellor's office'. By then, ironically enough, it had outlived its usefulness.

disaster overtook both himself and his ministry. Stalin's death, the fall of his old protector, Beria, and the uprising of June, 1953, in East Berlin had followed each other in quick succession. Ulbricht, unsure of his own position, had turned on his critics, one of whom was known to be Zaisser. Zaisser was dismissed and his Ministry downgraded to a State Secretariat of which, not Mielcke, but his other old colleague, Ernst Wollweber, was put in charge. It seemed for a moment as if the communists might have lost their nerve and the Federal Republic be able to enjoy some respite. This soon proved an illusion.

In spite of Khrushchev's denunciation of Stalin, his accession to power gave a new impetus to the campaign against the West. It was Ulbricht rather than the State Security Service with whom the Russians were displeased and, at their insistence, Wollweber was soon promoted and the whole East German subversive organisation reconstituted. With only minor changes it has endured to this day.

At the top stood the Central Committee of the Socialist Unity Party (S.E.D.) effectively the Communist Party of East Germany. This was a small, largely self-perpetuating body, whose composition was the result of hard bargaining between the party caucus and the Soviet authorities. It did not appoint the government, but no minister who lost its favour was likely to last long. Beneath it, two ministries and a special 'working bureau' of the Central Committee itself were charged with espionage and subversion.

The largest and most important was still the Ministry of State Security of which Wollweber was promoted Minister in 1954, to be succeeded a few years later by Mielcke who still held the post in 1972. The scope of Mielcke's operations was immense. His headquarters was staffed by three thousand people and a further 16,000 were employed in 16 regional and 220 district offices within the People's Republic. Internally he controlled the ordinary, frontier and secret police, ran espionage and counter espionage, looked after the 'security' of industry, transport and trade, of industrial and armaments research, controlled ciphers and censorship, was responsible for crime and prisons and the development, production and use of 'technical devices.'

Although every department of the ministry had a special section for West Germany and Western Europe, Mielcke also had under

him a 'Main Department of Intelligence' which dealt exclusively
with foreign countries, chiefly those belonging to N.A.T.O. run
by Major-General Marcus Wolf. Wolf, who was responsible for
sabotage, kidnapping and political murder among other things,
employed a further 1,000 people on his staff and from 18,000 to
20,000 agents in West Germany alone, some 2,000 of whom were
full-time.

The Ministry of Defence also had two departments which concentrated on the armed forces of West Germany and its N.A.T.O.
allies, the Department for Co-ordination, run by Colonel Willi
Sagebrecht, and the Independent Department under Colonel
Thomas Fröchen. To some extent they overlapped, since both
collected information and dealt with propaganda. But whereas
Fröchen's department was really concerned with psychological
warfare, issuing pamphlets and brochures, broadcasting over the
Deutschland-Sender, distributing forged call-up papers, leave passes
and even leaving love letters written on scented notepaper where
they might be picked up by West German soldiers' wives, Sagebrecht
was primarily concerned with gadgetry – radios, telephone-
tapping apparatus, quick action drugs, gas-guns, micro-film and a
whole range of forged documents such as passports, bank notes,
business letters, 'top secret' reports.

Between them therefore these two ministries supplied the
whole subversive organisation with the technical expertise it
needed. They produced the gimmickry necessary for kidnapping
(gas-guns disguised as cigarette lighters avoided the brutality shown
in the kidnapping of Dr Linse), ran a 'lie factory', a forgery centre,
a printing press comparable in size to any possessed by Europe's
largest publishing firms, and a series of 'think tanks', to produce
new ideas.

The 'Working Bureau' was quite separate and entirely controlled
by the Party. Up till 1972, when it was reorganised, it formed part
of the 'Western Section' of the Central Committee's Politburo
under Heinz Geggel, and was run by a former journalist, Erich
Gluckauf. With a staff of about a hundred, Gluckauf, who is still
believed to be in charge, co-ordinated all subversive operations
carried out by civilian organisations such as trade unions, the German Democratic League of Women or the Free German Youth.
The Bureau, being a political organisation, worked through East
German consulates abroad, could call on the help of thousands of

officials in the S.E.D. and, since 1969, on 30,000 members of the revived West German Communist Party.

Like the death watch beetle, this massive assembly of communist agents ate away from within at the fabric of West German society. Every year, according to police records, between 1,500 and 3,000 agents were caught or gave themselves up in the Federal Republic and every year at least as many others took their place. On this scale recruitment alone played a vital role in subversion, for it meant that thousands of West Germans were being watched, approached and often threatened so that they might be induced to indulge in treasonable action. The greatest demand came from Wolf's 'Main Department', for which the principal recruiting targets were the civil service, local or Federal departments of justice,[8] the police and officials of the political parties. For Wolf every agent gained was another nail in the coffin of the Federal Republic and he organised his assault with great thoroughness.

After 1961, the identity papers of everyone entering the People's Republic were checked; if a visitor happened to be a member of an important West German organisation, details were at once sent to Wolf's headquarters. If inquiries showed that the visitor might make a useful agent, the business of recruitment began.

The most frequent method was a threat to relations living in East Germany. A letter was forged or the relation forced to write inviting the intended victim for a visit. When he or she arrived, or sometimes as soon as they crossed the border, they were arrested and interrogated. During the interrogation the suggestion was made that they work for the East German 'Main Department' and it was plainly intimated that refusal could lead to harsh reprisals, perhaps against an old mother, a son or daughter. If the victim accepted (and understandably thousands did so), then they were made to sign an undertaking and warned that any failure to live up to their promise would have dire results, not only for their relations, but for themselves.

If the selected victim had no close relations, other methods were used. He might be accused of a petty crime like breaking a traffic law; he might be framed and accused of having helped someone

8 Employees of the Ministry of Justice are valuable agents because the East Germans like to keep track of all those serving sentences in West German prisons. If, on release, they find it difficult to get jobs, they may be tempted by lucrative offers; if they are hardened criminals they may make useful members of SMERSH.

escape from the People's Republic or of having committed some petty theft; the only way of being sure of returning home was to sign the service agreement. Many former prisoners of war in Russia signed undertakings in order to obtain their release and hundreds have since received letters reminding them of their obligations, sometimes enclosing facsimiles of the documents. Before 1969, people convicted of membership of the illegal Communist Party in West Germany were recruited after being released from prison on the promise of asylum in East Germany if they ran into trouble carrying out their work.

Mielcke's Ministry was particularly successful in penetrating the West Berlin police. Many of the 20,000 East German policemen who escaped to the West undoubtedly were 'plants' and began to act as agents as soon as they received their official registration as 'refugees'; others, who joined the police genuinely, were vulnerable either because they had relations in East Germany or through fear of reprisals for desertion.

In January, 1960, several members of the West Berlin force were arrested for having supplied information to the People's Republic and for having distributed a periodical, *Democratic Police*, published by Mielcke's Ministry but purporting to be the work of a dissatisfied group of West Berlin policemen. As a result of the trial it became clear that Mielcke had planted agents in all branches of the West Berlin police since 1946. These agents had supplied the addresses of all senior police officials, the registration numbers of their cars and also of the cars of the members of the Berlin administration. They had given particulars of the defence of the sector boundaries, the strength and pattern of the control of radio cars, a report on the registration law and details of the passport and identity system. One policeman used his own police station as a meeting place for East German agents and another, who worked in one of the large central police stations in West Berlin, had supplied German and Soviet spies with false papers for fifteen years.

But neither Mielcke nor Wolf confined themselves to particular categories; as innumerable confessions showed, no West German was safe from their attentions. 'A nursemaid employed in the Federal Republic,' ran one report, 'received a telegram ostensibly from her mother stating that the latter was ill and would like her to come at once. When she arrived in Glauchau in East Germany she found that her mother was not ill. On the following evening she was taken by several Russians to the Kommandatura where a Russian colonel questioned her about her work in West Germany. On the next day she was taken to Chemnitz and invited to work for the Russian intelligence service. She agreed to do so, fearing that some action might otherwise be taken against her mother or herself.'

Another police record states: 'A West Berlin customs official, who travelled through East Germany to spend his honeymoon in West Germany, was approached by the Ministry of State Security during his trip through East German territory. He was persuaded to agree in writing to meet a member of the Ministry at a later date. Afterwards he received several telephone calls from a woman and a threatening letter reminding him of his obligations. He ignored the warning. About fifteen months later his wife received a letter accusing her husband of adultery and containing a photograph of a nude woman.'[9]

Homosexuals were obvious targets, since homosexuality was still an offence in Germany. A typical case, taken from the files of the Berlin Department of the Interior, refers to a certain 'Gerhardt',[10] who had been a member of the West Berlin administration, but having been convicted of a homosexual offence, went to East Berlin at the end of 1948 where he joined the People's Police. By 1951, he had risen to the rank of Commissar, but was again convicted and lost his post. However, by exemplary behaviour in the riots of June, 1953, he so far rehabilitated himself as to attract the attention of the Ministry of State Security. On their instructions he fled to West Berlin and became registered as a 'refugee'. Still acting on instructions he joined the Social Democratic Party and used his homosexuality to establish contacts with its youth organisation and particularly with the staff of the youth magazine *Die Falken*. At this point he informed the West Berlin police of what he was doing and became a double agent.

However, Mielcke did not discriminate between the sexes. One of the specialities of his ministry was a 'finishing school' for girls drawn from all over Eastern Europe. They became skilled in the use of microfilm, telephone tapping apparatus, ciphers and codes and were also given special instruction in sexual acrobatics. When their

9 Ibid, p. 14.
10 Eastern Underground Activity against West Berlin. First Supplement, 1960, p. 45.

course was over they were given aristocratic-sounding names and sent out into the cities of Western Europe to found beauty parlours, photographic studios, fashion shops or night clubs from which they could do their work. As part of their routine they often wrote letters to members of the armed forces suggesting an assignation.

The 'Working Bureau' operated rather differently. While Mielcke and Wolf concentrated on spying and intimidation, the Party fomented revolution. For this purpose Gluckauf could issue instructions to every political, social and industrial organisation in the Peoples' Republic. With his encouragement the East German Federation of Trade Unions spent many million deutschmarks establishing contacts with trade unionists in the Federal Republic. Western German workers were offered courses at the training schools of the 'Free German Trade Union Federation' at Bernau, near Berlin, at Falkensee in the Nauen district and at Hermsdorfer-Muhle, near Königswuster-hausen. Other special schools gave training in underground organisation.

Both the communist controlled Society for Cultural Relations with Foreign Countries and the League for Friendship Between Peoples received detailed instructions on the use of culture for political purposes. An extract from the long term plan for the 'Study and Working Association for the Advancement of the German Folk and Amateur Arts', issued in 1956, reads: 'The media of folk art must give substantial support to the social and political struggle of the working class.

'The present political situation arising from the existence on German soil of two separate states with a differing social system, obliges us to ensure that the repertoire of all folk art troupes, particularly of those in West Germany, contain unmistakable objections to the revival of militarism and fascism and clear statements supporting the indivisibility of our national culture.' The instructions go on to say that this task can only be done 'in close collaboration with comrades and functionaries of the West German (then illegal) Communist Party.' Detailed estimates were made of the foreign currency needed for every exchange visit, for the setting up of special groups in West Germany, for their 'ideological and artistic direction', as well as for 'propaganda and agitation.'[11]

In 1958, a special direction was issued to local government officials and party branches 'regarding the improvement of political

11 Eastern Underground Activity, 1959, p. 56.

work in West Germany.'[12] Party workers were reminded that they must collaborate with government departments and trade unions. Work 'must contribute to the solidarity movement in large-scale strikes and the creation of a common workers' front'. Every district council and party committee must see that the fullest political use is made of every exchange of delegations. 'The purpose of the delegates is not the establishment of "technical contacts" in West Germany but of relations which further the struggle of the working class for Peace and Unity.'

The directions go on to say that the members of every delegation sent to West Germany must be carefully chosen, must be given clear instructions and make a detailed report on their return. Equal care must be taken about the reception of delegations from West Germany. 'Every member must be constantly and individually looked after.' The number of those invited 'must not overtax the political resources' of the organisations promoting the visits. In Berlin in this same year an 'Operational Plan for the Organisation of Political Work with Visitors from Western Germany during the Christmas Holiday' was printed and circulated in all the boroughs. Old-age pensioners must be invited by the National Solidarity movement to Christmas parties and taken to old people's homes. Political discussions must be arranged for labourers and skilled workers. The borough executives of the 'Free German Youth' must take charge of those under twenty-one. Professional men and women must have special seminars arranged for them. The object of these instructions, which have been frequently amended, is that 'every visitor to the People's Republic shall become a conscious agitator who, on his return home, will found a cell of national resistance in Western Germany'.

When a ballet or opera company or some trade union delegation arrived in East Berlin entertainment was lavish; no effort was spared to make the English, French or Scandinavian visitor feel at ease. But the impresario who returned to London, Paris or Oslo convinced that the East German brand of communism was more enlightened and humane than he may have supposed, did not know that within three days of his departure a report on himself and his mission had been filed with the Party Committee and that, in thousands of cases through the years, visitors had been blackmailed, bribed or cajoled into working for the 'Bureau' or the Ministry of

12 Ibid., pp. 64–6.

The Great Divide 237
State Security when they returned to their own countries. Outside
Germany these cases only came to light through occasional spy
trials or a defection to the East; the files of the West German police,
on the other hand, are stacked with confessions of those who have
later had the courage to denounce this abuse of hospitality. In 1960,
the year before the wall was built, 2,600 West Germans were invited to visit relations in the People's Republic and when they returned, 663 told the West German police that they had been
'persuaded' to serve East German news agencies, a first step
towards providing intelligence for the East German Government.

The weakness against which neither Mielcke nor his predecessors
were ever able to protect themselves was defection. The tensions
which the secret war built up among Germans were so great that
at any moment an agent, an official or even, in one case, a Minister
of State might crack and give himself up or start working for the
other side. The records show that the tension was greatest among
those who worked for the People's Republic partly, no doubt,
because they became painfully aware that East German communists were little more than Russian stooges. Former Nazis and
old-guard German communists who had fought in the underground
against Hitler, often suffered from revulsion. At the lower levels
this did not greatly matter because the individuals knew little, but
defectors from responsible positions could paralyse whole sections
of the security service for months and even years. In such cases
Mielcke (or the Russians) will go to any lengths to eliminate the
danger.

Robert Bialek was one of the earliest and most important examples. Bialek was an idealist who had led a guerrilla movement in
Breslau against the Nazis, become one of the leading spirits in the
Communist Youth Movement in the Russian zone and risen to be
Inspector General of the People's Republic. Deeply disillusioned
with the form that communism was taking under Walter Ulbricht
and the Russians he quarrelled first with Mielcke, whom he accused
of introducing Nazi forms of discipline into the Ministry of State
Security, and finally with Ulbricht himself. Bialek refused to recant
his 'errors' and was expelled from the party in 1952.

The revolt of June, 1953, was the last straw. Bialek knew that
its causes lay in the servility of the S.E.D. Central Committee which
not only agreed to rearmament at Russian insistence – no more

popular in East than in West Germany – but made no effort to prevent the scant rations from deteriorating even further as a result of the dislocation of the economic plan which rearmament caused. Local strikes had been taking place for months before the final explosion which occurred when the Russians insisted on a 10% increase on all 'norms' of work. During the revolt Bialek played a moderating role, trying to ensure that the factory committees passed reasonable resolutions in correct form so that the members should not be victimised when the revolt was suppressed. But he, like everyone else, knew that the uprising was not anti-communist, but on the contrary, was led by party members and connived at by local officials and People's Police. In other words it was a revolt within the Party against a leadership that was sacrificing East Germany in the interests of the Soviet Government.

The Central Committee was well aware of this. They knew that the Russians had deliberately waited until the régime was on the point of collapse before taking action and that unless Russian tanks had intervened the entire Party hierarchy would have been swept away. Stunned by the shock and seeking allies who had some standing among the sullen factory workers, the Committee invited Bialek to rejoin the party. When he refused, saying that it was the Central Committee itself that needed new blood, he knew that his days were numbered. He escaped to West Berlin in August, 1953.

Inevitably Bialek was regarded with suspicion, but the extent of his information and the depth of his opposition to Ulbricht's régime won him recognition. He joined the Social Democratic Party and worked for its Eastern Bureau, broadcasting daily to East German workers from the bureau's headquarters in West Berlin. Even if the broadcasts had not been effective, attempts to kidnap him would undoubtedly have been made, for he had too many sympathisers among the S.E.D. and his 'treason' had further undermined a discredited Central Committee; but the broadcasts not only kept alive the discontent in East Germany but constantly reminded the whole world of the true nature of Ulbricht's régime. Bialek had to be eliminated.

The N.K.V.D. had begun to lay its plans almost as soon as Bialek crossed the sector border. Within a few weeks a man called Paul Drzewiecke, who had been an officer in the People's Police under Bialek, ostensibly defected and persuaded the Western screening

committee to 'recognise' him as a refugee. He then struck up a
friendship with Bialek, pretending to have much in common with
him. For nearly eighteen months Drzewiecke cultivated Bialek, dis-
arming him of all suspicion. Then in February, 1956, Drzewiecke
gave a birthday party to which he invited Bialek and other 'friends',
three of whom were his accomplices. Bialek's champagne was
drugged. Reeling from the effects he managed to reach the bathroom, locked the door and collapsed inside. The landlord of the
flat found him and informed Drzewiecke, who expressed great concern, assured the landlord that he would drive Bialek straight to
hospital, and left with him in a car, only to take him straight to the
Russian sector. Bialek has not been heard of since.

It is, perhaps, not fair to label as defectors Wilhelm Kastner who,
as chairman of the puppet Liberal Democratic Party, rose to be
Vice-President of the People's Republic, or Elli Barczatis, Grotewohl's secretary; they remained at their posts and supplied the
Federal Republic with vital information for many years through
political conviction. Kastner, a believer in German neutralism,
was being canvassed by Semyonov, Political Adviser to the Soviet
Military Administration and an advocate of the 'soft' line towards
East Germany, as a successor to Ulbricht at the very moment of the
June uprising. The rising cut the ground from under Semyonov's
feet and forced the Russians to continue backing Ulbricht. However, Kastner retained the favour of the Russians and continued to
regale the Gehlen organisation with details of East German cabinet
meetings and other high level talks until 1955, when Wollweber
cracked the Liberal Democratic ring. Elli Barczatis was guillotined
and Kastner fled to the West.

Lieutenant-Colonel Siegfried Dombrowski, on the other hand,
was a straightforward victim of 'the miracle'. He liked good living,
spent too much time in the West and finally succumbed to one of
Gehlen's men. Warned in time that he was suspected, he fled in
1958. As a result of the inquiry which followed, a general, two
colonels and 67 officers of the East German Army were arrested
and another 200 officers dismissed. It took the East German Ministry
of Defence several years to rebuild the section.

The only comparable case in the West was the somewhat uncertain
one of Dr Otto John. John had been involved in the attempt on
Hitler's life on 20th July, 1944, but had used his position as a

Director of Lufthansa to escape to Portugal, and eventually to England. Having worked for Sefton Delmer in the Department of Psychological Warfare, he later became an interrogator of German prisoners of war, and particularly of generals. When he finally returned to West Germany he became head of the Federal Office for the Protection of the Constitution.

President Heuss, who knew John well, said that the object of the Office was to prevent a repetition of the events of 1933; in other words John was the Federal Government's watchdog against all anti-democratic movements. As there was no knowing where such movements might begin, John had a watching brief over all Government departments, the police, universities and youth organisations as well as the trade unions. It was a thankless task and John soon made enemies in high places including Gehlen. From his description of his work it is clear that John began to feel he was not getting the support he deserved. In particular he developed a pathological mistrust of Adenauer who had agreed to his appointment only after much hesitation and, as he confessed later in his memoirs, against his better judgement.

As an old 20th July conspirator, John was naturally hypersensitive about the employment of former Nazis by the Federal Republic. When some of Hitler's former generals emerged to help form the new West German army, he seems to have lost his mental balance. John claimed at his trial in December, 1956 (and in the book he wrote which was published in 1969), that in 1954, on the anniversary of the attempt on Hitler's life, he was drugged by a physician, Dr Wohlgemuth, whom he visited in West Berlin, and driven unconscious across the sector boundary. This claim was rejected by the court which was later to try him.

But if John went to East Berlin of his own free will, it is still not clear why he did so. He of all people must have known that Ulbricht was making even greater use than Adenauer of former Nazis in the government of the People's Republic, and although the Russians and East Germans did their utmost to make capital out of his defection, neither in the articles he wrote nor at the press conference he gave in East Berlin after his arrival, which was attended by many journalists from the West including Sefton Delmer, did he say anything particularly damaging to the Federal Republic or the Western Allies. He spoke about German unity and the evils of rearmament; he was clearly not a communist convert.

Had he been a convert, both Ulbricht and the Russians would have made further use of him. As it was, he was taken off to Russia and kept there for seventeen months in close but reasonably comfortable house arrest. To his own and everybody else's surprise he was then allowed back to East Berlin, from which he duly escaped.

Perhaps John's own explanation of this strange sequence of events is the correct one. The Russians, who interrogated him for weeks on end, were interested not so much in his work in the Federal Republic as in his connections with the British. They seemed to believe that he was a British agent who, at the time of the attempt on Hitler's life in 1944, had been trying to arrange for a separate peace between the Western Powers and any government that succeeded in overthrowing the Nazis. Had this been true it would have been useful propaganda. John was able to repeat, over and over again, that the reverse had been the case and that all the efforts he had made from Spain and Portugal prior to 1944 to interest the British in the German resistance to Hitler, had met with a blank refusal. What he did not know, until many years later, was that the man in the British Foreign Office who rejected all his overtures was Kim Philby, who had been a Soviet agent since 1933.

But in 1954, when John defected, Philby was under a cloud of suspicion in Moscow as well as London. The English rightly suspected him of being 'the third man' who had enabled Burgess and Maclean to flee to Moscow in 1951; the Russians feared all along that he might have been a double agent. Looking back on his imprisonment in Russia after the publication of Philby's book in 1968, John came to the conclusion that Philby must have suggested to the Russians that they interrogate him (John) so as to clear his own name. For Philby had certainly carried out Russian instructions faithfully in preventing communications from the German conspirators reaching the British government.

However, all this is speculation. The facts are that, on 12th December, 1955, Dr John managed to escape back into West Berlin with the help of a Danish journalist. A year later he stood his trial and was sentenced to four years' penal servitude for 'treasonable conspiracy.' He has always denied his guilt and is still working to clear his name. Probably the true explanation of his behaviour is that so many years of underground work were too much for a man who was always highly-strung and introspective. John became unbalanced and may well have suffered from the delusion that, because of the office he held in the Federal government, he alone might be able to bring rearmament to an end in both the German States and promote German unity. Luckily for him the Russians seem to have come to a similar conclusion about his mental state, or his name would certainly have been added to the list of those who have disappeared.

The secret war which this army of agents waged reached a climax in the early sixties. Although Khrushchev had denounced Stalin and was preaching co-existence, his passionate belief in the revolution pushed him inexorably towards direct confrontation with the West. In 1961, still confident that the Allies would give way if he pressed them hard enough, he installed his rockets in Cuba and issued an ultimatum over Berlin.

The East German security service took their cue. Since the Americans were the chief enemy, it was the Americans whom Mielcke and his colleagues set out to discredit. They possessed the ideal tool in Dr Alfred Norden, Professor of History at the Humboldt University in East Berlin and head of the propaganda section of the East German politburo. Dr Norden emigrated to America in 1933, and during the war, edited a magazine called *Germany To-day*. He returned to Berlin in 1945, became a member of the Socialist Unity Party and of its Central Committee in 1955.

Norden's brief was to persuade the West Germans not only that the Americans were depraved and undependable but that the whole Western way of life was decadent and on the point of collapse. Using his own knowledge of people in the American Administration and helped by up-to-date information supplied by agents in N.A.T.O. headquarters, he concocted a series of 'secret documents' which he issued at carefully timed intervals to the Press. The forgery centre and the lie factory excelled themselves. Within a few months they produced photostat copies of a secret 'order' issued to the American air force forbidding flights of aircraft carrying 'H' bombs over the United States (by inference permitting them over other countries including West Germany), a 'secret' medical report on the causes of frequent 'blackouts' of U.S. pilots, implying that they were either unfit or physical weaklings, a 'top secret' State Department document disclosing a plot to have Chiang Kai Shek accidentally killed and a letter on official paper from Rear Admiral Lawrence Frost, head of American Naval Intelligence, urging Sumatran rebels not to give up hope because, in spite of official U.S. policy, help would be forthcoming. All appeared first in East German press but the photostats were later reproduced in Western newspapers accompanied either by a demand to know whether they were authentic or by an official denial.

America's 'lackeys' in N.A.T.O. and particularly the West German leaders and military commanders came in for the same treatment. In 1961 a British 'cabinet document' was published in *Neues Deutschland*, East German newspaper, disclosing a plot to prevent trade unions in newly emerging African states from having any independent organisation. Here Norden fell below his usual standard as almost the only independent African states which did not have trade union federations of an aggressively independent character were those affiliated to the communist World Federation of Trade Unions. An attempt to sow discord between the United States and its N.A.T.O. allies was made in a 'letter' from Nelson Rockefeller, then Governor of New York, to President Eisenhower containing suggestions how 'the independent countries of the world and the former British, Dutch and French colonies might be brought under American control by economic aid.' This too was published in *Neues Deutschland*.

Any European who played a prominent part in the formation of the Common Market was also a target for Norden. Paul Henri Spaak, for many years Prime Minister or Foreign Secretary of Belgium and one of the great protagonists of the European idea, was the victim of a particularly elaborate forgery. A letter dated 22nd February, 1941, and purporting to be written from London to some friends of Spaak's in Vichy, in which Spaak apparently threw out suggestions for a separate peace between Belgium and Germany, was suddenly 'discovered' in the East German archives. Shortly afterwards another letter, apparently written in the same year, contained suggestions of business deals between Belgians and Germans. The signatures were a good imitation but, on examination, proved to be identical. This alone revealed a forgery.

For West Germans, Norden's department had an almost unlimited repertoire. During the early stages of rearmament an 'official document' was suddenly published in which it was stated that conscientious objectors in West Germany would have to wear special badges such as the Poles and Jews had had to wear in

4

244   *The Rise of Western Germany 1945-1972*

the Third Reich. A document apparently emanating from the
Foreign Office in Bonn contained a long interview with Erhard in
which, among other things, he stated that the only way to stop in-
flation was to decree an overall reduction in wages. Virulent cam-
paigns were launched in the East German press against General
Speidel, the Commander-in-Chief of N.A.T.O. land forces and
General Heusinger, the Commander of the German contingent.
Heusinger was accused of having 'betrayed' the men of the 20th
July. The climax of the campaign against Speidel came at a press
conference when Norden produced documents proving that
Speidel, on Göring's orders, had plotted the assassination of King
Alexander of Yugoslavia and the French Foreign Minister Louis
Barthou in 1939. Questioned by Western correspondents, Norden
said that the originals had been destroyed. These documents were
used as the basis for a film to be circulated behind the Iron Curtain;
but when Speidel threatened legal action they had to be cut from the
script.

Ordinary citizens and particularly the rank and file of the armed
forces were not neglected. At one time Norden's department
drafted a thousand different letters protesting against rearmament.
These were sent out at the rate of five thousand letters a day by
party members who picked out West German addresses from
telephone directories. East German pensioners were asked to sign
receipts for their pensions without realising that on the reverse side
was a statement supporting Russian proposals for Berlin as a 'demilitarised free city.' These also were sent into West Germany by
the tens of thousands.

Love letters sent to the homes of German soldiers, many of them
ending 'we'll marry after you get your divorce, darling,' were a
common gambit. One lady was particularly prolific. Soldiers in
units all over West Germany at one time received letters from the
nineteen-year-old girl who signed herself Countess von Bülow.
Some of the letters began: 'I saw you with some of your friends –
you must guess where. Dare I confess it? You came and conquered. But don't be too conceited. It often happens that way –
love at first sight.' The letter then went on to suggest a meeting and
told the soldier that he would find another letter at a *poste restante*.
When the soldiers went to collect the second letter, however, they
found the envelope full of communist propaganda.

To give credence to their forgeries communist intelligence

services frequently reported fictitious defections on the part of officials from the West or the theft of files from some government department, after which a new spate of 'secret' documents would appear in the East German press. To give one example, an orderly anti-American demonstration in Taiwan was reported as a riot during which the American Embassy was stormed and secret files taken. Afterwards a new series of 'documents' purporting to come from American official sources were published.

It was not the fault of the East Germans that Khrushchev's offensive failed. He had overplayed his hand and his bluff had been called. By allowing the Berlin Wall to be built he was conceding that Russian occupation of the whole city, with all that it might have brought in its train, was no longer a possibility and giving notice that Soviet policy would in future focus on a more distant objective. The campaign of subversion went on, but it changed its character. From being a prelude to victory it became a battle of psychological attrition whose object was to convince all Germans of the inevitability of the communist revolution.

West Germans who attacked the Soviet system or refugees who had 'betrayed' the cause by flight still suffered intimidation, although usually in a rather more subtle form. Both the K.G.B. (which the N.K.V.D. had now become) and the S.S.D. had realised that ugly scenes in the streets were not the best way of convincing Berliners of the superiority of the communist way of life; if someone had to be kidnapped it was easier and more discreet to entice them into East Berlin and arrest them where no one would dare protest. A forged letter or a telephone call were usually enough to do the trick. Sixteen people have disappeared in this way since the Wall was built.

If the intended victim was suspicious it was still occasionally necessary to take drastic action. On 21st January, 1967, a West German car with a woman's legs sticking out of the window drove through 'Check Point Charlie' at high speed straight into the Eastern sector. The woman was seen to be screaming and struggling, but the Western guards were too late to stop the car and dared not shoot. The woman's handbag fell out as she passed and she was identified as the wife of a Syrian named Sammat, who had fled from East Germany two years earlier. Apparently her husband had helped to kidnap her. It was a bad week during which George McGhee, the

United States Ambassador to the Federal Republic, had to protest against five shooting incidents in West Berlin. A little more than three years later, in the summer of 1970, a defector told the West German police that a former woman colleague of his, Gudrun Heidel, who also had defected, had been run down and killed in the streets of West Berlin eighteen months earlier. Until then her death had been thought to be accidental.

But the emphasis now was on psychological rather than physical intimidation. Since 1961, agents had been instructed to supply 'short candid reports on everyday difficulties in West German life, to collect statistics on fertility rates, the incidence of venereal disease, the condition of old people, students, children and anything else which might be used to show the decadence of Western society.' This information was used throughout the past decade in a massive poster, letter and press campaign drawing comparisons between the two Germanies and vilifying certain prominent individuals in industry, the armed forces, and the police in Western Germany.

At one time in the early sixties the government in Bonn estimated that 12,000,000 leaflets a month, costing some £3 m ($7.5 m) a year, had been distributed. Before the closing of the frontiers the leaflets were posted mainly in West Berlin; agents then stuck up the posters all over Germany. After the building of the wall some leaflets were sent across by rocket; but this proved an unsatisfactory method of distribution and there has been no record of it since 1966.

The character of the leaflets has changed with the political climate. In the early sixties many were addressed to the Social and Christian Democratic Parties urging them to stop West German rearmament which would only bring Soviet retribution upon their heads. Others harped on the high taxation and rising prices which membership of N.A.T.O. had caused. As the People's Republic became more stable its propaganda became more confident. 'How rich are we?' 'Who Lives Best?' proudly asked two leaflets that were dropped by rocket. They claimed that social services and stable prices in Eastern Germany were worth far more than the mythical West German 'miracle'. 'Atom-bombs On The Frontier' proclaimed another pamphlet drawing a frightening picture of the danger to Western Germany of tactical nuclear weapons. The theme of Nazis in high places was constant. A leaflet entitled

'Murderers in Judge's Robes' stated that fifty-two members of the West German judiciary were former Nazis and named them all.

Forged letters and 'identity' cards were, perhaps, more telling because they were aimed at individuals many of whom might well have lived a double life at some time. Politicians, particularly socialists who had taken a strong anti-communist line, frequently received threatening letters or found that letters accusing them of being communist agents had been sent to their colleagues. Army and police officers were more often sent hand-written letters from women accusing them of licentiousness or sometimes of procuring abortions for their mistresses. Several of these have been reproduced in the spurious magazine *Democratic Police* or in *Links Um* (Left Turn), a paper produced openly by the revived West German Communist Party which, among other things, had issued instructions on how to get out of the army or sabotage the training programme.

'Identity Cards', often carrying the photograph of the person to whom they were addressed and accusing them of working for the British or American secret service, of having been Nazis or of being Russian or East German agents who are not living up to their promises, were pushed through letter boxes or sent through the post. 'Citizens, when will criminals like this be brought to justice?' ran the caption under the photograph of a man named Benedict, alias Kallweit, who was alleged to work for the Americans. Karl Heinz Wahl's identity card, which was dropped through the letter boxes of houses in the district in which he lived, ironically warned his fellow-Berliners that, as a British agent, he hated both mankind and peace.

The only light-hearted aspects of this sinister campaign were the practical jokes. It was difficult not to laugh when a large consignment of whisky was delivered to a company manager's office with an invoice implying that he had ordered it, or an expensive fur coat arrived at a politician's home in similar circumstances. Yet the organisation behind these jokes was frighteningly thorough. Unordered furniture or machinery was delivered to offices and factories in a manner which defied detection; civil servants received letters informing them of promotion or telling them they might take extra leave, soldiers were sent false demobilisation papers and local government officials papers calling them up to the army. All such letters were typewritten on official notepaper with printed headings and inevitably caused irritation and confusion. They also conveyed an unpleasant feeling of powerlessness in face of an omnipresent enemy.

By contrast, the work of conventional spies might seem tame if it had not been so ubiquitous. The list of those who have been caught or have confessed to being communist agents since 1961, comprises journalists, photographers, every kind of skilled craftsmen, telephone engineers, electronic experts, businessmen large and small, army, navy and air force officers, including an admiral and a submarine navigator, several groups of scientists, a West German judge, political party workers, a member of the Federal Parliament, economists, agriculturists, teachers, opinion pollsters and a diminishing number of civil servants and policemen.

In 1962, Dr Ursula Henninger, a forty-one-year-old woman biologist, who had been trained as a spy when she moved to East Germany in 1948, was sentenced for a whole series of operations first as a secretary in the Max Planck Scientific Institute in Heidelberg, then in an industrial institute for nuclear research in Mannheim, and finally from January, 1961 onwards, while working as librarian in the Euratom organisation in Brussels.

In 1970, Hans Heinz Porst, owner of a multi-million mark mailorder photographic business, was convicted after fourteen years' collaboration with East German intelligence. He had formerly been a member of the communist party in East Germany and had remained a dedicated revolutionary. The mystery of Rear-Admiral Hermann Lüdke, the Deputy Chief of Logistics at N.A.T.O.'s military headquarters in Europe, has never been cleared up. He was found dead in his car in October, 1968, having been shot in the back. At the time he was under suspicion of spying for the Russians but he could equally well have been framed. Either way his death had serious repercussions because he had detailed knowledge of all N.A.T.O. tactical nuclear weapons, ammunition and refuelling depots, as well as of the harbour, railway and road logistics of the Allied forces in time of war. He could even have given away N.A.T.O.'s strike plan in the event of a Soviet attack in the West. Several tactical nuclear weapons had to be relocated as a result of his death.

In February, 1970, came an almost equally disturbing revelation. An eighty-one-year-old retired West German judge, Dr Heinrich

Wiedermann and two women, Liane Lindener, a psychologist, and Irene Schültz who, after being the judge's secretary, had become confidential secretary to successive Ministers of State for Science and Education in Western Germany, were all found to have been working for the East German government for thirteen years. Judge Wiedermann had in fact been dismissed for 'irregularities' in 1950 by Dr Heinemann (then Minister of the Interior in Adenauer's government and later President of the Federal Republic), and subsequently offered his services to the communists. For a salary of about £300 ($750) a month from the Ministry of State Security he proceeded to found and run a company which arranged private loans for West German civil servants; through the hold this gave him over them he then extracted information.

Irene Schültz, described as 'a charming middle-aged lady, popular with her superiors and all her colleagues, trusted by everyone,' had access to top secret cabinet and scientific papers and passed them on to Liane Lindener who ran the group. Photostat copies of the minutes of two cabinet meetings were in her handbag when she was arrested and it is believed that all cabinet minutes for the previous five years have been passed on to the East German government as well as the blueprint of the West German scientific programme for the next decade.

Over and over again the West German government announced that this or that subversive ring had been broken, yet always new rings emerged. Six Germans in Bavaria working for the Polish intelligence service and sixteen agents of the East German trade unions were all arrested in January, 1961; five spy rings comprising 514 agents were uncovered in April and May, 1962, and four more groups, of three agents each, later that same year; five more rings were 'smashed' in 1967; a network of scientists including five nuclear physicists, a microbiologist, and a jet propulsion expert disclosed in January, 1969, at a press conference in East Berlin that they had been sending secret information from West to East Germany for ten years and accused West Germany of planning to use nuclear weapons in conjunction with Israel and South Africa.

The Western Allies claimed that the year 1970 was a bad one for the Communists and that spy rings were broken up in Switzerland, Belgium, Italy, Latin America, Yugoslavia as well as in West Germany; yet at the end of that same year Hubert Schrübbers, head of the Office for the Defence of the Constitution in the Federal Republic, said in an interview on the radio that two agents a day were still being recruited in West Germany by foreign intelligence services, eighty per cent of them by the East German Ministry of State Security.

The student unrest which swept the world in the late 1960s was an opportunity of which the East Germans were quick to take advantage. Ulbricht himself not only wrote an open letter in support of West German extremist 'extra-parliamentary groups', cynically protesting against the infringement of individuals' rights when students were arrested or expelled from their universities, but offered some of their leaders scholarships at the Humboldt University in East Berlin. In the People's Republic such dissident groups get short shrift, but to-day in West Germany they are more numerous than in any other European country.

The League of Democratic Women conducted a relentless campaign to win over the West German housewife. A stream of leaflets and letters sympathising over rises in the cost of living or harping on the terrors of nuclear war was addressed to women in their homes. Invitations to mothers to bring their children to cheap holiday camps in the People's Republic were issued by the thousand. When accepted, as they often were, women and children found their pleasures interlarded with political indoctrination which was part of the camp routine. Even children were made to write letters to their fellow pupils in Western Germany: 'This year I am going to the Baltic coast for a fortnight's holiday. That costs us only 15 deutschmarks. What is the position with you? If the Federal government would do without atomic arms it could use the milliards it spends on them for your holidays . . .' read a letter written in a partly formed handwriting.

It is difficult to assess accurately the effects of this relentless psychological bombardment. The Federal Republic is still thriving, and it can be argued that the communists are no nearer success than they were when Adenauer resolutely set his face against any accommodation with the Russians. Yet opinion has changed dramatically during the last ten years. There is always an argument for reaching an understanding with one's enemy, even if it means appeasement, but it is difficult to believe that the support which Chancellor Brandt received for his *Ost Politik* was not motivated as much by fear as by any genuine hope of rapprochement; and fear is the commodity the communists have extended so much effort to instil.

Perhaps, in this instance, statistics are a significant pointer. According to a report published by the Ministry of the Interior in Bonn in 1971, there have been 35,000 known attempts to recruit agents in the Federal Republic since it came into existence and more than 100,000 recorded assignments connected with espionage, sabotage or other forms of subversion. For every known assignment at least five others are believed to have been carried out. The Federal Government's estimate of the amount of money the Russians spend on espionage and subversion varies from £500m to £800m ($1,250-2,000 m) a year, of which a disproportionate amount finds its way into Germany. The People's Republic consistently spends another £50m ($125 m) and the Poles, Czechs and other East European satellites perhaps £10m ($25 m) between them. At a conservative guess, therefore, the Federal Republic has had to withstand a persistent effort to overthrow its constitution, directed from behind the Iron Curtain, costing about £5m ($12.50 m a week. With the possible exception of Israel, no other country has been subjected to a comparable onslaught. It is no small part of 'the miracle' that, so far, West Germany has not succumbed.

CHAPTER XIV

The End of the Affair

Adenauer's decline began almost as soon as he had celebrated his greatest triumph. In March, 1957, along with the Prime Ministers of five other countries, he signed the Treaty of Rome and took the Federal Republic into the European Community. Marshal Bulganin, the Soviet Prime Minister, thundered against the Treaty as a plan 'designed to serve the interests of Western circles who want to supply West German revenge-seekers with weapons'; the British Government, having failed to get acceptance for its alternative proposal for a Free Trade Area, went ahead with its peripheral Free Trade Association; President Eisenhower, alarmed by the violence of the Soviet reaction, put forward a plan for an 'inner zone of security' either side of the Iron Curtain which would have condemned Germany to a fatal neutrality. But the parliaments of 'The Six' ratified the treaty and a few months later the West German people, for the first time, gave the Christian Democrats a clear majority at a general election. Adenauer's dream of the twenties, so often misunderstood by his own people, had come true at last.

The clouds that rolled up in 1958 were not of Adenauer's making and came from an unexpected quarter. All through 1957, successive French governments had wrestled ineffectively with the Algerian problem. Mollet, the Socialist leader, who began as a reformer and ended by doing what the army told him, was brought down in May. Bourgès-Maunoury, the Defence Minister who succeeded him, followed in September, after which France was without a government for five weeks. By 5th November, when forty-four-year-old Felix Gaillard took office, the situation had passed beyond the control of any coalition government. It had become clear that only de Gaulle could save France from civil war. Suddenly the future of the fledgling European Community hung in the balance once more.

Adenauer did not know de Gaulle, but much that he knew about him was disturbing. He had read de Gaulle's memoirs carefully and, while recognising the services he had rendered France, had few illusions about his character. He seemed to be a nationalist whose vision of France belonged to another century. Adenauer realised that de Gaulle had clung to his belief in the dismemberment of Germany until the last possible moment,[1] and was apprehensive about de Gaulle's extreme touchiness. He remembered the General's bitter opposition to the 'half-baked idea' of a European Defence Community and recalled that he had promised, if he were ever returned to power, to repeal the Treaty of Rome. 'France shall not be Germany's valet,' the General had growled to Debré, who had been only too willing to broadcast the insult. De Gaulle's hatred of the Americans boded ill for N.A.T.O. and therefore for West Germany's security.

Above all Adenauer was apprehensive of the General's ambivalence towards the Soviet Union. His war-time flirtation with Stalin, his constant reiteration of the theme of a Europe from the Atlantic to the Urals, his assertion that the reunification of Germany could only be brought about, if at all, by negotiation with both East and West, all suggested not only that the traditional leanings of France towards Russia might be revived under a Gaullist régime, but that the General might well contemplate an alliance with the Soviet Union as a substitute for dependence upon the United States.

Adenauer's fears were confirmed by some of the inquiries he made during the summer. He had been puzzled by the failure of the French communists to do anything effective to prevent de Gaulle's restoration and even more by the silence of the Kremlin. He asked his Intelligence services for an explanation. The answer came back that the communist world regarded de Gaulle as an asset and possible ally. Khrushchev apparently entertained the hope that the General's contempt for supra-national organisations would break the newly-formed European Community and his jealousy of the United States wreck N.A.T.O. And since none of the Western Powers was backing France in Algeria the Russians, who had only tardily recognised the F.L.N., were seriously considering switching once more in the hope that de Gaulle might turn to them in his isolation. Looked at from almost any angle the arrival of de Gaulle on the scene threatened Adenauer's life-work at the moment of fruition.

1 He could not know that the first question de Gaulle was to put to Couve de Murville when he appointed him Foreign Secretary a few weeks later was: 'How much still remains of my policy for the dismemberment of Germany?' Couve de Murville replied: 'Nothing.'

De Gaulle had read Adenauer's mind and had seen the chink in the formidable old Chancellor's armour. 'By a stroke of good fortune,' he wrote later in his memoirs, 'Konrad Adenauer, of all Germans the most capable and most willing to commit his country alongside France was still at the head of the Bonn government . . . This Rhinelander was imbued with the sense of the complementary nature of Gauls and Teutons which once fortified the presence of the Roman Empire on the Rhine . . . This patriot was aware of the barriers of hatred and distrust which the frenzied ambitions of Hitler, passionately obeyed by the German masses and their élite, had raised between this country and all its neighbours and which France alone, he knew, by offering the hand of friendship to the hereditary enemy, could succeed in breaking down.'[2] De Gaulle wasted no time in putting 'this Rhinelander' to the test.

In his *Memoirs*, de Gaulle goes on to say that, 'As soon as he (Adenauer) realised that my return was something more than an interlude, the Chancellor asked to see me.' Adenauer did nothing of the sort. What happened was that de Gaulle, having failed to bully Eisenhower and Macmillan into accepting France as the third member of a triumvirate which should rule N.A.T.O. (a demand that could only have been met by relegating all the other member countries, including the Federal Republic, to an inferior status) was now embarking on the long journey which he intended should end by shedding all dependence on the Anglo-Saxons and making France the undisputed leader of an independent Western Europe. His first step was the seduction of the German Chancellor.

Throughout the summer of 1958, de Gaulle sent a steady stream of emissaries to Bonn. To begin with, they were mostly politicians who came unofficially to sound out opinion. However, from the middle of July, the visits became more serious. First came Maurice Picard, Prefect of the Department of Yonne and a man close enough to de Gaulle to be able to tell Adenauer that, although the General did not feel he could issue a formal invitation since there was no specific reason for an exchange of ideas at that moment, he hoped the Chancellor might follow the example of Eisenhower and Macmillan and invite himself.

Picard was followed in the same month by Couve de Murville who had just relinquished his post as Ambassador in Bonn to become

2 *Memoirs of Hope*, Charles de Gaulle. Trs. Terence Kilmartin, Weidenfeld & Nicolson, London, 1971, pp. 173–4; Simon and Schuster, New York, 1972.

Foreign Secretary. De Murville suggested that Adenauer's visit might attract less attention if he stopped in on his way back from the holiday he was about to take at Cadennabia, on Lake Como. Then, at the beginning of August, de Gaulle himself spoke to von Maltzan, the German Ambassador in Paris, and suggested that the Chancellor might prefer to pay a private visit to La Boisserie, de Gaulle's country house on the Marne, rather than go to the Elysée. Had Adenauer been the world's greatest heiress and de Gaulle a penniless suitor, no more elaborate precautions could have been taken to make sure that the first meeting was a success.

After much hesitation Adenauer agreed and said that on his way back from Lake Como he would stop at Baden-Baden and from there motor to Colombey-les-Deux-Eglises.[3] Finally Antoine Pinay, a former critic of de Gaulle but the first politician of the Fourth Republic to approach the General in that fateful May of 1958, and now Vice-President of France, paid Adenauer a visit while he was at Cadennabia. Adenauer liked and trusted Pinay who was able to dispel some of his worst fears. At last the stage was set.

De Gaulle's thoroughness paid off. On Sunday, 14th September, as Adenauer drove through Strasbourg to the Marne, he was still nervously wondering whether de Gaulle's whole outlook was not so different from his own that a meeting of minds would prove impossible. However, no sooner had he stepped out of the car at La Boisserie, to be greeted at the front door only by de Gaulle and his wife, than the spell was cast. De Gaulle invited Adenauer and his companions to sit down immediately to lunch and, when the meal was over, suggested that Couve de Murville take Von Brentano, the German Foreign Secretary, and those who were with him for a drive, not to return before supper. Then, in the presence only of an interpreter, who was seldom called upon since each understood the other's language, the two leaders sat down in the library for four hours of talk, interrupted only by a short walk in the garden in the middle of the afternoon.

De Gaulle began by asking Adenauer if he would like to describe the international situation as he saw it, adding the hope that they might be able to help each other. Adenauer replied at length, saying in particular that he thought extreme nationalism in Germany was no longer a danger, expressing high hopes of the new Europe and gratitude to the United States from whom, nonetheless, Europe

3 *Erinnerungen* 1958–1959, Konrad Adenauer, Deutsche Verlags-Anstalt, Stuttgart, p. 425.

must make itself independent as soon as possible. He went on to say that the Soviet Union must be regarded as an Asiatic dictatorship and quoted an American's remark that Britain was like a rich man who had lost all his property but did not know it. For his host it was the perfect cue.

De Gaulle at once seized upon the points that would please Adenauer. He agreed that there had been a change in Germany, but added that if Teutonic drum-beating was no longer a danger, it was quite otherwise in France. His most difficult task, he continued, with an oblique reference to Algeria, was to bring French nationalists down from the clouds to face reality. With infinite tact he then went on to describe the 'sickness' through which the French people were passing. A people who had been great but, even more important, had always believed themselves destined to play a leading part in the world, had failed to understand that they no longer had the means with which to fulfil such a role. As a result they tended to turn to communism or escape into intellectual anarchy.

Since de Gaulle had spent his whole life trying to convince his countrymen of exactly the opposite and was to employ the decade of power which lay ahead of him to give France just the role he was then decrying, this whole passage was a sublime example of hypocrisy. Adenauer however, failed to notice it. Although later he would occasionally recall these words and express surprise that the General did not seem to be behaving quite consistently, at the time he was overwhelmed.[4] 'De Gaulle in no way resembled the conception of him that one must have gained from reading the press in the last few months,' he wrote later. 'He was a totally different man . . . as a politician I did not get the impression during our talks of a nationalist such as he had always been depicted.' The spell had not only begun to work, it endured.

Some differences emerged from their conversation. Adenauer set more store by N.A.T.O. and the American military presence in Europe than the General, although de Gaulle was by no means yet ready to dispense with them. Adenauer was openly hostile to the Soviet Union and saw the European Community as the only means of survival, whereas de Gaulle was still dreaming of a Europe from the Atlantic to the Urals and, although accepting the Treaty of Rome in principle, was utterly opposed to the supra-national character the Community had so far assumed. But the area of agree-

4 *Erinnerungen* 1955–1959, Konrad Adenauer, pp. 425–6.

ment was wide. Although Adenauer had shed crocodile tears over Britain's refusal to join 'The Six', it is plain from both accounts of the conversations that he and his host were equally relieved at her absence. Above all they were united in the conviction that Europe could only be rebuilt, and the world saved, by the closest possible understanding between France and Germany. Although Adenauer had been warned by his colleagues and officials against making any definite commitments, the two men began there and then to formulate the method of their future collaboration.

Two months later de Gaulle returned Adenauer's visit. Accompanied by Debré and Couve de Murville, he met Adenauer, Von Brentano and, surprisingly, Erhard, at Bad Kreuznach. Here 'the direct and special links' were established which, as de Gaulle later recounted, were to lead to fifteen meetings between the two leaders in the next two years involving more than a hundred hours of conversation 'either in private or with ministers in attendance or in the company of our families.'[5] In the same period they exchanged letters on more than forty occasions. In other words the Franco-German Treaty was in operation, and from de Gaulle's point of view at its most effective, five years before it was formally signed.

But although the desire to end the centuries-old enmity between the two peoples was deep and genuine in both men, Adenauer never really understood de Gaulle or the game he was playing. Amazed and delighted at the General's 'simplicity and naturalness' during their first meeting, he could never bring himself to admit afterwards that his new friend was capable of dissimulation, far less duplicity. To Adenauer friendship with France literally meant turning the Rhine into 'a street' instead of 'the ditch' across which the two peoples had fought each other for so long; but de Gaulle saw it as a means to an end. He had gauged accurately the sense of guilt and inferiority under which the Germans still laboured and the gratitude they would feel at his gesture; he saw clearly how to turn both to the advantage of France.

The General immediately put the Chancellor to the test. Although Adenauer was well aware that the French were no substitute for the Americans as the defenders of Europe, he made no serious protest when de Gaulle withdrew the French Mediterranean Fleet and several fighter squadrons from the N.A.T.O. command in February, 1959, nor when, in June, the General refused to allow the United

States to stock-pile nuclear weapons on French soil. He did not even comment publicly when, in November, de Gaulle told the officers of the Centre for Advanced Military Studies in Paris that if a country like France had to make war, it must be *her* war and that the 'system known as integration' was dead. Yet by the other N.A.T.O. partners this speech was taken as formal notice that France was about to leave the organisation.

Admittedly Adenauer had some excuse for reticence. Ever since November, 1958, when Khrushchev had threatened to make a separate peace with East Germany and hand over control of all routes into Berlin to the People's Republic, the Russians had been putting extreme pressure on the Western Allies to sign a Peace Treaty for the whole of a neutralised Germany. The pressure was well-timed because, apart from de Gaulle's refractoriness, the whole North Atlantic Treaty was due to be revised at the end of its first ten years and both a Presidential election in the United States and a general election in Britain were in the offing. As Adenauer knew only too well, the leaders of Anglo-Saxon democracies were always susceptible to talk of 'peace' at such times. Both Eisenhower and Macmillan had already shown that they were prepared to consider some fresh arrangement over Berlin which would affect the relations between the Federal and People's Republics. In February, 1959, much against Adenauer's advice, Macmillan had paid a sudden visit to Moscow; since when he had been pressing his allies to agree to a 'summit' meeting at which the whole German question could be discussed.

Adenauer was convinced that any compromise with Khrushchev would be fatal both to Berlin and the Federal Republic and ultimately to the newly-born European Community as well. To his surprise, he found an ally in de Gaulle. The General was still deeply embroiled in Algeria and, whatever his feelings towards N.A.T.O., was not yet in a position to dispense with the American umbrella. In his talks with Adenauer, therefore, he had agreed that they must together 'stiffen' the Anglo-Saxons. When, in December, the three Western leaders met in Paris, de Gaulle supported Adenauer against Eisenhower when the latter suggested that the rights of the Allies in Berlin were of little value and should be used as bargaining counters. Eisenhower backed down.

Yet, within a month, de Gaulle was showing how fickle he could be. Although maintaining in public that the American Alliance was essential to Europe and that France would sustain it, he authorised Debré and Couve de Murville to tell Adenauer, during the talks preparatory to the projected 'summit', that France and Germany must be ready to share the responsibility for the defence of Europe because the Americans were definitely going to pull out. A few weeks later the General forced Pinay to resign because of his open opposition to de Gaulle's European policies and then, in March, 1960, to Adenauer's consternation, received Khrushchev in Paris for a visit preparatory to the 'summit' which was scheduled for May. Adenauer was seriously perturbed and was considering writing a special letter to de Gaulle deploring the deterioration in their relations when Pinay arrived in Bonn. Once more, Adenauer poured out his heart to him.

The Chancellor could not bring himself to believe that de Gaulle was playing a double game. He admitted to Pinay that he sometimes found it difficult to understand his friend's mind but, with touching credulity, said that he thought the contradictions in the General's behaviour sprang from the fact that two ideas struggled for supremacy, the greatness of France on the one hand and Europe on the other. Pinay had no such illusions. The robust old politician told Adenauer that de Gaulle suffered from overweening pride and wanted always to be in control. Adenauer demurred. He had found the General neither proud nor devious. Pinay stuck to his guns and shocked Adenauer by explaining that he had not resigned but had been sacked by de Gaulle.

Nevertheless, Pinay not only reassured Adenauer but dissuaded him from sending his letter. He argued that, once the Algerian question was out of the way, de Gaulle would become more amenable to public opinion because he needed the support of the masses in his struggle with Parliament; and public opinion was against a deal with Khrushchev and wholly in favour of close Franco-German understanding. Adenauer allowed himself to share this wishful thinking.

Yet from the Chancellor's point of view, things were going from bad to worse. The French had successfully exploded their first atomic device in the Sahara (on which Adenauer had congratulated de Gaulle) and now, shortly after Pinay's visit, the General presented his prodigiously expensive plan for an independent nuclear striking force to the French Parliament. He followed it up with a speech delivered at Grenoble in October, 1960, in which he asserted that no nuclear bombs should be dropped in the Free World without French consent and that if ever such bombs were launched from French soil it would only be because France herself had taken the decision.

But although both the plan and the speech struck at the very roots of the North Atlantic Alliance, upon which the security of the Federal Republic depended, Adenauer's attitude remained equivocal. In one breath, when addressing the Foreign Press Association in Bonn on 10th November, he said the Atlantic Alliance could not be allowed to dissolve into a coalition of national armies and that United States leadership was necessary and natural; in the next – a week later when speaking to a gathering of Christian Democrats – he was emphasising that differences over N.A.T.O. in no way affected the friendship between France and Germany which was now so firm it could overcome all obstacles. When, in private, he raised with the General the cost of the nuclear striking force, he allowed his objections to be brushed aside.

And so the dialogue or, as the General called it, the 'love affair', went on. While Khrushchev was building up the pressure over Berlin in the spring and summer of 1961, General Norstad, the N.A.T.O. Commander, was doing his utmost to counter de Gaulle's wrecking tactics by getting Eisenhower to agree that the Atlantic Alliance should be the fourth independent nuclear power. He got little support from Adenauer though the Chancellor did protest to de Gaulle that the reform of N.A.T.O., about which he assumed they agreed, would be impossible unless France played a leading part. He announced publicly that if France left N.A.T.O. the Federal Republic would follow suit.

But Adenauer warmly supported de Gaulle's plan for a 'European Europe' which would have transformed the Community into a loose confederation of states held together only by 'regular consultations' between governments, although it was opposed by both Benelux and Italy. He seemed crestfallen when it finally ran into the sands in the spring of 1962. In public the Chancellor continued to make polite references to Britain's application to join the Common Market; in private he outdid de Gaulle in deploring the length of time the negotiations were taking and in emphasising that Britain's entry needed the most careful consideration. He echoed Von Brentano's remark that Britain seemed to be made of a 'different wood' from the countries of the continent and not even newly-elected President Kennedy's denunciations of 'national' as opposed to N.A.T.O. nuclear forces could deter him from following the path de Gaulle was so skilfully plotting.

The climax came in 1962. As if to emphasise that the two principal countries would put their ideas about the Community into practice whether their partners liked it or not, Adenauer paid de Gaulle a State Visit in July, and de Gaulle returned the compliment in September. Both were euphoric occasions during which each visitor was visibly moved by the warmth of his carefully prepared and well-publicised reception. 'The backbone of all developments in Europe is the Franco-German relationship,' said the Chancellor to his guest, and assured him that the German people desired a formal Treaty of Friendship as much as he did himself.

De Gaulle was at his most oracular. France and Germany must combine, he said, because they lived under a common threat from the Soviet Union; they must also combine because together they could form the core of a Europe united from the Atlantic to the Urals. His German hosts cheered both thoughts indiscriminately and when he descended into the crowds shaking hands and making little impromptu speeches in their language, he experienced the same sense of mystical communion as he sometimes did among his own *vaches* or *canaille* in the French provinces.

Perhaps in answer to these mutual protestations of undying friendship and admiration, fate suddenly conspired to bring de Gaulle's long courtship to a triumphal conclusion. On 22nd October, 1962, Khrushchev retreated from his wild gamble in Cuba. Next day, by referendum, the French accepted de Gaulle's proposal that in future their President should be elected directly by the people. A month later the General's party won an overall majority in the French Parliament, a feat that had never before been achieved. De Gaulle's last hesitations vanished. Earlier in the summer the French people had endorsed the Evian Agreements through which Algeria gained her independence; now they had confirmed that they wished the General to continue governing them, apparently indefinitely. He himself was finally convinced by Khrushchev's retreat that the Russians would never risk a nuclear war in Europe and that the time had come to throw off the American yoke and rule Europe through the Bonn-Paris axis.

Already Adenauer had become his willing accomplice. Soon after returning from his state visit to Germany, de Gaulle had sent the

Chancellor his proposals for a formal Treaty of Co-operation. Although the monthly, two- and three-monthly meetings of senior Civil Servants, Ministers and Heads of State, which the French envisaged, implied a collaboration so close that the other members of the Community must realise that they had to deal in future with a common front rather than with two equal and separate partners; although such an intimate relationship must make it infinitely more difficult for the Germans to withstand de Gaulle's designs upon N.A.T.O., Adenauer raised no objections. The terms were agreed early in the new year of 1963.

One minor difficulty still had to be overcome. In Brussels the negotiations for Britain's entry were nearing completion. Neither de Gaulle nor Adenauer was in any doubt that, if they reached a successful conclusion, the underlying object of their Treaty would be undone because Britain, by coming to an understanding with Italy and Benelux, could form a counterbalancing axis. Adenauer's own account of his conversations with de Gaulle gives the impression that this would have been as unwelcome to him as to the General. In any case, as soon as de Gaulle knew that the terms of the Treaty were agreed, he called a press conference and, on 14th January, 1963, dismissed Britain's application on the grounds that it would 'completely change' the nature of the Community. As things then stood between himself and Adenauer, this was certainly true.

A week later Adenauer was again in Paris and, on 22nd January, signed the Treaty of Co-operation between France and Germany. Broadly speaking it meant that in future the two countries would try to act as one in all questions of foreign policy and defence (which, of course, included N.A.T.O.), and in everything that concerned the European Community. Each country would encourage its children to learn the other's language in schools and universities; the Departments of Education would co-ordinate their curricula and standards and promote an exchange of students on the largest possible scale. Both Adenauer and de Gaulle were deeply moved by the ceremony. De Gaulle felt that 'the gates of a new Europe' had been opened 'for France, Germany, Europe and in consequence, the whole world.' 'You have expressed the feelings of all those who . . . have shared in this work in such a perfect manner,' replied Adenauer, 'I have nothing to add. Each of your words corresponds to our hopes.'[6] As the two old men embraced tears came into Adenauer's eyes.

However, de Gaulle's triumph was hollow and Adenauer's satisfaction short-lived. There was no country outside the communist bloc that was not glad to see France and Germany reach a genuine understanding; on the other hand, except in France, there was scarcely a parliament or a government in which serious misgivings were not expressed about the manner in which the treaty had been negotiated. Not only had Adenauer's other partners in the Community not been consulted during the negotiations, but Adenauer himself no longer truly represented the German people or even his own party. For the past eighteen months he had been under sentence of retirement. It had only been on condition that he would not remain Chancellor for the full parliamentary term that the Free Democrats had agreed to join his coalition in 1961; now they demanded to know the date on which he would leave office. And the man who had already been chosen by the Christian Democrats to succeed him had been the most consistent and outspoken critic of his dealings with de Gaulle.

Ludwig Erhard had uttered his first threat against de Gaulle even before the French Assembly had confirmed the General in the office of Prime Minister in June, 1958. Germany, he said, might refuse to continue guaranteeing the French deficit in the European Payments Union if the General came to power. Although the threat did not materialise, Erhard's antagonism remained. The following year, in Rome, he made a speech which disturbed not only Adenauer and de Gaulle but some other members of the Community as well. The Common Market, he said, must be considered only as a first step towards a wider free trade area which should include not only Britain but Switzerland and Sweden as well. This was music indeed to Eden and Macmillan and quite consistent with Erhard's thinking, but, according to Adenauer, it so shocked the Italian Prime Minister, Signor Segni, that he told Erhard after the meeting that he could not accept his thesis. Adenauer himself was outraged and wrote Erhard a letter begging him to keep within the bounds of party policy, especially when speaking abroad. Erhard blandly replied that he had always urged the Chancellor to take other members of the cabinet more into his confidence over

6 Keesings Archives, Col. 19209.A.

foreign affairs, but that he was sure that, when the Chancellor read the text of the speech, he would be wholly reassured. In fact Adenauer was more alarmed than ever.

Erhard's indiscretion came at a critical time. According to the Basic Law, Professor Theodor Heuss, who had been President of the Federal Republic since its foundation, must retire in September, 1959, after his second term of office. Heuss's relationship with Adenauer had been so close that the Chancellor would have liked him to stand again, but Heuss was adamant that the Constitution should not be tampered with. A successor had to be found and one, moreover, who would not prejudice the chances of the Christian Democrats at the general election which was due in the autumn of 1961.

Under the Constitution, the President is elected by a college of more than a thousand members drawn equally from the Federal and State parliaments. The Social Democrats chose as their candidate Professor Carlo Schmid, one of the ablest and most engaging men in German public life. But Schmid had always tended towards neutralism and Adenauer was afraid that, if he were elected, the whole fabric, not only of the Federal Republic, but of the European Community as well, would be at risk. He had to find a candidate who would carry both the Christian Democratic Union, which was one short of a majority in the Federal Parliament, and the minority parties as well.

In February, Adenauer set up a small committee of the party drawn both from the Bundestag and the provinces to consider the whole question. The day before it met, Dr Gerhard Schröder, the Minister of the Interior, came to see Adenauer and suggested Erhard as the man. Schröder said he had spoken to Erhard and he seemed to be willing. Adenauer was taken aback. He conceded that Erhard would beat Schmid, for he was popular with both the Christian and Free Democrats, but he had doubts about his suitability as a person.

Adenauer had a genuine admiration for Erhard and gave him full credit for his part in 'the miracle', but he had never thought highly of his political judgement, particularly in foreign affairs. On reflection however, he came to the conclusion that it would be safer to have him as President, where he would have little power and be subject to the Chancellor's influence, than have him perpetrating the sort of gaffes of which he had recently been guilty, with a strong chance of his attaining to the Chancellorship later. Next day the party committee announced that it would propose Erhard for the Presidency.

Erhard, however, was having second thoughts. His popularity in the party was not only due to his economic achievements; he was far closer to the rank and file in his attitude towards Britain and America than Adenauer. Also his great value as an electoral asset would be lost to the party if he became President. His friends, therefore, begged him strongly not to stand for the Presidency but to wait for the reversion of the Chancellorship which would surely be his when Adenauer retired. Astonishingly, Erhard sought Adenauer's advice. The Chancellor urged him to take time for reflection and, above all, to say nothing in public until the full parliamentary committee met on 3rd March. But Erhard was over-persuaded and on that very day, but before the committee could meet, announced to the Press that he would not run for the Presidency. Adenauer was back where he started.

The next move came from the party. On 6th April, the day before the parliamentary committee was to hold its postponed meeting, Dr Heinrich Krone, the leader of the C.D.U. in the Federal Parliament, and three other prominent party members went to see Adenauer and told him that, after carefully considering all possible alternatives, they had come to the unanimous conclusion that he, the Chancellor, was the only man who could be certain of beating Schmid and that he must therefore stand for the Presidency. For Adenauer everything depended upon the choice of Chancellor. The Presidency was tempting because it offered him the certainty of five and the probability of ten further years of office, and no President was likely to wield greater power than he, provided his Chancellor was amenable. When he asked his visitors whom they had in mind for Chancellor they replied unanimously, 'Etzel'. This suited Adenauer perfectly. Etzel, a convinced European but not a particularly forceful man, had been Finance Minister since 1957 but was far closer to Adenauer than to Erhard.

Next day Adenauer met the parliamentary committee and laid before them his ideas of how the President should act. In order to keep informed he should be able to attend cabinet meetings and even take the chair. He should not be bound automatically to follow his Chancellor's advice in home or foreign affairs and had a special responsibility in questions of war and peace. The committee did not demur and later, on its behalf, Eugen Gerstenmeier, the Chairman, asked him formally to run. Adenauer accepted and that afternoon broadcast his acceptance on television saying significantly that he intended 'to safeguard the continuity of our policy for years to come'. Next day he went on holiday to Cadennabia.

But Adenauer was already out of touch. No sooner had he left Bonn than a lively debate broke out in Parliament and Press over the question of his successor as Chancellor. The longer it went on, the stronger the support for Erhard became. On his return Heuss recommended him to have a frank discussion with Erhard and this Adenauer did on 13th April. But Erhard brushed aside his objections, assured him they held the same views and that he would faithfully follow Adenauer's advice in all things except economics, which he could oversee as Chancellor with only 'ten per cent of his working time.' Adenauer was more depressed than ever.

It was a gap that could not be bridged. Erhard was perfectly genuine in thinking that he shared Adenauer's view; he had not only welcomed but made excellent use of the opportunities offered by the Common Market. He saw it, however, as a step to something bigger. On the other hand, although Adenauer never failed to stress the importance of the American Alliance, he had already so far committed himself to de Gaulle's conception of 'The Six' as a 'European Europe' excluding the Anglo-Saxons, that he regarded any more flexible view as treason.

Adenauer was now in a cleft stick. The world had taken it for granted that he would become President and it would be extremely embarrassing to have to withdraw; yet, as he told Krone, if after he had accepted the Presidency, Erhard were chosen as Chancellor, he, Adenauer, would feel obliged to resign. In his heart Adenauer did not accept Erhard's assurances and was not prepared to be a party to any arrangement which might weaken his liaison with de Gaulle. The struggle and heart-searching went on throughout May and into June. Against the advice of his party colleagues Adenauer put his thoughts on paper and sent them to Erhard with a covering letter begging him once more to withdraw his candidature. Erhard came to see him and said bluntly that he wished to be Chancellor and that if Adenauer made it impossible he would resign. Even those who agreed with Adenauer, like Krone, implored him to stick to his decision, stand for the Presidency and accept whatever Chancellor the party chose because of the great damage a withdrawal would do to his reputation. Adenauer would not agree.

On 4th June he wrote formally to Krone withdrawing his candidature. On 5th June, less than a month before the date when a new
President had to be chosen, he published his letter. Using as an
excuse for his action the dangerous international situation which
had arisen as a result of the apparent failure of the Foreign Ministers'
Conference in Geneva, he said that he did not feel it right to shed
his responsibilities at such a moment.

The party leaders were in despair. For three and a half hours they
tried to persuade Adenauer to change his mind; he not only refused,
but said openly that his real reason for staying on was the un-
suitability of Erhard for the Chancellorship. Although Gerstenmeier, the Speaker of the Bundestag, said afterwards that scarcely
one of those present agreed with Adenauer's reasoning, there was
nothing to do but accept his decision. Adenauer's quarrel with
Erhard had already done enough damage; if the C.D.U. leaders now
rejected Adenauer himself they would tear the party to shreds and
make a Social Democratic victory in the coming election a certainty. The meeting, therefore, announced on behalf of the
Christian Democrats, that they accepted Adenauer's decision, had
'unlimited confidence' in him and would continue unreservedly
to support the policies he had pursued for the past ten years. On
1st July, Dr Heinrich Lübke, a Roman Catholic and Minister of
Food and Agriculture in Adenauer's cabinet, was elected President
of the Republic.

Adenauer had done himself irreparable harm. To the world he
appeared as an old man clinging obstinately to power; even to his
own supporters he seemed to be treating with contempt the democratic institutions he himself had created. The charge that he was
behaving like a Nazi, levelled at him by the Opposition, found
echoes far beyond the ranks of the Social Democrats. Not surprisingly, his actions had the opposite effect to that which he intended. Instead of preventing Erhard becoming Chancellor he had
made certain that, if the Christian Democrats were returned to
power, Erhard inevitably would succeed him. By suggesting that he
alone was capable of conducting foreign policy he had confirmed
the suspicions of all those who regarded his intimacy with de Gaulle
as a threat to West German security. Retribution came swiftly.

Erhard had behaved with considerable dignity. He was in
America when Adenauer announced his decision and although he
said that he regretted it because it cast doubt on Germany's capacity

to work democratic procedures, he refused to be drawn into out-right opposition. He pointed out that he would never have been a candidate for the Chancellorship if Adenauer had not decided to run for the Presidency and that he had been a loyal supporter for ten years. Only in regard to Adenauer's assertions that he was an 'opponent' of European integration and 'unfit' for the Chancellor-ship did he demand 'rectification'.

The party saw that he got it. On 10th June, the Parliamentary Group, in the presence of both Erhard and Adenauer, passed a resolution welcoming Adenauer's assurance 'that he had never meant to imply any disqualification of Erhard,' expressing 'special confidence' in Erhard and deploring 'statements likely to damage his reputation.' Adenauer knew it was a slap in the face, but had to accept it. A week later, after giving an interview to the *New York Times* which repeated the imputations, Adenauer was again forced to withdraw.

The general election brought a further humiliation. Throughout 1960 and 1961, when the tension over Berlin was at its height, it was Willy Brandt, the Socialist Lord Mayor who became the national hero rather than the Chancellor who so seldom left his beloved Rhine to visit the beleaguered city. When the votes were counted in October, 1961, the Christian Democrats had lost heavily and the Free Democrats, who like the Social Democrats, had increased their representation, could only be induced to con-tinue the coalition with the C.D.U. on the understanding that Adenauer would not remain Chancellor for the full term of the new Parliament. The old man was becoming a liability.

The end came as a result of the notorious affair of *Der Spiegel*. In October, 1962, *Der Spiegel* published an article under the heading 'Fallex '62', the code-name for the first N.A.T.O. exercise held on the assumption that the Soviet Union had launched a nuclear attack on the West. The author cast serious doubt on the efficacy of N.A.T.O.'s defences and in particular on France's role within them. The article, which was too detailed and authentic to have come from other than official sources, stated that although two-thirds of N.A.T.O.'s nuclear weapons remained intact after the first communist onslaught, its nuclear counter-attack had failed to stem the advance of the 'decimated' communist divisions, which occupied a large part of Germany including Schleswig-Holstein and Hamburg. Of N.A.T.O.'s forty divisions, only the five American were at full strength and there had been a complete breakdown of civil defence and communications.

N.A.T.O.'s battle plan had been based on the assumption that its nuclear counter-attack would be supported by orthodox forces which would strike at the long lines of Russian communication, but because of weak divisions and even more, of de Gaulle's refusal to ascribe to N.A.T.O. the troops which had returned from Algeria, there was insufficient strength to carry the plan out. The general conclusion was that, as the nuclear umbrella was not by itself a sufficient defence, there should be a large increase in orthodox (and particularly West German) forces which should work in future in close harmony with the Americans.

Such an article, appearing just after de Gaulle and Adenauer had exchanged state visits, was doubly unwelcome to the Chancellor because it exposed the hollowness of de Gaulle's claim that he stood by the N.A.T.O. Alliance; for a different reason it also in-validated the whole basis of the strategy of his Defence Minister, Franz Joseph Strauss. For Strauss had been resisting American demands for larger orthodox forces in the belief that nuclear weapons could do the job more effectively and more cheaply. 'A single bomb is worth a whole brigade,' he had often said. Now it seemed that Strauss was wrong and Adenauer must face the pro-spect of nearly doubling the strength of the German Army which would be distasteful to his own people and even more to de Gaulle, who would accuse him of kow-towing to the Americans and acquiescing in the exposure of France as the weak link in the Alliance.

Whether or not Adenauer ordered the proceedings which fol-lowed, he certainly connived at them and could have stopped them had he so wished. On the day after publication of the article, Federal Police searched and sealed the offices of *Der Spiegel* in Hamburg and Bonn and arrested Rudolf Augstein, the proprietor, Claus Jacobi, one of his Managing Editors, and several other members of the staff. The following day Dr Conrad Ahlers, the author of the article, was detained by Spanish police at Torremolinos, where he was on holiday with his wife, and escorted back to Germany by air. Be-tween then and the end of the year several others, including two Colonels of the Federal Military Intelligence Service, were also arrested. On 2nd November, the Federal Prosecutor announced that the charge against *Der Spiegel* had been laid by a Professor

Freidrich August Freiherr von der Heydte, a Würzburg Professor of Constitutional Law, a Brigadier of the Army Reserve and several other private persons. On 20th December, a preparatory judicial examination on allegations of treason and disclosure of State secrets was opened by the Federal Prosecutor against Rudolf Augstein and others.

The outcry was tremendous. Dr Wolfgang Stammberger, the Federal Minister of Justice and one of the five Free Democrats in the cabinet, resigned because he had not been told of the impending action. The State Ministers of the Interior asked for a conference because state police had been used by the Federal Authorities without permission of the State Governments. The Chief Burgomaster of Hamburg threatened to investigate the legality of the steps taken by Federal officials and the Hamburg Senate protested against the way the investigation was being conducted.

Der Spiegel reacted vigorously. A manager, who was also arrested shortly afterwards, said that all the material published had been submitted to and passed by the appropriate authorities and that in any case most of it had appeared before in different papers; it also, unsuccessfully, challenged the actions of the Federal Government in the courts. However, the magazine continued to appear, to defend itself and to attack the Government.

The details of the case are no longer of great importance because, one by one, the charges were withdrawn for lack of evidence. But Adenauer's role is significant. At first it seemed that neither he nor Strauss had played any part in the proceedings. On 2nd November, in a speech at Nuremberg, Strauss rebutted accusations that he had initiated the action to avenge himself for the attacks which *Der Spiegel* had made on him saying; 'I have had nothing to do with the matter in the truest sense of the word.' In the debate in the Bundestag which began on 7th November, Dr Hocherl, the Minister of the Interior, said that neither Adenauer nor Globke, his State Secretary, had known in advance of the action against *Der Spiegel*. However, later in the debate Strauss admitted that he had instructed the German Military Attaché in Madrid, without informing Schröder, the Foreign Secretary, to tell the Spanish police that a warrant for the arrest of Dr Ahlers had been issued in the Federal Republic. Later that month, after Strauss had been forced to resign, he and Adenauer issued an agreed statement in which it was said, in defence of Strauss, that the Chancellor had especially emphasised the need for secrecy about any moves against *Der Spiegel*. Then, on 6th December, in reply to questions tabled by the Opposition, the Federal Government stated that the reason why the then Minister of Justice, Dr Stammberger, had not been informed of the intended action by the Federal Prosecutor was that the Chancellor had issued instructions that the number of those to be informed was to be kept to a minimum. That same day, in contradiction to the previous statement made in agreement with Strauss, Adenauer's office denied that he had issued any instructions at all.

Out of this welter of assertions and denials two things emerged. Both Adenauer and Strauss did know in advance of the action to be taken against *Der Spiegel*. Adenauer not only approved of it but was particularly anxious to preserve secrecy, presumably because it had been arranged that the charges should be laid by private individuals and he hoped to make it appear that the Government was neutral. Yet in spite of saying in the Bundestag debate that it was wrong for Parliament to interfere in matters that were sub-judice, he went on to declare that the country was 'faced with an abyss of treason' systematically practised by a publication 'for the sake of financial gain.' 'Who is this Herr Augstein who prospers on treason?' he asked, and repeated much the same charge outside the Chamber when campaigning for Strauss in the Bavarian elections which took place later that month.

As fifty-three professors and lecturers of Tübingen University remarked in one of a series of protests from academic bodies, in the old-established democracies a crisis of the dimensions then facing Adenauer would have brought about the resignation of the Cabinet. But Adenauer had an exceptional reason for hanging on. Throughout those tumultuous days when he was accusing Augstein and defending Strauss, the terms of his treaty with de Gaulle were being agreed. If he had resigned, as he was pressed to do, the treaty might never have been signed. When, therefore, Dr Mende, the leader of the Free Democrats, said that his party would not re-enter the coalition unless the Chancellor named a date for his retirement, Adenauer set it nine months ahead, in September or October, 1963.

But by now not only the Opposition but his own party and the other partners in the European Community and N.A.T.O. were thoroughly alarmed. In March the Socialist parties of 'The Six' issued a statement saying that the Franco-German Treaty was unacceptable as it stood and that its aims could have been better achieved within the framework of the Community and without a bilateral pact. Professor Hallstein, President of the European Commission, feared that the co-ordination of the policies of 'The Six' might be retarded by bilateral consultation, particularly if it meant a bloc vote within the organisation.

When the Treaty came to the German Parliament, the Upper House, consisting of members of the State Governments, insisted on amending the Ratification Act of the Bundestag by a resolution which might have been drafted by Erhard himself. While welcoming reconciliation and friendship between the two peoples, it requested the Federal Government to implement the Treaty so as to strengthen 'the close partnership between Europe and the United States', the common defence within N.A.T.O. and the integration of the Allied forces; to achieve the unification of Europe through the integration of Britain and other countries, the reduction of trade barriers between the Community, Britain and the United States within G.A.T.T., and the realisation of German reunification. In other words the Bundesrat qualified the Treaty by restoring all the elements of Federal foreign policy which de Gaulle had sought, and Adenauer had agreed, to eliminate.

Before the Treaty reached the Lower House, a delegation of Adenauer's own party, led by Schröder, his Foreign Secretary, visited him at Cadennabia where he was on holiday, and demanded that the Bundesrat's resolution should become the formal Preamble. Although he knew that in de Gaulle's eyes this would undermine the Treaty's whole purpose, he could do no more than meekly accept. On the condition laid down by Carlo Schmid that the Preamble had the same force as the rest of the Treaty, the Lower House unanimously ratified it.

Adenauer was now a pathetic figure. The foreign policy for which he had refused the Presidency had been taken out of his hands by the supporters of the man he had rejected as his successor but who was waiting to step into his shoes. Adenauer could preside over the first meeting of French and German Ministers in Bonn and say that it had been almost a 'joint Franco-German Cabinet meeting,' but except for the creation of a Youth Office to facilitate student exchanges, no progress was made on any important subject. Secretly even de Gaulle must have been glad to say good-bye when Adenauer visited him at Rambouillet in September; he had already noticed Adenauer's loss of influence in Bonn and knew that the old man would have soon become an obstacle to the new course of action he was planning.

For it was de Gaulle who first violated the Treaty. Piqued by the Preamble, which Erhard strictly observed as soon as he became Chancellor, de Gaulle began to act in total disregard of the clauses he had so carefully drafted. The most important stipulated that neither government would take any major decision on foreign policy without consulting the other. In January, 1964, de Gaulle, without formally consulting even his own Cabinet, suddenly recognised China. This was a major shock to the whole of the Western world. He followed it by a whole series of gestures, taken entirely on his own initiative, which were calculated to show the Germans that, as far as he was concerned, the Treaty was a dead letter. In the spring of 1964, he sent a Parliamentary Delegation to East Germany, an act of blatant provocation. Soon afterwards he received Nicholas Podgorny, one of the more important Russian leaders, in Paris. Knowing that the Germans had aligned themselves with the Americans over Vietnam, he came out with a plan for the unification of the two halves of that country under a pledge of neutrality.

To drive home these lessons de Gaulle then went on his rogue-elephant tour of the Americas during which he stimulated every conceivable brand of opposition to the United States, adding Britain and Canada to his list of injured friends when, at the end, he advocated the secession of Quebec. He courted the countries of Eastern Europe and concluded extensive agreements with them and with the Soviet Union, as a result of which they relieved him of his surplus wheat, enabling him to bully his partners in the Common Market the more effectively to accept the French agricultural policy. In February, 1965, de Gaulle pronounced that the reunification of Germany could only come about within a Europe from the Atlantic to the Urals and followed his statement by receiving Andrei Gromyko, the Soviet Foreign Minister, in Paris and then paying an eleven-day visit to the Soviet Union himself later in the summer.

Erhard kept his head. He protested against de Gaulle's actions but continued to meet him at regular intervals according to the terms of the Treaty. When, in the summer of 1964, the General made a frontal attack, listing the 'sins of omission' committed by the Germans and threatening to 'change the direction' of French policy unless they mended their ways, Erhard replied with dignity that his country was dependent neither on France nor America, and could not be relegated to a political no-man's-land or to the inferior rank of a country without a history. In the spring of 1965, even Adenauer, who was still Chairman of the Christian Democratic Union, wrote a letter of protest to de Gaulle. Although he had previously criticised Erhard for trying to achieve political collaboration with 'The Six' instead of with France alone, he now felt that de Gaulle was endangering the whole concept of Western Europe.

Erhard, therefore, can claim credit for having restored German foreign policy to what it was before Adenauer met de Gaulle, but he also fulfilled another of Adenauer's prophecies. He was not a successful Chancellor. This was due partly to Adenauer himself, who did not hesitate to snipe from the wings and keep alive a 'Gaullist' faction, but also to a faulty sense of timing. Erhard's efforts to galvanise 'The Six' into close political collaboration came at a time when the Community was engaged in a life and death struggle over one of the Treaty's basic principles, a common agricultural policy. A modern Moses preaching unity to Jews and Arabs could scarcely have had less impact. Neither his geniality, optimism nor brilliance as an economist could disguise, even from himself, the fact that he was not a politician. When in October, 1966, the five Free Democratic members of his Cabinet resigned over his budget proposals – ironically the great free marketeer had increased taxes – he wisely said he would not stand in the way of a new coalition.

But the coalition which followed, although it was called 'Grand', was little more than an interregnum. The Free Democrats overplayed their hand and Dr Kurt Kiesinger, the Prime Minister of Baden-Wurttemberg, who had succeeded Erhard as Chancellor, invited the Social Democrats to join him. For three years Kiesinger and Willy Brandt, the Socialist leader who became Vice-Chancellor and Foreign Secretary, worked in uneasy partnership with only the splinter parties in opposition. As almost always happens with such coalitions, they achieved less together than either would have done alone or with a less powerful running mate, but they earned one melancholy distinction. It was during their joint term of office that the final curtain was rung down on the great Franco-German 'Affair'.

As a loyal disciple of Adenauer, Kiesinger tried to revive the old intimacy, but although de Gaulle rewarded him by saying that he 'had breathed new life into the Treaty,' in reality the General was only disguising his own defection. Already he had withdrawn from the N.A.T.O. Command; now, in November, 1967, as the first elements of his nuclear striking force came into being, he threw off all pretence that he had ever regarded the American Alliance as anything but a temporary convenience and casually declared that, if France was to be truly independent, her defence in future must be directed against 'all points of the azimuth,' including, of course, those which indicated her partners in N.A.T.O., the Community and her special friend, the Federal Republic. De Gaulle had 'changed direction' too far. There was never the slightest hope that the Axis could be revived.

By then Adenauer was dead and a year later de Gaulle had once more resigned through pique rather than policy. Ironically it was only in the hands of new men with new horizons that the Treaty, which the two gnarled old statesmen had concocted as a plot, became of true value as a genuine reconciliation of peoples. To-day, Adenauer at least, would acknowledge that his work had not been wholly wasted. Yet while he lived the Treaty had been a digression which had cost his country much of the influence his earlier achievements and its economic strength had earned it. In 1969 there was a political vacuum, not only in Germany but in Europe, waiting to be filled.

CHAPTER XV

Dancing with the Bear

Willy Brandt brought a breath of fresh air into European politics. Until he became Foreign Secretary at the end of 1966, almost all the leaders of the Free World had either been politicians in the thirties or had made their mark in the war. Harold Wilson had brought new men to lead Britain, but their role still seemed indeterminate; of the new generation only John Kennedy had flashed across the political firmament like a meteor, to be suddenly and tragically extinguished.

Brandt was different. He had glamour, but of another kind than Kennedy's. He was only fifty-three years old but the lines on his face and round his eyes spoke of suffering and struggle. Yet his smile transformed his expression and his blue eyes looked directly but kindly at those to whom he spoke. He possessed great vigour but in some ways seemed prematurely old.

Brandt had been born in Lübeck at the beginning of the First World War, the illegitimate son of a nineteen-year-old shop assistant to whom he was an embarrassment. He never knew his father and never tried to find him. The baby was given his mother's name, Herbert Ernst Karl Frahm, and was brought up by his grandfather, a lorry driver and a passionate socialist who later was to take his own life partly through illness but also in horror at what Germany had become under the Nazis. Besides his grandfather the strongest influence in Brandt's early life was Dr Julius Leber, leader of the Social Democrats in Lübeck, later to be hanged for his part in the plot against Hitler. When Leber was arrested in 1933 Frahm, as he still called himself, organised a demonstration and later that year went to Berlin for the first time as a member of the anti-Nazi underground. There he was given the code name 'Willy Brandt' which he has used ever since. He was then nineteen years old.

Within a few weeks of arriving in Berlin, Brandt had to take the first major decision of his life. The Nazi round-up of communists and socialists had begun and he was a marked man; he had to decide whether to stay in Germany or flee. He escaped from the little port of Travemunde on the Baltic coast and reached Oslo in Norway. The decision, for which he is still criticised and has even been called a traitor, was one made only by those who believed deeply in communism or democracy and could therefore reject the battle cry 'my country right or wrong'; since organised opposition had already crumbled, it was also a decision which each individual had to take for himself. Brandt not only had the courage to escape, he came back to Berlin before the war broke out to continue his work in the underground, and escaped again. By this time he had been deprived of his nationality by Hitler and, having become bilingual, took Norwegian citizenship. Brandt earned his living as a journalist, among other assignments reporting the Spanish civil war, and at the same time ran a socialist anti-Nazi bureau in Oslo. He had become quite well known and, had the Germans caught him when they occupied Norway in 1940, would undoubtedly have been executed. Once again, however, Brandt escaped, this time putting on Norwegian army uniform and becoming a prisoner of war. His fellow prisoners not only protected him but helped him cross the frontier into Sweden where he remained until after the German surrender.

In 1947, Brandt made the second crucial decision of his career. He was well liked in Norway, had married a Norwegian wife, and had excellent prospects either as a journalist or in the Norwegian foreign service which he considered entering. But he was sent back to Germany to report the Nuremberg trials for a Norwegian newspaper and decided to stay. In face of so much misery and devastation he felt it impossible to return to the comparative ease and security of Oslo and, within a year, had resumed his German citizenship. Politics were still his main interest and, believing that Berlin would soon again be the capital of a new and reunited Germany, he settled there.

Brandt's stay in Scandinavia had tempered his socialism. 'I think I learned that there is not only one answer . . . and many things have to be put together if one is to help people,'[1] he was to say later. He had discarded the orthodox interpretations of Marx as too rigid, and become a convinced democrat and reformer. Within ten years he was elected Lord Mayor, not of the capital of a re-

1 In a talk with Lord Chalfont on B.B.C. Television 1st December, 1970.

united Germany but of the world's most tormented city. It was then that the world first heard of him.

Adenauer had never liked Berlin, even in its days of greatness, and after the war seldom went there; it was Brandt who epitomised the City's spirit of resistance during those three years when Khrushchev was deliberately building up tension in a final effort to drive out the Western Allies. In speech after speech the Lord Mayor assailed the Russians for their failure to live up to their promises at Potsdam and the German Communists for the odious tyranny they were imposing on a third of the German people. He also sometimes attacked the Allies for not taking a stronger political initiative although, had he been asked to specify what he meant, he might have found it difficult to say, for he was well aware that any military retaliation meant the risk of a third world war. It was Brandt who organised the reception of the flood of refugees and saw to it that, however crowded the transit camps became, the fugitives were passed safely on into the Federal Republic. When in June, 1963, President Kennedy made his lightning visit to the city, it was to Brandt rather than Adenauer that he paid his famous compliment: 'Two thousand years ago the proudest boast in the world was "*Civis Romanus Sum*". To-day in the world of freedom the proudest boast is "*Ich bin Ein Berliner*".'

Already in 1961, Brandt had been chosen by the Social Democrats as their candidate to fight Adenauer for the Chancellorship; six months after Kennedy's visit they elected him leader of the party. The road to the highest office lay open. Yet how could he induce the electorate to change their allegiance in face of the continuing 'miracle' on the one hand and the persistent Russian threat on the other?

Brandt's chance came unexpectedly. In 1965, he again stood for the Chancellorship and again was defeated, this time by Erhard. But although Erhard claimed the result as a great personal triumph, the tide had already begun to run against him. The Free Democrats, like the Liberal Party in Britain, were divided between those who believed in free enterprise almost to the point of *laissez-faire* and those who put social reform before further increased prosperity; neither faction was satisfied with Erhard's middle course. Within little more than a year the coalition had dissolved, Kiesinger had replaced Erhard and invited Brandt to join him in a Grand Coalition of the two main parties.

Once again Brandt was faced with a sudden and dramatic decision. Many of the most prominent Social Democrats urged him to refuse Kiesinger's offer, partly because of the new Chancellor's early association with the Nazi Party but also because they mistrusted Strauss, who was to be a member of the cabinet. Their stand was upheld in the country as a whole when seven out of eleven state parties voted against acceptance. But Brandt and a small inner caucus believed that for the sake of the parliamentary party, which had been in opposition for seventeen years, the opportunity of changing the emphasis of German policy should be grasped. After a debate which lasted twenty hours and spread over three days they won a decisive vote. On 1st December, 1966, the Grand Coalition came into existence and Willy Brandt became Vice-Chancellor of the Federal Republic and Foreign Secretary.[2] Although few people suspected it, a new phase of German history had begun.

When the Grand Coalition took office German politics were becalmed. Internal reform was circumscribed by an almost mystical fear of interfering with 'the Miracle' and initiative abroad by the obsessive need to resist communist pressure. Adenauer's shadow hovered over the unexciting programme which Kiesinger and Brandt put forward. There seemed little scope for innovation.

But Brandt was biding his time. He knew that the changes he wanted to make were fundamental and would probably provoke a clash with his coalition partners. He therefore avoided a clash over foreign policy but prepared the ground for future action by encouraging one of those 'experiments in democracy' which he had so often advocated as the best method of strengthening a free society.

Under Article 21 of the Basic Law 'parties which in their aims or attitudes seek to restrict or remove the free democratic order' could be declared unconstitutional in the Federal Republic. As the Communist Party of Germany (K.P.D.) had faithfully followed the policies of the S.E.D. and worked openly to bring all Germany under Communist rule, no one was surprised when, in 1956, the Constitutional Court had declared it illegal. Communists were driven underground and the more prominent fled to the People's Republic. Those who continued the party's work were frequently arrested and tried. But although it was impossible to question the

2 Brandt was succeeded as Lord Mayor of Berlin by his deputy, Heinrich Albertz, an evangelical pastor who had been imprisoned for preaching against the Nazis.

validity of the court's decision, there were many who questioned its wisdom. Social Democrats in particular, had never abandoned their dream of persuading the Russians to be reasonable and felt that the ban on the K.P.D. was just one more obstacle in the way of an understanding.

As soon as the Grand Coalition was formed, an agitation began, instigated by Communists but fanned by Liberals and Socialists, to have the ban removed. Both Brandt and Herbert Wehner, a former communist who had become Minister for All German Affairs, listened sympathetically. The wave of student unrest which spread across the world from China to California and hit Germany in the beginning of 1968, swelled the agitation almost into a revolutionary movement. West German citizens who had begun to feel secure in their prosperity and freedom were suddenly shocked to find that not even the example of Ulbricht's tyranny, from which so many students had fled a few years earlier to found their own Free University in West Berlin, had destroyed their belief in Marxist philosophy.

Yet neither Brandt nor Wehner were deterred. Both held that one of the reasons for unrest was the disappearance of serious parliamentary opposition as a result of the formation of the Grand Coalition, and argued that 'more democracy' was preferable to suppression. Taking their stand on the classical doctrine that a democratic government shows strength when it allows the widest possible discussion on any and every subject, they urged their Coalition colleagues to reconsider the ban.

Dr Heinemann, the Minister of Justice, announced that he saw no legal obstacle to the re-establishment of a communist party provided it was clearly a new party and not the old K.P.D. refurbished; whereupon Kiesinger, the Chancellor, anxious not to be outdone by Brandt in the run-up to the general election of 1969, adopted the palpable subterfuge of accepting a new communist party provided it changed its name. In September, 1968, the German Communist Party (D.K.P.) took the place of the Communist Party of Germany (K.P.D.) as a legal political organisation with Kurt Bachmann, editor of the left-wing Frankfurt weekly *Die Tat* (Action) as its Chairman in place of Max Reimann, the former Chairman of the K.P.D. who remained in East Berlin.[3] Under cover

3 Max Reimann was later allowed to return to the Federal Republic and became an ordinary party member.

of the coalition Brandt had made what he believed to be an unavoidable move towards an improvement in relations between the two Germanies and a better understanding between Western and Eastern Europe.

The sequel seemed to indicate that the people were on his side. Votes began to swing towards the Social Democrats in sufficient numbers to ensure that in March, 1969, Heinemann beat Schröder, the former Foreign Secretary and C.D.U. candidate, in the contest for the Presidency. By the autumn the swing had increased and, at the General Election, the Social Democrats polled nearly two-million more votes than in 1965, winning twenty-two more seats in parliament and becoming the largest party in North-Rhine-Westphalia for the first time.

Brandt felt that he was on the crest of a wave and wasted no time. Although the Christian Democrats were still the largest party in parliament, the Free Democrats, with thirty seats, held the balance. As they had quarrelled with their coalition partners three years before, Brandt had every reason for thinking they might prefer to join him rather than Kiesinger. Within twelve hours of the results being declared he had informed the President that he intended to form a government and, within a week, had reached agreement with Herr Walter Scheel, the Free Democrat leader. On 21st October, 1969, Willy Brandt was elected Federal Chancellor. In the Bundestag his coalition government had a paper majority of twelve which, in view of the questionable loyalty of several Free Democrats, was no better than a working majority of six.[4]

Once Chancellor, Brandt threw off all restraint. As Foreign Secretary he had spoken of Germany's role as a 'bridge' between East and West; now he made a series of proposals which, if successful, would transform that dream into reality. To Poland and the Soviet Union he offered treaties based on a renunciation of force as a means of settling disputes, respect for each other's territorial integrity and a mutual undertaking not to try and change the 'social structure' or interfere with the alliances of their respective states. To Czechoslovakia he offered extra compensation to the victims of Nazism and a trade agreement. At the same time he urged his Western Allies to re-negotiate with the Soviet Union the Four Power Agreement by which they had controlled Berlin. In other

4 Three Free Democrats defected to the Christian Democrats shortly afterwards.

words in return for a resumption of Allied authority he was conceding the *status quo* and reversing more than twenty years of West
German foreign policy.

All Brandt's proposals were accepted. Negotiations between
West Germany and the Soviet Union took place in Moscow and
were quickly completed. The Russians sacrificed nothing, but won
de facto recognition of the Federal Republic's existing frontiers, the
right to a Consulate General in Hamburg in exchange for a similar
West German office in Leningrad, and the promise of a further one
in West Berlin once the Four Power Agreement was concluded. A
treaty to expand trade would follow. The Poles, who desperately
needed to do business with West Germany to offset the economic
consequences of being a satellite, gained almost all they desired,
including *de facto* acceptance of the Oder-Neisse line. They too
signed a treaty before the end of 1970.

Although the Americans, British and French had welcomed
Brandt's initiative and agreed to a Four Power Conference, these
negotiations took longer. It was not the Western Allies who were
obstructive. They agreed, and Brandt accepted, that if the Four
Powers were to resume control of Berlin, the Western Sectors
could no longer be treated as part of the Federal Republic. Those
parts of the Basic Law which asserted the contrary, therefore, had
to be suspended and official functions, such as the election of the
West German President, could no longer take place in West Berlin.[5]
But the Russians had considerable difficulty with the East Germans.
For them the reversion of Berlin to its Potsdam status meant surrendering the control over access to the city which the Soviet
Union had ostentatiously granted them by treaty and accepting once
more Russian control over their capital. This was a bitter pill
which they could be forced to swallow only after Ulbricht had been
replaced as Party Secretary by Erich Honecker, a hardliner for
whom obedience to Moscow was an article of faith.[6]

But although the Agreement was eventually signed in December,
1970, Brandt was already running into difficulties. He had always
stipulated that he could not present the treaties to Parliament for
ratification until the detailed arrangements for the new régime in
Berlin had been agreed with the East Germans. These negotiations
made little progress. Brandt had won many concessions for West

5 According to the East Germans, 166 laws and bye-laws would have to be amended.
6 Ulbricht remained Chairman of the Council of Ministers.

Berliners. Instead of being subject to constant delays and searches, traffic 'by road, rail and water across the People's Republic into Berlin was not only to be unimpeded but to be given preferential treatment so that it moved in the most simple and expeditious manner.' But when it came to interpreting these clauses the East Germans, resentful of their loss of sovereignty, made every conceivable difficulty. For example, if there was 'sufficient evidence' that lorries or railway wagons contained propaganda or other material which the communists might consider 'subversive', then search was to be allowed. But who was to decide what the evidence was? In each case the East Germans claimed that the sole responsibility was theirs and the talks broke down.

Meanwhile trouble for Brandt was brewing at home. Although the Christian Democrats had backed Brandt's early Eastern approaches they had never been more than half-hearted and, when the terms of the Russian treaty were published in August, 1970, had expressed 'decisive reservations'. Dr Rainer Barzel, leader of the Parliamentary party, pointed out that whatever concessions had been won for the citizens of the Federal Republic or West Berliners, none had been granted to the East Germans who remained as strictly incarcerated behind the Iron Curtain as before. He was 'unable to detect an equal balance of concessions by both sides.'

Kiesinger, the party leader, said in an interview on Swiss television that the 'overall conception' of the treaty was wrong because it would 'replace the West European concept by the Soviet concept for Europe.' 'We continue to believe,' he went on, 'that the Soviet Union aims at the gradual extension of its rule over the whole of Europe . . . in whatever form and manner this opportunity offers itself . . .' The Federal Government was showing 'completely unjustified optimism' in assuming that the treaty might deflect the Soviet Union from its purpose.

When the arrangements for West Berlin finally were completed in December, 1971, Barzel, who by then had succeeded Kiesinger as leader of the Christian Democratic Union, went into outright opposition. He was supported by Schröder, the former Foreign Secretary, who believed that the treaties would extend the influence of the Soviet Union in Europe and encourage the 'growing shift to the left' in West German politics, which was exactly what the Russians wanted. The *Bavarian Courier*, a weekly journal of which Franz Joseph Strauss was the proprietor, went even farther and accused Brandt of having concluded a secret agreement with the Soviet Government on his visit to Moscow under which West Germany would withdraw from her Western alliances and become neutral.

Brandt was unrepentant. He described the allegations in Strauss' paper as a totally unfounded 'smear' and gave fresh point to his refutation by going on a second visit to Moscow a few weeks later. There, in a joint communiqué issued by himself and Brezhnev, he defended the treaty as opening 'extensive opportunities' for co-operation in trade, scientific, technical, cultural and sporting 'ties' and in youth exchanges. Both leaders pledged themselves to work for a conference on European Security as soon as possible.

But this announcement only hardened the opposition. Brandt's difficulty was that he was flying in the face of all post-war experience. There was really no evidence that the nature and purpose of the Russian Government had changed. On the contrary, its recent aggression in Czechoslovakia and naval penetration in the Mediterranean and Indian Ocean, suggested a fresh determination to maintain and expand the doctrine of World Revolution. Observers with less roseate spectacles than Brandt's could be excused for regarding the Soviet renunciation of the use of force and the undertaking not to try and change the 'social structure' of the Federal Republic as pure eyewash.

In the view of his opponents, Brandt's case had been further weakened by his resurrection of the West German Communist Party. Certainly all the traditional liberal arguments were in favour of such a course, but it was one thing for a country like Britain, with a long history of democratic evolution behind it, or even for Italy or France, which had buffers between themselves and the Russians, to indulge in liberal purism; it was quite another for West Germany which not only had the Russian Army on its doorstep but was subject to a relentless subversive campaign.

Notwithstanding the denials of socialist and trade union leaders, the Party was daily becoming more effective. Many young socialists were collaborating with the communists rather than with the S.P.D. and evidence published by the Ministry of the Interior in North-Rhine-Westphalia in December, 1970, showed that, within a year of the founding of the D.K.P., left-wing factory newspapers had trebled, reaching a circulation of more than 100,000 in that province alone, and factory cells had more than doubled; 12,000 copies of *The Red Beetle*, which the Party supported, were distributed free to Volkswagen workers at Wolfsburg.

The fears of the Christian Democrats, therefore, were not imaginary. In pursuing his *Ost Politik*, Brandt was running a risk that the campaign to intimidate the West German people into accepting the inevitability of communism would become increasingly effective. The new Consulates General in Hamburg and West Berlin, although they would no doubt increase trade, would also improve espionage and subversion, for it is through such consulates that communist penetration is most effectively carried out. However flagrantly the new Party flouted the Basic Law and sought 'to remove the free democratic order,' it was clear that it would not again be suppressed; and although no one could impugn Brandt's personal devotion to democracy, it was already evident that Ulbricht, Honecker and their colleagues regarded the whole sequence of events which the *Ost Politik* had set in motion as a shot-in-the-arm for the communist cause. There was a new confidence and a new slant in their speeches and writing. At his Party Congress in April, 1970, Ulbricht was already envisaging an 'anti-imperialist' West Germany which, in the not too distant future, would unite with the Peoples' Republic in a single Socialist country. Brandt's programme for the redistribution of property, the extension of co-determination and public ownership, were steps which the Party could support on its road to power. For the first time since the war, a peaceful take-over of West Germany by the communists had become a possibility.

CHAPTER XVI

The Riddle of the Future

Nevertheless, in spite of the risks, Brandt probably was right to take the gamble. If democracy was to take root in Germany, the one thing the political parties could not afford to do was to stand still. After twenty years of Christian Democratic rule the Federal Republic was in danger of becoming a one-party régime. Adenauer and Erhard, each with a touch of genius in his own field, had given the majority of the German people a chance to develop a society free from the crude tyrannies to which they had become accustomed. The people had seized the chance and by a combination of technical skill and hard work had created a community in which poverty had become relative and life unexpectedly secure. And yet the security was partly illusion. No mere police system, subject to the law, can indefinitely hold at bay hostile ideas relentlessly impregnated into the society it protects. If the Federal Republic was to survive, it had to generate a faith in the civilised ideals of a liberal democracy which would inspire its humblest citizens.

Brandt possessed this faith and was deliberately trying to impart it. He was an astute party leader, as he showed when forming the Grand Coalition in 1966 and in seizing power in 1969. He admitted that he was once an ambitious politician. But in 1966 he was dangerously ill and thought he would die; the experience humbled him and left him without burning personal desires and a deeper, more patient resolve. His answer to the Christian Democrats, therefore, was not simply that he had to be different for political reasons; he believed, and said, that the way to meet the communist threat was not by suppression but with 'more democracy.' It was no good being 'afraid of' communism; it was an idea that had to be met and defeated openly. Communists had to be allowed to organise even though they were bent on the destruction of the society in which they lived. The leaders of West German opinion had to develop convictions which could triumph through their own depth. Certainly the liberal society had to defend itself against violent revolution, but the only true security lay in its own self-evident superiority. The West German people had to be sure enough of themselves not only to argue with the communists in their midst but to negotiate unafraid with their communist neighbours. Brandt believed that unless they could do this, the Federal Republic was doomed.

Only time will show whether Brandt's faith is justified. After a tense parliamentary struggle during which he missed being supplanted as Chancellor by two votes, he got his treaties ratified in the summer of 1972. But as the subsequent vote on the budget of the Chancellor's office showed, he had lost his working majority and could continue to govern only at the whim of some fickle back-benchers. Schiller, his able Secretary of the Treasury and Minister of Economic Affairs, resigned. Whereas, in the spring, opinion polls had suggested that Brandt could win a general election handsomely, by the end of July the pendulum had swung against him. His chances in the election which he was forced to accept in December seemed no better than even.

However, Brandt, far from making any concession to public opinion, instructed his negotiator, Egon Bahr, to put a coping stone on the *Ost Politik* by negotiating a final General Relations Treaty with East Germany in the weeks before the election. Bahr succeeded, as the treaty, as a result of which the People's Republic was expected to win international recognition as a sovereign state, was ready for signature before the election campaign was concluded.

Once again Brandt's boldness paid off. When the votes were counted on 19th November, the government coalition emerged with a majority of 48, one of the largest in the history of the Federal Republic. For the first time the Social Democrats became the largest party in Parliament and their partners, the Free Democrats, scored handsomely against the Christian Democratic Opposition; the minor parties were swept into oblivion.

But although Brandt's victory set the seal on his *Ost Politik*, there is no doubt that the real struggle still lies ahead. Brandt has launched West Germany on to a new course of collaboration with its communist neighbours from which neither Barzel nor any other successor will easily be able to turn back unless the communists themselves give them good cause. Whether the West Germans will be able to withstand the pressures to which that collaboration must subject them is another matter.

It would be naïve to suppose that the Russians will desist from their purpose of bringing all Germany under communist control. The treaty formula of altering the frontier of the two German states only 'by agreement' must stimulate rather than diminish communist propaganda, and there is no sign of any relaxation in underground warfare. The solution which many moderate Germans fear is the 'Finlandising' of their country, in other words, Russian insistence on a 'friendly' West German Government which, although not directly under Moscow's control, will be susceptible to Russian influence. Since the United States has supported the *Ost Politik*, is not over enthusiastic about an enlarged Western European Community and is anxious to withdraw some of its troops, American acquiescence is at least a possibility. Some such plan will certainly be in the forefront of Russian minds if and when the Soviet Government gets a European Security Conference off the ground.

The answer to the riddle depends upon the degree to which the ideals of liberal democracy have taken root among West Germans. It is easy to be pessimistic. 'It's all the same to them if they manage the deportation of the Jews from Hungary, a defamation campaign against nuns or the sale of canned chicken. They handle everything beautifully,' says a character in *Halbzeit*, a mammoth novel by the West German author Martin Balser. It is difficult for any of Germany's former enemies over the age of forty-five not to share the feeling that, despite the zeal that has gone into the building of the Federal Republic, West Germany is still a country without a soul.

It can scarcely be a criticism to say that Germans love efficiency for its own sake. The young man who cleans your windscreen and spurns a tip, the girls in the bookshop who so kindly and carefully go through school text books to see if they contain the material you want, the trade union official who insists on your visiting a works council, all give a service which is admirable and ungrudging. And yet, all the time, in the lobbies of the Bundeshaus, on the floor of a factory, in shops, hotels and even in private houses, one feels that the courtesy which is shown (except on the roads) is somehow professional, the result of training rather than instinct.

Of course, such judgements are superficial and highly subjective, yet the feeling is widely shared, even among Germans themselves. Many German writers have tried to analyse what some describe as 'this brittleness' in the German character. Sociologists point to the intellectual schizophrenia which has enabled Germans in the past to develop profound moral philosophies which left untouched their own and their countrymen's lives. Certainly under Hitler, German scholars, bereft of the leavening of the Jews, found little difficulty in providing a moral basis even for the worst aberrations of National Socialism. When they now praise democracy, it is difficult to avoid the suspicion that they are performing the same professional function for new masters. It was the German historian, Hannah Arendt, now an American, who wrote in 1963: 'Even to-day, eighteen years after the collapse of the Nazi régime, it is sometimes difficult not to believe that mendacity and "living a lie" are an integral part of the German national character.'[1]

In trying to answer the question why, until now, liberal democracy has not caught the German imagination, Ralf Dahrendorf, now a German member of the European Commission, suggests that there is a basic inhumanity in his countrymen which is still evident in their patronising attitude to women, their treatment of children and indifference to the aged. Where else, he asks, could the untranslatable expression '*untermensch*' (literally, sub-human being) have been coined? But when he and others see alarming signs of the '*Herrenvolk*' complex in the behaviour of West Germans towards their two million foreign 'guest' workers, they are probably being unjust to themselves. It is certainly not difficult to hear comments such as 'filthy bastards' or 'smelly brutes chasing our girls' in Cologne bars or Munich beer cellars where foreign workers abound but in this Germans are certainly no worse than Anglo-Saxons, and it is worth recording that Cologne Cathedral has been opened to Turkish workers for use as a mosque.

Respect for authority is undoubtedly less supine to-day than under Hitler or the Kaiser, and the importance of status is gradually losing its hold on German society. Opinion polls suggest that professors are now the most revered figures and a respect for titles still lingers in the universities. A professor at Freiburg, who married an English wife and has spent many years in Britain, was concerned about the manner in which two English guests[2] should address the Dean of his faculty. 'You really ought to call him *Spectabilität* and address him in the third person,' he said, 'but I suppose, as you are foreigners, it won't matter if you call him *Herr Professor*.' Although

1 Quoted by Amos Elon, Op. Cit., p. 26.

the modern undergraduate is gradually breaking down the tradition there is still something faintly ludicrous about addressing the Rector (Vice-Chancellor) as *Magnifizenz*.

West Germans often speak of the 'Rule of Law' as if it were a newly discovered talisman capable of exorcising the past and leading the righteous unaided into the paths of true democracy; yet to most of the public the law is still regarded as a weapon of authority rather than as a means of protection for the individual. Of the 50,000 to 60,000 West Germans taken into custody in any year the majority are under interrogation without appearing in court for at least two months and a quarter are usually found to have been wrongly arrested. When a judge remarked casually that of course he assumed that the person in the dock was guilty 'or he would never have got there,' he was making an improper observation; yet he was also reflecting the way the system works. On the other hand there are comparatively few complaints against magistrates and German judges have been fearless in dealing with crimes against humanity, in resisting communist intimidation and in standing up to government pressure in the *Spiegel* and other cases.

It would be possible to lengthen almost indefinitely the list of national weaknesses which, in the eyes of the Germans themselves, make the future of democracy precarious. They complain that the Federal Republic lacks a true capital or any acceptable élite which can set the tone for a democratic society. Admittedly Bonn was an odd choice and any of the thirty-five larger towns would have had more character. Hamburg, Bremen, Dusseldorf, Cologne, Frankfurt and Munich are all great cities in their own right and focal points for separate but distinct societies; but in a Federal State such a dispersal of attraction is not necessarily a disadvantage.

The upheavals of the past century have undoubtedly destroyed the traditional élite of the officer corps and civil service; the aristocracy, which might have filled the gap, has commercialised itself and counts for little. The great West German landowners have turned their castles into hotels instead of inhabited museums as in England, and many have made millions out of real estate and are among the richest of European families. The majority of those who appear in the *Almanach de Gotha* work hard as bankers or businessmen, take little part in public life and marry and entertain each

2 The author and his wife.

other. Titled Germans become consuls for foreign countries but an eccentric prince, championing the liberalisation of laws relating to homosexuality or abortion, upholding the rights of hippies or workers on strike, such as may be found in Italy, Spain or Britain, has yet to emerge.

Some economists and sociologists emphasise that West Germany has undergone a bourgeois revolution and that the middle classes now dominate not only industry but the land as well. Their reaction to catastrophe, so say these writers, has been an orgy of philistinism in which a love of the arts or a passion for ideologies has given way to consumption. 'Eat, drink, travel and spend while the mark is worth so much of other people's money and let the men in Bonn look after the morrow,' is allegedly the middle class motto.

But all these strictures are half-truths and could apply to the people of many other countries. It would be absurd to expect all disturbing German characteristics suddenly to have disappeared; what is important is that they are balanced, and perhaps outweighed, by the changes that have taken place. Federalism, which never really succeeded in eighteenth and nineteenth-century Germany, has worked surprisingly well in West Germany. Besides decentralising authority it has enabled the Social Democrats, who failed for twenty years to win power at Bonn, to exercise it in many of the States. When Brandt finally took office he could form his cabinet of men who had held posts of high responsibility for many years. The new State civil service is gradually training men to take the place of the old Prussian-trained bureaucracy.

Even if there is not yet any widespread or passionate belief in the principles of democracy, its techniques are being practised with considerable skill. In the past an exaggerated respect for authority led to apathy towards politics as a whole and even to-day many people complain that the young, in particular, refuse to take an interest unless they hold extreme views. Yet by British standards the West Germans seem to have arrived at about the right mixture of getting on with their own lives while asserting themselves when it matters. To say this is not to be cynical. The ideal projected by undergraduates of a society in which everyone is directly concerned with every decision affecting their common life could only produce anarchy which, in turn, would lead once more to tyranny. Democracy can only work through representation. The people elect some tens of thousands of their fellow citizens to look after their local and national interests and, if they do not like the results, elect new representatives when the time comes, and try again. The essence of the system is patience and forbearance, coupled with a lively awareness of where one's own interests lie.

The inhabitants of the Federal Republic seem to possess these qualities in at least as great a degree as those of any other advanced industrial country. When extremists of right or left have attempted to persuade West Germans to return to an authoritarian régime, the people have rejected them so overwhelmingly that none has ever won a seat in the Federal Parliament. On the other hand, the large turn-out for the democratic parties at elections is impressive and shows that the people not only wish to use their votes but are prepared to change their allegiance. In the elections of November 1972, no fewer than 91.2% of the electorate voted, a massive turn-out for any democratic country. The six minor parties, which included the Communists and the neo-Nazis, only gained 0.7% of the votes between them.

Once elected, West German representatives have shown that they intend to lead their constituents rather than be their mouthpiece. No doubt as a reaction against the mass murders of the Nazis, the death penalty was abolished by the Basic Law. At the time the reform had overwhelming public support. But as violence and intimidation reappeared, largely as a result of communist subversion, public opinion changed. Yet although something like 80% of the electorate is now believed to be in favour of restoring the penalty, Parliament has steadfastly refused to make a move. It is the same with the trials of war criminals. The public, by a large majority, wishes to bury the past; Parliament, this time supported by a significant section of the Press, insists on continuing them.

The media themselves show a healthy independence. Although, like Axel Springer, a majority of newspapers support the Christian Democratic establishment, there are several critical provincial newspapers and radio and television maintain a high standard of public debate. There is no commercial broadcasting in West Germany, but all efforts by the Federal authorities to convert the public services into an arm of government, as in France, have failed. The nine regional television stations remain autonomous and arrange their networking among themselves. The second channel, which is nation-wide, is run by a public corporation responsible to the State governments.

Not only do television and radio broadcast harrowing documentaries about Nazi crimes, refusing to allow the Germans to forget their past, but the discussions they have mounted on such questions as the Eastern Frontiers, the Common Market, the Berlin Wall (of which Thomas Mann's son Golo, as the chief commentator, said that Hitler rather than the communists was the true mason), have often been more searching than the debates in parliament.

Partly as a result of this mass education, public opinion in West Germany has been evolving in an encouraging manner. No country is so thoroughly cross-examined by opinion polls and the questions are often of a broad political and sociological character. The answers have shown that whereas in 1951, 42% of the people felt that 'Germany's best time' was under Hitler, by 1963 a large majority voted for the present day. That majority has continued to increase.[3] In 1953 as many as 15% of those asked said that they would still vote for a man like Hitler. To-day the number is fewer than 5%. Faith in parliamentary government, in a plurality of political parties and in freedom of speech as the chief bulwark of democracy has grown likewise.

Militarism has receded to an almost unbelievable extent. When the German contingent for N.A.T.O. was constituted it is not too much to say that officers were loathed and soldiers despised. To-day this is no longer the case, but all ranks prefer to be in civilian dress when off duty and, if anything, officers feel themselves too little of an élite; morale and discipline have sometimes suffered. Policemen are still accused of being officious and deal harshly with rioting students, but visitors praise them for their courtesy and at least they are trained to think of themselves as the citizen's friend rather than as his corrector.

Above all, democracy has spread into industrial life to a greater degree than in other European countries. American and British employers may deride *Mitbestimmung* and Works Councils, but the truth is that in West Germany the rigid hierarchical control of industry has been broken down. Trade Union representatives do share in decision making at all levels and there is no doubt that co-determination will soon be the general law of the land. Since it becomes increasingly obvious that a mixed economy cannot preserve a free society if unions and management persist in archaic

3 In April, 1970, eighty-one per cent voted for the present day. Institut für Demoskopie. Allansbach.

antagonism, the West German system offers a hopeful example. This alone goes a long way to justify Brandt's optimism.

Finally, for all the mud that has been thrown at it, 'the miracle' has provided the West Germans with a prosperity which even the most militant trade-unionist hesitates to disturb. It is still possible to find poverty in West Germany, in the caravan sites outside big cities, in the back streets of some of the murkier Ruhr towns and among small farmers; but many of the poor are foreign workers who send a large part of their earnings home to their less fortunate relations. The vast majority of the people live in well-built, well-equipped houses or flats, have secure well-paid jobs and enjoy good holidays. There are almost as many cars per family as in the United States and more West Germans go abroad each year than do the inhabitants of any other European country. They own twice as many colour television sets as the British, and besides schnapps and beer consume more than 12,000,000 bottles of whisky and drink more champagne than the French. Germans of both sexes eat expensively, and pay dearly for the clothes with which they attempt to disguise the fact. They like to organise their leisure and, as in Anglo-Saxon countries, associations exist for every conceivable purpose from butterfly-catching to opera. They have a membership of more than fifteen million people.

It is a vigorous but rather vulgar life without much style or distinctive taste. A rich man's house in the Federal Republic may be full of expensive furniture, good pictures and china; but one rarely sees an attractive room unless it was built before the middle of the nineteenth century. Perhaps to foreigners West Germans lack warmth and humour, but this is true of many races; among themselves they are affectionate and laugh uproariously. The scene in a great Bavarian beer cellar on almost any evening, with every bench packed and an orchestra playing under the vaulted ceiling while men and women wave their mugs and sing, has a spontaneity which many people might envy.

Were West Germany an old established country doubts about its future might well be less disturbing than those felt by the British or Americans about their own. Yet two question marks persist. There is a chasm between the generation which fought the war and its children which will probably never be bridged and which makes prediction more than usually difficult. A week-end spent among students, even at so conservative a university as Freidburg, leaves the visitor perplexed. It is not the *Korporationen*, the duelling clubs, which are disquieting, even though these have staged a mild revival; it is the simple fact that so many intelligent and charming young people of both sexes confess that they cannot talk to their parents. 'We do not understand how they allowed Hitler to happen and we cannot bear to listen to their excuses,' they say, and usually refuse to be drawn farther.

The older generation is acutely aware of this gulf. Many books have been written about it, seminars and discussions in which it is the main theme are constantly held. But the gulf remains.

> 'The Fathers don't count
> They have flopped
> I speak to students
> Girls and boys
> Who think.'[4]

ran a verse in a poem published by *Die Welt* in 1963, and that is still how many quite dutiful sons and daughters feel. Older critics retort that the students are 'withdrawn 'or 'escapist', but the truth is that no one really knows what the new generation believes or whether any belief is possible for it. The danger is that, without self-confidence or guidance at home, they will be easily led by the small but articulate groups of extremists of right or left.

The second question mark related to the pull of the East. The Germans have always been the 'people in the middle' whose eastern frontiers have been indeterminate and who have never seemed to be quite sure where they belonged. In spite of the threat of communism, many Germans still have a closer affinity with the Slavs than with the Franks and Teutons. Brandt's *Ost Politik*, therefore, is not simply the product of one ardent socialist trying to get on terms with another of a different type, it strikes a historical chord which, under favourable circumstances, could reverberate in a manner which would transcend all political creeds. Unless Western Europe provides West Germans with an ideal to take the place of nationalism, the pull of the East may be decisive.[5]

4 *Amos Elon*, Op. Cit., p. 198.
5 The number of those wishing to 'work closely with' the Soviet Union has risen steadily from 18% in 1953 to 52% in November, 1970. Only a fifth of those ·ked showed any concern at the flying of the East German flag at the Olympic games in Munich in 1972. Institut fur Demoskopie, Allensbach.

Nevertheless, there is surely more cause for hope than fear. The least that one can say is that in the short space of a quarter of a century the West Germans have made as good an attempt at running a democracy as many other peoples in ten times as long. Bearing in mind the violence and intimidation which are increasingly manifesting themselves in other Western countries, it would be curmudgeonly to suggest that the West Germans are less likely to continue on that road than their Western neighbours. The evidence is overwhelming that at last they have learned that life organised through the ballot box can give them more of what they want than a system dominated by the bullet, the jackboot or the concentration camp.

It is fortunate for Western Europe that this is so. For it is not just the future of West Germany that is at stake. Democracy is under heavier attack in every Western country than it has been since the introduction of adult suffrage. It needs strengthening and expanding within and between the nations which practise it. Although the internal problems of the United States have not yet destroyed the nuclear umbrella under which Western Europe lives, they threaten its credibility and have eroded much of America's moral leadership. It is from Western Europe that new inspiration must come. And whether or not the Germans are prepared to admit it or the other countries of Western Europe are aware of it, the Federal Republic is now Western Europe's natural leader, politically and economically. Brandt took the initiative which neither N.A.T.O. nor the European Community dared risk and the members of both organisations must either support and strengthen the *Ost Politik* or risk a deterioration in their relations, not only with the communist world, but with the Federal Republic as well. The result could wreck the whole concept of Western European Union. The West Germans to-day have an alternative foreign policy and if democracy cannot be extended in the way they wish, they might well settle for some less exacting form of society.

But whatever the future brings, for a people to have risen from the degradation into which they had sunk under Hitler, to a point where their former victims and enemies look to them for an example and for help, is no mean achievement. The West Germans have more than fulfilled Roosevelt's demand that they work themselves back into the family of civilised nations.

Bibliography

In attempting to tell the story of the rise of Western Germany since the catastrophe of 1945 I have relied partly on personal experience, on innumerable interviews, on contemporary newspaper reports and published documents and books. Since a list of the latter would add little to the knowledge of those versed in the subject, I mention here only those which I found particularly helpful or illuminating.

THE DEFEAT AND OCCUPATION OF GERMANY

I refer in the footnotes to the histories, memoirs and biographies of the Second World War from which I have quoted. Of the others, *The Forrestal Diaries* (Cassell, London, 1952; Viking, New York, 1951), and Stettinius' *Roosevelt and the Russians* (Jonathan Cape, London, 1950; Doubleday, New York, 1949), state more bluntly than is usual a view that was unfashionable at the time.

The background to the demand for Unconditional Surrender and the fateful decisions taken at the Yalta Conference is still most vividly presented in the last volume of Sir Winston Churchill's, *The Second World War. Triumph and Tragedy* (Cassell, London, 1954; Houghton, Mifflin, Boston, 1953), Herbert Feis's *Churchill, Roosevelt and Stalin* (Princeton University Press, 1957), Chester Wilmot's *The Struggle for Europe* (Collins, London, 1952; Harper & Row, New York, 1952), and Robert Sherwood's *Roosevelt and Hopkins* (Harper Bros., New York, 1945). Christopher Sykes' *Troubled Loyalty* (Collins, London, 1969), a biography of Adam von Trott, puts the case for a conditional surrender urged by the German 'resistance.'

Civil Affairs and Military Government, N.W. Europe 1944/6, by F. S. V. Donnisson (H.M.S.O., London, 1961), and Michael Balfour's contribution to *Four Power Control in Germany and Austria 1945–9* (Royal Institute of International Affairs, 1956), describes the failure of the Allies to reach agreement about the administration of the zones of occupation.

The Occupation itself is brilliantly described both by Michael Balfour in the work already mentioned and by Eugene Davidson in *The Death and Life of Germany* (Jonathan Cape, London, 1959). Of the autobiographical accounts *Decision in Germany* (Heinemann, London, 1950), by General Lucius Clay, Eisenhower's deputy and then successor as American Military Governor in Germany, is probably the most authoritative record of the workings of the Control Commission as seen by the Western Allies. Brigadier Frank Howley's *Berlin Command* (Putnam, New York, 1950), gives by far the most graphic first-hand account of the difficulties thrown up by the attempt at Four-power control of the former Reich capital. William Shirer's *The End of a Berlin Diary* (Hamish Hamilton, London, 1947; Alfred A. Knopf, New York, 1947), contains a haunting picture of the ruined city after the surrender. Ewan Butler's *Divided City* (Sidgwick and Jackson, London, 1955; Praeger, New York, 1955), describes the growing tension in the years before the wall was built.

THE OCCUPATION

Besides Victor Gollancz's books and pamphlets to which I have referred in the text, *The Monthly Report of the Control Commission* (British Element), *The Background Letter*, emanating from the same source, the *Monthly British Zone Review*, all of which are available in the library of the Ministry of Defence, provide a contemporary account of the collapse of organised life in Germany and the way in which Military Government attempted to deal with the resulting chaos. *Europe 1945, Germany Under Allied Occupation*, a digest of German newspapers edited by the Wiener Library, contains the glimmerings of a revived German interest in their own fate. Hans Dollinger's *Deutschland unter den Besatzungs-Machten* (Kurt Desch, Munchen, 1967) and Hans Schlange-Schoningen's *Im Schatten des Hungers* (Parry, Hamburg, 1955), present a factual but moving picture of German life under the Occupation. Ernst von Salomon's novel *Der Fragebogen* (Rowolt Verlag, Hamburg, 1951), and Hans Habe's *Off Limits* (Desch, Munich, 1955), portray the despair of the ordinary German trying to survive the chaos and the disillusion of the idealist intellectual at the way in which the representatives of democracy succumbed to the temptations of absolute power.

THE REFUGEES

There are a great many books dealing with the experiences and problems of German refugees from Eastern Europe as well as a succession of official reports and a large body of legislation all of which was debated in Parliament. One of the most dramatic books is Wolfgang Leonard's *Die Revolution entläst ihre Kinder*, abbreviated and translated by C. M. Woodhouse as *Child of the Revolution* (Collins, London, 1956). Leonard, a Russian-trained German Communist, returned with Ulbricht to found the People's Republic but defected and escaped. The refugee problem as a whole is put in perspective by the same author in *This Germany* (translated by Catherine Hutton, New York Geographical Society, Greenwich, Connecticut, 1964), Amos Elon in *Journey through a Haunted Land* (André Deutsch, London, 1967; Holt, Rinehart & Winston, New York, 1967), and Professor Alfred Grosser in *Western Germany, from Defeat to Rearmament*, translated by Richard Rees (Allen and Unwin, London, 1955; Praeger, New York, 1955). The books written by refugees themselves are understandably partisan and often bitter. The *Rebirth of the German Church* by Stewart Herman (S.C.M. Press, London, 1946; Harper & Row, New York, 1946), describes the sufferings of the millions who fled from the East and attempts an analysis of numbers. Elizabeth Wiskemann in *Germany's Eastern Neighbours* does her utmost to be objective over the problems both of the refugees and the Eastern frontiers.

THE BEGINNINGS OF THE FEDERAL REPUBLIC

Professor Grosser has condensed much of what he has written on Germany into a single book, *Germany In Our Time*, translated by Paul Stephenson (Pall Mall, London, 1971; Praeger, New York, 1972). He writes as an avowed French Socialist but the breadth of his knowledge is matched by his fairmindedness. Terence Prittie's *Germany Divided* (Hutchinson, London, 1961; Little, Brown, Boston, 1960), is a straightforward account of the events leading up to the foundation of the two Germanies by one of the best postwar British foreign correspondents.

There is an interesting psychological study of Kurt Schumacher by Lewis Edinger (Stanford University Press, 1965). Of the many

biographies of Konrad Adenauer, Paul Weymar's is the most
intimate and adulatory, *Konrad Adenauer*, (André Deutsch, London,
1957), and Terence Prittie's the most informative and objective,
Adenauer (Tom Stacey, London, 1972; Cowles, New York, 1971).
Adenauer's memoirs, although turgid and confined almost entirely
to foreign affairs in the last three volumes, are more rewarding than
is generally supposed. Adenauer's total domination of his government during his first ten years of office, his brilliant handling of the
Western Allies and the patience and consistency with which he
pursued his foreign policy all emerge. The way the memoirs are
written is itself a mirror of Adenauer's method and mind. Only
the first volume has been translated: *Adenauer Memoirs 1945–53*.
Translated by Beate Ruhm von Oppen (Weidenfeld and Nicolson,
London, 1966; Henry Regnery, Chicago, 1966). The other three
volumes, of which the last is incomplete, carry the story to 1963.
Konrad Adenauer, Erinnerungen (Deutsch Verlags-Anstalt, Stuttgart,
1966).

RECONSTRUCTION AND 'THE MIRACLE'

The four volumes of *The Survey of International Affairs 1949–52* by
Peter Calvocaressi (The Royal Institute of International Affairs and
Oxford University Press, 1953–5), provide the context in which the
recovery began in comprehensive if unexciting terms. None of the
books written by or about Ludwig Erhard are as impressive or
revealing as the speeches he made as he preached his gospel of the
Social Market Economy over the years. These have been collected
in *Der Weg der Sozialen Wirtschaft* (Econ Knapp, Düsseldorf, 1962).
A selection has been translated as *The Economics of Success* (Thames
and Hudson, London, 1963; Van Nostrand Reinhold, New York,
1963). *Wirtschaftsordnung und Wirtschaftspolitik* (Rombach, Freiburg,
1966), by Müller-Armack, one of Erhard's two State Secretaries,
fills in many gaps particularly in regard to the social content of
Erhard's policies. Henry Wallich's *Mainsprings of the German Revival*
(Yale University Press, Newhaven, 1960), sets out clearly the different roles of public and private financial agencies and the contributions of different industries. *Gott Erhält die Machtigen*, by
Kurt Pritxholeit (Karl Runch Verlag, Dusseldorf, 1968), is a more
critical appraisal of the phases and mechanism of reconstruction.
Karl Jasper's *Wohin Treibt die Bundesrepublik* (R. Piper and Co.,

Munich, 1966), is interesting because it shows how distorted by political prejudice an eminent writer's judgement can become. His prophecies were proved false almost before the book appeared.

There are biographies of several of the leading industrialists and financiers, but as so many are still alive and active, the human side of 'The Miracle' is best culled from conversations, newspapers and magazine articles, the published records of private firms, official year-books, and reports. The Germans are plainly fascinated by their new breed of millionaire and perhaps the liveliest sketches are to be found in Bert Englemann's *Meine Freunde die Millionaire* (Deutsche Taschenbuch Verlag, Munich, 1966), *Meine Freunde die Manager*, produced by the same publisher in 1959, and Jorg Andreas Elten's *Die Junge Millionaire* (Nannen Verlag, Hamburg, 1966).

TRADE UNIONS

The History of the German Labour Movement, by Helga Grebing, abridged by Mary Saran and translated by Edith Korner (Oswald Wolf, London, 1969), is a useful text book, but as the most interesting developments have occurred since 1945 the story is told most fully in the pamphlets and reports published by the Deutsche Gewerkschaftsbund (D.G.B.) and its Institute of Research in the Hans Böckler Strasse in Dusseldorf, in the Parliamentary debates on the whole complex of Industrial Legislation of the last twenty years and the comments in the press. Both the German Embassy in London and the British Embassy in Bonn have a great deal of up-to-date information on the workings of the various Acts of Parliament. Walter Hesselbach has himself condensed the essence of his book, *Die Gewerkschaftlichen Unternehmen*, into a small pamphlet, which is available at the German Embassy in London, entitled *The Importance of Commonweal Enterprise within the German Economy*.

SUBVERSION AND ESPIONAGE

The Office for the Defence of the Constitution in Cologne and that of the Senator for the Interior in Berlin have published an extensive sample of the information available on the subversive campaign waged by the communists against West Germany. There are several valuable collections of newspaper cuttings containing reports of the cases of espionage and subversion which have come before the courts. The Public Information Office of the Federal Republic issues a regular bulletin which contains detailed summaries of subversive activity and periodical appreciations of the overall situation.

EAST GERMANY AND OST POLITIK

I have deliberately refrained from any attempt to describe the founding or progress of the People's Republic of East Germany, but its existence constantly impinges on the story I have tried to tell. Among authors to whom I have referred in the footnotes, J. P. Nettl, Eugene Davidson and Alfred Grosser all write objectively about the development of the Communist State: Amos Elon and Wolfgang Leonard convey accurately the impressions one receives in conversation with sensitive West Germans who pay frequent visits across the 'frontier'. *Die D.D.R. ist Keine Zone Mehr* by Hans Werner Schwarze (Kiepenheurer and Wisch, Cologne, 1969), is an example of the well-judged and perhaps well-founded propaganda which has gained such wide acceptance for the *Ost Politik* in the Western World.

The *Ost Politik* itself is likely to remain such a live issue that it will continue to be the subject of debate in Parliament and Press, on radio and television for many years. A concise summary of the main arguments which led Willy Brandt to make his attempt to establish a new relationship with Russia and Eastern Europe and of the early stages of the negotiations is given in *Germany's Ost Politik* by Lawrence Whetten (Royal Institute of International Affairs, Oxford University Press, 1971).

GENERAL BOOKS ON POST-WAR GERMANY

I was relieved to find that Professor Grosser considers Ralf Dahrendorf's *Society and Democracy in Germany* (Weidenfeld and Nicolson, London, 1968, translated by the author; Doubleday, New York, 1967) as 'fundamental' to a study of modern Germany; some Germans whose judgement I respect had spoken disparagingly of it. Professor Grosser's books and Eugene Davidson's *Death and Life of Germany* are equally indispensable. The most sensitive impression of a return visit by someone who once lived in Germany is contained in Amos Elon's *Journey Through a Haunted Land*. Wolfgang Leonhard's *This Germany* is the intelligent man's political and gastronomic guide written by a former German communist who now lives in the West.

Index